Jeffrey Watson is a broadcaster, author and journalist who has worked for nearly forty years in the print and electronic media both in Australia and England. This is his third book.

A documentary film on Sidney Cotton—*The Last Plane Out of Berlin*—is available on video.

*For Robin*

# Sidney Cotton

## The Last Plane Out of Berlin

Jeffrey Watson

HODDER

A Hodder Book

Published in Australia and New Zealand in 2002
by Hodder Headline Australia Pty Limited
(A member of the Hodder Headline Group)
Level 22, 201 Kent Street, Sydney NSW 2000
Website: www.hha.com.au



**National Library of Australia**
**Cataloguing-in-Publication data**

Watson, Jeffrey.

Sidney Cotton : the last plane out of Berlin.

ISBN 0 7336 1516 3.

1. Cotton, Sidney, 1894-1969. 2. Air pilots - Biography. 3. Air pilots - Australia - Biography. 4. Air pilots, Military - Biography. 5. World War, 1939-1945 - Reconnaissance operations, British. I. Title.

629.13092

Cover design by Danielle Cairis
Text design and typesetting by Bookhouse, Sydney
Printed in Australia by Griffin Press, Adelaide

# Contents

# Author's note

In telling this story I have relied significantly on the dramatic techniques of television—many conversations and events have been reconstructed. I have certainly not written a conventional biography or a formal history of events. But it is based on research into the era and the man, and on what is on the record.

I am indebted to a great many people in the writing of this book; in particular Ralph Barker, who co-wrote Sidney's book, *Aviator Extraordinary*, and who gave me permission to use extracts from it; to Sally and Charles Cotton who, although they were only young when he died have vivid memories of this extraordinary man and who gave me access to his letters and photographs; to Joan Hopkinson who, after she gave me an interview, passed away in her 94th year; to Jill Cotton in Calgary; to Pat Martin in Hawaii; to Joan Astley; Gill Drake, Rhoda Fraser; Sadika Tancred, Brian Brooke-Smith, Jack Eggleston; Leslie Axon and the late Desmond Sheen in England.

For the background to the operations in France I have to thank Edward Leaf and his excellent book *Above Us Unseen*; and to the staff at the Australian War Memorial for access to Sidney's papers; and to the Public Record Office in London; to Omar Khalidi for background information on Hyderabad; Heiderose Leopold in Berlin who made it easier for me to visit the Karinhalle, Hermann Goering's country house, or what is left of it, despite obstacles placed in my way by the authorities; to Group Captain Stephen Lloyd, the commanding officer of JARIC (the Joint Aerial Reconnaissance Intelligence Centre) at Brampton in England; and to David Humphrey, curator of the Museum of Photography at RAF Cosford. Above all, my gratitude to my wife, Robin d'Arcy, whose exhaustive researches in many public archives unearthed a great deal of fresh information.

Cotton's own book, published in 1969, seems to lead to a series of dead ends. Names of the rich and famous are sprinkled like glitter dust as if to impress; many of them may well have been friends who subsequently deserted him when the going got tough. Cotton glosses over the more controversial aspects of his career and passes effortlessly from one chapter to the next, pausing only to vilify the bureaucrats and career officers who stood in his way.

I was also intrigued to know more about Herr Schoene and Herr Traeder, the two German pilots who, according to Sidney, served on the staff of Hermann Goering. Despite exhaustive research, it was not possible to trace either—-although there is a record of a Herr Traeger of Goering's staff. In his dealings with the Nazis, was Sidney Cotton dealing with men with assumed names?

After I made a documentary film about Sidney, a number of people contacted me to say that I had only told half the story. I am also aware that a number of people I interviewed sought to protect his reputation.

Even now, it is clear that there may be a lot more to say.

Jeffrey Watson

# Introduction

I left it rather late in the day to write a book about Sidney Cotton. After all he had been dead for thirty years and the trail was cold. Most of the people who knew him during the early days were dead and gone.

I first heard about him in 1980, not in his native Australia but in Newfoundland.

Cotton spent most of his life overseas, in Europe, in North America and in the Middle East and his adventures were rarely reported. And because of the secret nature of his wartime work, he preferred to be behind the camera rather than in front of it.

My enquiries took me to the librarian at the Royal Aeronautical Society in London.

'How may I help you?' he enquired.

'I want to know everything about a man called Frederick Sidney Cotton.'

'Oh,' said the librarian, with a sharp inrush of breath, 'he caused a lot of trouble over here you know.'

That was an example of English understatement at its best.

The search to find more took me to a great many places. It took me down a road through a pine forest in Germany to the house of

Hitler's deputy Hermann Goering. It took me to a dusty archive in Canberra Australia and a colour picture of a woman he called Mata Hari.

It took me to the top of a hill on the island of Kauai in Hawaii to meet his mistress. It took me on a long drive along the shores of Lake Ontario to drink gin with an old lady who could imitate the cry of the loon.

Australians love taking the British down a peg. When I made a film about Sidney Cotton many people wanted to believe that Sidney was a rough colonial who had bested the effete and class-conscious English. It is a nice idea, but it is wrong.

Sidney neither looked nor sounded like an Australian and, despite what some academics have said, he was certainly no rough diamond. He was debonair, quietly spoken and articulate—what the French call soigné. More significantly, he could play the British at their own game and win.

By the time I started writing this book, the cars and yachts and private planes had all gone. The bureaucrats and politicians and military men he either befriended or offended were all dead.

All that remained was a photograph of a tall rather bland man in a suit.

The most memorable thing about the picture was the barely perceptible smile that played around the lips. Like the smile on the Cheshire cat, it was there long after he was gone.

# Chapter 1

## Spy in the Sky

The aeroplane is painted a pale blue-green. Against the sky over north Germany it can hardly be seen. At the controls is a middle-aged man with eyes the colour of cornflowers. He flies the Lockheed like he is caressing it, the fingers of his left hand resting lightly on the oval control column, his right hand occasionally touching the two throttle levers.

In the co-pilot's seat is another man, his head bent low over an aviator's chart. The map is a quilt of coloured squares and rectangles. It is the purple patches they are interested in—for these are the forbidden no-fly zones, containing sensitive military installations that would be of interest to a foreign power. The sensitive areas are those of the Greater German Reich. The foreign power is Great Britain.

Behind them in the passenger cabin of the aeroplane five of the six seats have been removed to make way for extra fuel tanks—big grey metal boxes. There is only one passenger seat and a pretty girl in a pink angora sweater occupies it.

The hairs on the sweater normally stand out in a fuzzy ball

making her look plumper than she really is, but at this altitude—14 000 feet—the drop in pressure causes them to lie flat like cat's fur.

From time to time she sniffs from a tube attached to an oxygen bottle. But the girl has a job to do. She lies on her stomach, her face close to the lurching metal cabin and busies herself with a large camera, its lens facing downwards, mounted in a hole in the floor. It is noisy in the back of the aircraft but she seems not to notice. Her jawline is set and she is preoccupied with the task in hand.

The man with the silver hair turns round from his seat in the cockpit and shouts above the booming engines.

'Over target now. Start the cameras.'

She crouches low to the floor and cocks and fires the cameras.

Three miles below in the dockyards of the German navy, a welder pulls off his mask and wipes the sweat from his brow. High above him he hears the drone of an aeroplane, but even on this bright clear day he cannot see it. Its undersides have been painted the same colour as the sky, so to all intents and purposes it is invisible.

He loses interest and returns to his work, unaware of the fact that he has just had his photograph taken from 14 000 feet.

In the sunroom of her house in Perth, Ontario, Joan Henry Cotton Hopkinson wishes to talk about her first husband, Sidney, the businessman.

Her home is the ground floor of a three-storey sandstone house in Gore Street West, almost in the centre of town. She is sitting in a wheelchair on the deck which overlooks the car park of St Paul's Uniting church next door. A pink plastic band straddles her head holding hearing aids in both ears. She is ninety-four but it is easy to see that Joan Henry, as she was when Sidney met her, was a great beauty.

I have flown halfway across the world to see her. As it happens this will be the last interview she will give.

A sigh. Was it from Joan or from the railway track at the end of the garden? It is from both. A freight train hoots mournfully as it clatters over the tracks on its way to Ottawa. She summons lunch: 'Mr Watson has come a long way and would like to eat.' It is not yet twelve.

From the depths of the house emerges Heather, a cheerful vague woman in her forties who offers boiled ham, potato and sweet corn served on white plates. Coffee is brought and Heather retreats below stairs although one gets the impression she is not far away.

'Oh Sid, dear Sid,' Joan says, and begins.

A month before the outbreak of World War II, a luxurious private aeroplane landed at an aerodrome in Frankfurt, Germany. Stepping down from the door at the rear of the aircraft was a tall wolfish man with flowing white hair and blue eyes. A grey double-breasted suit and heavy spectacles completed the picture. The urbane British businessman.

The aeroplane bore a civilian registration and stood out among the rows of more mundane private aircraft. Moreover, it was painted a pale blue-green, a curious colour scheme at a time when most private planes were silver. Only the most observant would have noticed that when airborne the Lockheed appeared to disappear without trace into the sky. Taking off into the gloaming or into the light of early dawn the aircraft was invisible.

The man in the suit was Frederick Sidney Cotton. He was forty-five years old, the son of a prosperous grazier from Queensland Australia. Cotton had left his native land after World War I, hardly ever to return. He had flown as a pilot in the Great War and had then set up a number of business ventures in Canada. None of them had been especially successful, but Cotton had acquired a reputation as a focused and driven individual, an adventurer and a buccaneer, a man to whom officialdom and red tape were anathema.

A group of Luftwaffe officers in their grey dress uniforms gathered around Cotton and *der Kolossal* Lockheed. Cotton noticed the yellow collar tabs denoting they were aircrew and black arm-bands bearing the names of their *geschwader* or squadrons.

The Lockheed was a modern airliner, fast and sleek and made of metal at a time when many aeroplanes were still covered in doped fabric. It was state of the art in 1939; there was a murmur of approval from the fliers. It was almost as good as the new breed of Luftwaffe aircraft on display, the Heinkels and Messerschmitts. Mr Cotton must be a rich man indeed to afford such an expensive toy.

Mr Cotton was occasionally a rich man. Like all entrepreneurs his fortunes expanded and contracted like the bellows of a concertina. He made and lost huge sums of money.

The truth was that the pale blue-green aeroplane was not really his. It had been paid for jointly by the Secret Intelligence Service of the British government and the French Deuxième Bureau, the money laundered through a private company, the Aeronautical Research and Sales Corporation with offices in Piccadilly. Chairman Sidney Cotton.

Although at first glance the Lockheed might appear to be a gentleman's luxury carriage it was a spy plane which was in Germany with one express purpose—to photograph from the air the military secrets of the Third Reich. If the Luftwaffe officers had examined the aircraft more closely they would have been shocked to discover that it carried hidden cameras in the wings. Embarrassingly they were German cameras, the best in the world—Leicas. And the reason it was painted an eggshell blue-green was so it could not be seen against the sky.

Sidney Cotton was a man of many talents. He was an experienced pilot with a combat record in World War I. He was an inventor who knew about machines, metals and engines. He was a pioneer of colour photography. But perhaps his greatest talent was his single-minded determination to do things his way, even if it meant treading on a lot of toes. He was known as a charming and generous man and commanded enormous loyalty among the people who worked for him. But to some members of the British establishment, he was a colonial upstart.

## Chapter 2

# A Hidden Vale

Motorists who venture south of Brisbane on the Cunningham Highway might find themselves in an outer suburb with the splendid name of Grandchester. Despite being named after Rupert Brooke's famous poem, this is nothing like rural England. Flat farming land gives way to a long straight road flanked by eucalypts, which climbs steadily uphill to the entrance to the old Hidden Vale homestead, with its paved drive and Moreton Bay fig trees.

Here in 1900 came Alfred Cotton, Sidney's father, an imposing man with a moustache worn thick and long in the style of Lord Kitchener. Alfred J. Cotton had made his money further north and had bought this property from an Ipswich butcher, Philip Jost. In 1908 he replaced the Jost home with a splendid two-storey house with wide verandahs. In 1911 he sold it to return to England to educate his children, but bought it back again in 1914 for £27 500. The four Cotton children adored the freedom and mystery of Hidden Vale and this was where Sidney Cotton spent some of his happiest days.

'I shall never forget the magnificent view as we emerged from the trees into open country approaching the property,' he wrote. 'We had driven about four miles from the railway station by buggy when we suddenly found ourselves on the top of a hill looking down across a valley.'

Cotton had been born on a cattle station at Goorganga near Proserpine. He was six when the family moved to Hidden Vale. Sidney loved riding and working the cattle, and was fascinated by the new machines that were being invented, like motor cars and aeroplanes.

When Sidney Cotton was born, Queen Victoria was still on the throne and the sun had yet to set on the British Empire. During his lifetime Cotton was to see the introduction of electricity and the telephone, of radio, television, nuclear energy and space flight. A high point of his own life was a bringing together of two of the most important developments of the twentieth century—photography and the aeroplane.

Sidney Cotton had an insatiable appetite for new technology. How he applied that technology became one long adventure that took him to most countries of the world.

Not much of Sidney Cotton survives in Australia, unlike some pioneer fliers. In Melbourne there is an aerodrome named after the great Harry Hawker. In Bundaberg there is a plaque to Bert Hinkler. Sydney's international airport is named after Sir Charles Kingsford Smith. But the only memorial to Sidney is a metal plate in a cemetery in a place called Tallegalla.

Sidney Cotton exchanged the featureless Queensland bush for an office in Piccadilly and a brown pinstripe suit. He could have stayed in Australia and played the gentleman farmer. Instead he went to Europe and America and acquired a circle of friends that included royalty, heads of state, and shadowy figures from the world of espionage. It was all a wonderful game.

Who was Sidney Cotton? A great aviator or a confidence trickster? A brilliant innovator or a self-seeking social climber? A patriot or a war profiteer? Or all of the above?

Sidney's father, Alfred John Cotton, was one of Queensland's pioneering pastoralists and could trace his ancestry back before the Norman Conquest. A. J. Cotton, according to one account, was one of the pioneers who blazed their tracks through the state of Queensland when it was 'a wild and dangerous land inhabited only by treacherous blacks'.

Alfred Cotton was born in St Helier in the Channel Islands on 21 June 1861 and went to school in Brighton and at the Taplow Grammar School in Bristol. He was the only son of Charles Nelson Cotton, a London merchant. An uncle, Sir Richmond Cotton, was Lord Mayor of London in 1875. The library of an ancestor, Sir Robert Bruce Cotton, was one of three collections which started the British Museum Library and is known as the Cottonian Library.

Orphaned at fourteen, after his father had lost his money in South Africa, Alfred Cotton went to sea and served his indentures on the barque *Edeline*, a coal ship on the China run. It was a tough life for a boy in his early teens. The cabin he shared with a shipmate measured only six feet six inches square. Later he served on the barque *Clara*, which carried large numbers of immigrants between England and Queensland.

In 1879 while the ship was in Hong Kong he completed his indentures and was promoted to third mate. With five hundred Chinese coolies on board the *Clara* set sail for Antigua in the Caribbean. The coolies mutinied but somehow Alfred Cotton regained control and the ship reached its destination. Alfred Cotton spent six years at sea before settling in Australia. He arrived in Australia when he was twenty years old and worked as a jackeroo at Yaleroi station in New South Wales.

He soon developed a flair for handling horses and cattle and travelled all over Queensland droving cattle from one station to another. He arrived one day at Bromby Park near Bowen and met Annie Bode. Annie Bode was one of four daughters of Frederick Bode, a family with a German name and Teutonic roots. Cotton was not the only settler with aristocratic roots who farmed in Proserpine. Three other families were listed in *Burke's Peerage*.

Alfred Cotton had financed some of his early property deals by rounding up brumbies and selling them to the British Army for service in the Boer War. He got eight pounds a piece for the horses. After the war was over he exported the horses from South Africa and resold them for four pounds a piece.

Alfred Cotton was a man 'of frugal temperament' and saved enough money to buy Goorganga station in 1894, the same year that Sidney was born. Goorganga is Aboriginal for 'home of the waters and of the crocodile'.

Six years later he sold Goorganga to the Lascelles family and bought, successively, Hidden Vale Grandchester (later the family home), Inkerman, Lawn Hill, Bohemia Downs, Springfield, Brunette Downs and Canobie near Normanton in North Queensland.

Alfred Cotton bought and sold stations and won and lost fortunes. He was an expert in the cattle market.

At one time he had 53 000 cattle on the road. He tells the story in his book *With the Big Herds in Australia*. Another time he took five contracts simultaneously to deliver 7600 cattle from North Queensland to New South Wales.

Like many pioneer pastoralists A. J. had good years and lean years and his life was a constant struggle against drought. In 1914 at the Sydney Agricultural Show he had met another pioneer pastoralist the Honourable James White of Muswellbrook in New South Wales. The Whites had acquired the enormous Brunette Downs station in the Northern Territory but it was not a success. They asked Cotton if he wanted to go into the venture on a 50:50 basis. Cotton agreed but had to sell all his other properties to buy into Brunette Downs and this weakened him.When the stock market crash came in 1929 he had nothing to fall back on. It had all gone. He lost millions. It was a pattern that was to be repeated with his eldest son.

Sidney Cotton was born into this old money in 1894, the third of the five Cotton children. Alfred and Annie Cotton's first child was a daughter, Lilian, born in Proserpine in 1891; she died in early childhood. Vera arrived next, followed by Sidney, Victor and Douglas.

Today floatplanes and helicopters full of tourists fly over Goorganga on their way to the islands of the Great Barrier Reef. Down the road is Airlie Beach, a steadily growing tourist destination with its bars and backpacker hostels. Significantly, it is the aeroplane which has brought this part of Queensland just a few hours from the major capital cities.

But in 1894 there were no aeroplanes or cars. A journey to Goorganga was by horse-drawn coach or steamer. Goorganga was just a speck on the map at the edge of a vast dry continent. It was more than five hundred miles to Brisbane, a journey that by road would take five days. The little settlements clung to the coastline, their only lifeline the steamer. The ocean looked placid enough but the estuaries were full of crocodiles and the dry inland teemed with snakes.

Sidney's earliest childhood memories were of Goorganga. The house was a Queenslander, a large wooden mansion with wide airy verandahs. It was here that baby Sidney would crawl around on his hands and knees playing with his toddler brother Victor. One day they put their hands through a hole in the edge of the verandah and found some fluffy white balls. 'They were great to play with,' wrote Sidney 'and we always put them back in the hole after the game.' The fluffy balls were the eggs of a tiger snake, one of the most dangerous of the twenty-eight varieties of poisonous serpents in Australia. Later Annie Bode drew her infant sons away with a shudder. The tiger snake had been crawling along the verandah and Victor had been crawling after it.

It is not certain when Sidney Cotton saw his first aeroplane. The Wright Brothers had made their historic flight at Kittyhawk in 1903 and Louis Blériot had flown the English Channel in 1909, but Australia was largely isolated from the mainstream of aeronautical research. Even by 1910 there were few aeroplanes in Australia.

Five months after Sidney Cotton was born in 1894, an

Englishman called Lawrence Hargrave had successfully lifted himself into the air in a kite at Stanwell Park in New South Wales. Hargrave is acknowledged as one of the pioneers of flight. He had the machine but not the means to lift it into the air. Unlike the Wrights he failed to develop a successful engine to power his machine. Years later, however, the design of aeroplanes in Europe was dominated by Hargrave's box kites.

When he was nine or ten, Sidney sketched a design for his own aeroplane which looked surprisingly like the Caudron Type A of 1911. It was a twin boom biplane powered somewhat optimistically by a twenty horsepower motor. The rudder, curiously, was suspended between the struts of the underslung fuselage rather than above it, and carried Sidney's initials S. C. It was surprisingly advanced for a country boy still at primary school.

In 1904 when Sidney was ten he was sent to Southport Grammar School on the Gold Coast about seventy-five miles from Hidden Vale. Today its glorious white beaches are swarming with tourists but in those days Southport was a sleepy hollow. The journey from here to Hidden Vale would take the best part of a day so Sidney became a boarder. Six years as a boarder bred in Sidney a self-confidence and independence that was to serve him well in later years. But although Sidney was popular at school he had few close friends and developed a reputation as a loner.

In 1910 Alfred Cotton decided to put all four children through their final schooling in England. The family sailed to England and checked into Berners Hotel just off Oxford Street in central London. Aviation was the talk of the town. All London was agog with talk of the Frenchman Louis Blériot who had flown the English Channel in an aeroplane of his own design a few months earlier. Most people were more interested in the personal details—the fact that he had broken both ankles in a previous crash and had roped his crutches to the fuselage.

The French seemed to be doing it better than the English. However, if you were interested in aeroplanes in England in 1910, there was only one place to be. Brooklands. This famous aerodrome was not only the cradle of flying but of motor racing. Flying machines were built in the big black sheds and flown from the field at the centre of the famous banked racing track. Men in goggles drove around the perimeter in cars with names like Napier, Bentley and de Lage. All the great aviation names were here too—T. O. M. Sopwith, Alliot Verdon-Roe (Avro), and Harry Hawker, Cotton's fellow countryman.

Sidney wasted no time in cultivating the doorman at the hotel who told him how to find his way to Brooklands aerodrome—in those days a formidable journey from central London. Brooklands was near Weybridge in Surrey, about two hours by road. But Sidney did not have a car, although he harboured a desire to build one.

'I was much too shy to do more than help push the machines out of their sheds and watch them trying to take off but I became thoroughly obsessed with aeroplanes.'

His father meanwhile had rented Warthill Castle near Aberdeen. This was a property of some twelve hundred acres owned by the Patrick Leslie family, who also had properties in Australia.

Business was booming. In October 1910 Alfred Cotton was rich enough to place an order with Chivas Bros of Aberdeen, spirit merchant, for two ten gallon drums of Chivas Regal whisky. Chivas Bros wrote to him: 'We beg to acknowledge return of deposits on the empties; two 2 gallon jars 3s 6d, one 1 gallon jar, which is placed to your credit.'

Aviation was as much a novelty in Scotland as it was in England but the opportunities to see aeroplanes in flight were fewer. Cotton senior had heard that there was a flying meeting at Lanark but this was a long way from Aberdeen. He grudgingly decided to treat the three boys to an outing. Sidney was thrilled to discover that the aviators included two of the most famous pioneers, Colonel Samuel Franklin Cody and Henri Farman. Cody came straight out of the Wild West. Born in Texas the flamboyant Cody was a crack shot and expert horseman as well as an aviator. In 1908 he had made the first sustained powered flight in Great Britain. Farman and Cody were on a tour of Britain to popularise flying.

'Colonel Cody was the hero of the meeting, and headlines in the local paper reported that he had got up into the clouds,' wrote Sidney. Henri Farman the Frenchman, however, could not get very much lift and his aircraft crashed into the top of a tall tree. 'There he stayed until someone got a ladder and fetched him down.'

Sidney, Victor and Douglas were boarded at Cheltenham College in Gloucestershire and Vera went to school at the exclusive Wickham Abbey. During the two years that Cotton spent at Cheltenham he devoted much of his spare time to building model aeroplanes. With the help of the carpenter from the school carpentry shop he built a six foot model of bamboo and linen powered by a small single cylinder petrol engine.

The model was ready to fly in time for the summer holidays and after a few short test flights on the school cricket field Sidney packed it up carefully and sent it up to Aberdeen. Tragically the beautiful model was lost on its first flight.

'I set the rudder so that the plane would fly in a wide circle. It took off beautifully but instead of going into a turn it flew on and on and was soon lost from view.' Sidney thought that the plane had ended up in the branches of one of the many fir trees on the estate. 'I was inconsolable. I had lost the toy on which I had lavished six months of my school life.'

At the end of 1911, Alfred Cotton returned to Australia. The four children remained behind at school in England. Sidney hated the long winters and chafed at the strict discipline of an English private school. He missed his father very much and pined for the freedom of Hidden Vale. 'We could not adjust ourselves more than temporarily to what we felt was the restricted life in England' wrote Sid. All four children petitioned their father to return to Australia and in 1912 he agreed.

That strange machine, the motor car, was starting to appear on the streets of Australia, and Alfred Cotton was not slow to realise its potential. He needed a tough utilitarian vehicle which could handle the bad roads on his vast properties. But there was nothing available in the fifth continent.

While he was in England Alfred Cotton had investigated all the motor companies to find someone who would build him a car suitable for the bush. He decided to build his own.

Alfred Cotton's car was the Land Rover of its day. An old Sunbeam was the prototype with many of the parts supplied by the Dennis brothers. It stood fifteen inches above the ground, high enough to ford the erratic creeks of Far North Queensland. There was a winch on the front so it could pull itself out of trouble. The radiator could be swung sideways so that grass seeds could be picked out of the core.

Sidney, too, was to build his own car. In 1914 his father sent him off to Cassilis near Dalkeith in New South Wales to work for Frederick McMaster, a family friend. McMaster allowed him to use the equipment in the workshop and he ordered the parts to build a cycle car. This was a basic vehicle, registered as a motor cycle in some countries, and powered by a single cylinder engine. But, rudimentary though the car was, it had some revolutionary features.

Sydney drove the car back from Cassilis to Brisbane for his holidays. In the absence of a driver's seat he used a soap box. 'My father was not at all pleased when he realised how I had been spending my time at Cassilis. It was our first real clash of wills,' wrote Sidney. 'There were many more to come.'

But Alfred Cotton had to grudgingly admit that Sidney was showing aptitude as an engineer. The car was sent off to the Willys Overland agent in Brisbane to have a streamlined body fitted. Sidney was not to know it at this stage in his life but he would go on to own a number of most exotic motor cars—a crimson Hotchkiss, an ERA racing car and a beige drophead Rolls Royce. But all this was to come.

## Chapter 3

# Unsuitable for Employment

On 4 August 1914 Sidney Cotton's life was to change forever. On that day Britain declared war on Germany, and Australia, being a dominion of the Empire, followed suit. At last here was an opportunity to get into uniform and, more importantly, learn to fly an aeroplane. Australia had no air force, but in Britain both the Royal Flying Corps and the newly formed Royal Naval Air Service were looking for pilots. Sidney asked his father if he could go off to war. The answer was no. Alfred Cotton believed the war would last only a few months. In fact it was to last for four years and cost ten million lives.

In April 1915 Sidney and his father drove the car which bore both their names on the twelve hundred mile drive to Brunette Downs station. On the way there they stopped in a small country town and Sidney bought a newspaper. The paper was a week old but it told of the sinking of the *Lusitania* by a German submarine.

'The news so incensed me that I told my father I was determined to go to England when I got back.' Sidney was close to twenty-one. His father and mother could not stop him. 'My mother drew me aside and told me that she wouldn't stand in my way,' said Sidney.

Reluctantly, Alfred Cotton booked Sidney a passage to England on the *Maloja*. On board the P&O liner he met other young Australians who had volunteered for duty and were ready to die for their king. The early mood of elation soon evaporated, and they whiled away the time during the long sea voyage by learning Morse code and signalling. Sidney liked the sea almost as much as he liked aeroplanes and was a competent yachtsman. This fact was not lost on the ship's officers who advised him to join the newly formed Royal Naval Air Service rather than the Royal Flying Corps.

These were interesting times for naval aviation. Three years earlier Commander Charles Sampson had made the first flights from the deck of the HMS *Hibernia*. By the end of World War I the Royal Navy would have the first real aircraft carrier, the *Argus*. There were ways, reasoned Sidney, of combining his two passions, flying and the sea.

A few weeks after the *Maloja* docked in Southampton, Sidney Cotton was standing on a freezing flying field at Chingford in Essex. He was now Flight SubLieutenant Cotton. On the left sleeve of his uniform appeared the insignia of an eagle, its wings outstretched and its head inclined to the right. The Royal Naval Air Service (RNAS), Britain's newest military force was barely twelve months old.

His flying instructor was a man called Warren Merriam whose somewhat eccentric behaviour was the result of a serious accident which had affected his sight and, it was said, his mind. Sidney Cotton's first flight was to be a case of the partially sighted leading the blind. Also, unlike most pilots, Sidney went solo on his first flight. Merriam was under the impression that Sidney had some flying experience. In fact he had barely looked inside the cockpit of an aeroplane much less flown one.

Novice pilots were trained by doing hops. A number of spark plugs were removed from the engine to reduce its power. Then the students taxied about on the airfield and by fully opening the throttle were able to lift themselves into the air a few feet before settling the aircraft onto the ground. It was considered a safe way of training without exposing the students to too much danger.

By today's standards Sidney's aeroplane was a hideous thing. The Maurice Farman Longhorn took its name from the the two wooden outriggers which jutted out in front of the aircraft to stop it turning over in the event of a bad landing. The pilot sat ahead of the wing in a plywood nacelle shaped like a bathtub and the student sat behind him. A huge mahogany propeller rotated between the spindly twin booms of the uncovered fuselage. There were no dual controls. Once the aircraft was in the air, Sidney leaned over Merriam's shoulder and grasped the handelbar controls.

A cold wind blew across the airfield and Sidney Cotton's teeth chattered in his head. Below the wings the small green fields looked too close for comfort. Sid was terrified.

Merriam flew Sidney around the airfield a few times, then showed him how to line the aircraft up over a tree to land just inside the aerodrome. He taxied the clattering Farman to a stop and strode off to eat. After lunch, it would be Sidney's turn. Normally, novice pilots would have made at least a dozen or so hops before flying solo. Sidney was to make his first flight—and possibly his last one—without any flying experience at all.

'I knew that if I tried to go solo now I should almost certainly break my neck,' he wrote. Playing for time, he asked the mechanics to change the plugs and replace a few rusty bracing wires. Sidney had no appetite for lunch. When he came out of the mess, Merriam was sitting in the bathtub cockpit running up the big eight cylinder Renault engine. Sidney offered up a silent prayer that Merriam had forgotten all about him. But it was not to be. The instructor had simply been warming up the engine.

The reluctant aviator climbed into the pilot's seat and Merriam leaned over the side to strap him in. The Farman would do about sixty-eight miles per hour flat out. It would unstick from the ground at forty miles an hour. Merriam disappeared over the side of the cockpit and walked round to the rear to swing the propellor.

Pointing the aircraft into the wind Sidney opened the throttle and charged across the airfield.

The Longhorn was unusual in that the elevator was in front of the pilot instead of behind him. As the aircraft gathered speed it wobbled uncontrollably. Sidney did everything wrong. Pilots were supposed to have a light touch on the controls. Instead he grasped the strange handlebar stick as if his life depended upon it.

The hedge which bordered the field was getting uncomfortably close. Cotton froze and awaited the inevitable impact. Instead, nothing happened. Scarcely daring to look down he realised that he had cleared the hedge by a few feet. Being so tense he had slid to the back of the seat and in doing so pulled back on the controls. It was enough to get this collection of wires and sticks off the ground.

For the first time in his life Sidney Cotton was at the controls of a flying machine that was heavier than air. Not bad considering the only other aeroplanes he had ever flown were models. Once Sidney was in the air he started to gain confidence. At three hundred feet he pushed the stick forward and the Farman nosed over, diving towards the hangars. He pulled it out of the dive at fifty feet. He decided not to stray too far from the aerodrome and to try a few gentle turns.

To receive his pilot's ticket Sidney had to prove that he could take off, climb, control the aircraft, make figures of eight and land safely. The bracing wires sang as did Sidney's heart. Now all that remained was to demonstrate the figures of eight. Sidney banked the Farman steeply and using the forward mounted elevator now as a rudder slewed the aircraft from side to side in what pilots somewhat indelicately referred to as a split arse turn. By now a small knot of students was watching him from the ground.

The terror had evaporated into euphoria but Sidney was becoming overconfident. It was time to set the machine down. He was too high over the tree and opened the throttle to go round again. Finally on his second attempt he made a perfect landing in the centre of the circle.

The big mahogany propeller swung to a stop. Half deafened by the noise of the engine Sidney swung his leg over the side of the cockpit and dropped to the ground. Merriam grasped his hand and offered his congratulations. If he had realised that Cotton had no previous flying experience he was not about to let on.

The incident, said Cotton later, taught him how far it was possible to go on sheer bluff. In later years it would be something he would use to his advantage.

Early in 1916 Sidney was posted to the Central Flying School at Upavon in Wiltshire. Upavon, in the middle of Salisbury Plain, was the cradle of military aviation in Britain and an attractive posting after the dullness of Chingford. It was surrounded by pretty villages and rolling plains. Here Sidney learned to fly the BE 2c, a slightly more advanced machine which was armed with a rearward facing Lewis gun and could carry bombs under the wings.

After he had five hours solo flying in his log book Sidney was posted to the BE 2c flight at Dover. Here he was to try another new aeroplane, a French designed Breguet. The Breguet was a handful to fly because it had an all flying tail . . . in other words there was no fixed part to the elevator. This meant that movements of the stick had to be very small to stop the aircraft oscillating up and down. Sidney found that by clenching the stick tightly between his knees he could get the aircraft off the ground but that was only the start of his troubles.

The engine of the Breguet was notoriously unreliable. Sidney was barely airborne when it started missing and he made a forced landing in a field so that he could clear the carburettor. He was to make several more unscheduled stops before he finally coaxed the aircraft back to Dover.

'Where the devil have you been with my aeroplane, Cotton?' asked the squadron commander. But Cotton had impressed the officer with his airmanship. Shortly afterwards he was to graduate to No. 5 Wing of the RNAS, flying the dreadful and cumbersome Breguets.

Sidney had been in England for ten months. Finally he was

going to war! His chances of survival were not good but considerably better than those fighting in the mud of Flanders. By now he was based at Couderquerque near Dunkirk and flew on several bombing missions against docks and airfields near Ostend.

On 25 July Cotton requested permission to return to No. 5 Wing based in France. A few days later he was on patrol in the Breguet over the English Channel when he saw a large ocean liner stopped in mid ocean. As he watched he saw the waterspout of an explosion alongside the ship. Shortly afterwards it started to sink. Sidney realised with sudden shock that it was the *Maloja*, the very liner which had brought him from Australia to England.

From his aerial vantage point he watched in horror as people jumped over the sides. More than a hundred were drowned, many of whom, like Sidney, were Australians who had volunteered to join up. 'It made me determined to get into the fighting,' he said.

The opportunity would not be long in coming. A few days later Sidney was on patrol near Dunkirk when he saw little black clouds forming up beneath his wings. 'I had never seen clouds form so quickly before, nor had I seen them form such strange shapes. Then one appeared suddenly very close to me and in the centre was a purple flash which was followed by the sound of an explosion.'

Flight Sublieutenant Cotton was being shot at!

Sidney pushed the stick forward and hedge hopped the Breguet all the way back to Dunkirk. The aircraft had not been hit but his nerves were shattered.

The Germans were becoming more bold and were bombing targets in broad daylight. On the afternoon of 19 March 1916 a mixed formation of Friederichshafen, Hansa-Brandenburg, and Gotha bombers crossed the English Channel to bomb the coastal towns of Dover, Deal and Ramsgate.

The Gotha was a large plywood aeroplane which could mount no less than four defensive guns including one that covered its blind spot below and to the rear. It was the product of the Gotha Wagon Works which previously had not made aeroplanes but rolling stock for the railways. For an aircraft of its day it was unusually well defended with guns in the nose, belly and amidships. Sidney and his observer Reg Soar were outclassed.

Five minutes after 2 p.m., Sidney's Breguet lumbered into the air, Sidney flying the aircraft from the rear cockpit, his mane of dark hair perilously close to the underside of the torpedo-shaped fuel tank. As the big Gotha headed back across the Channel they gave chase but it was to no avail.

There was one other momentous episode in Sidney's life at the time. He was to invent a flying suit that bore his name—the Sidcot. In some ways it looks like a scuba diver's dry suit and it could be used anywhere to protect the wearer from cold and wet. It was a simple garment and it was strange that no one had thought of it before. In 1916 enclosed cockpits were unheard of and most pilots sat exposed to the icy slipstream. Aircraft engines sprayed castor oil over their pilots and required constant attention.

Cotton had been flying bombing missions into Germany based at an airfield called Ochey near Nancy. He had always preferred to personally supervise the maintenance of his aircraft. The winter of 1916 was bitterly cold. One day he had been tuning the engine, wearing only his old blue overalls, which quickly became smeared with oil and grease. The squadron received word that enemy aircraft were approaching. Cotton did not have time to get into his flying suit, and took off in his greasy overalls. Curiously, when they landed back at the airfield, the rest of the squadron were frozen stiff but Cotton was quite warm. 'I concluded that my overalls, which were thick with oil and grease, must have acted as an airtight bag and kept the body heat in,' he said.

On his next leave in London Cotton called on the outfitters, Robinson and Cleaver, with the design for a flying suit. A lining of thin fur, a layer of airproof silk and an outside layer of waterproof cotton. There were deep pockets below the knees and the neck, and the cuffs were lined with fur to keep the warm air from escaping. The Sidcot became *de rigueur* with bomber pilots who flew longer, higher and colder missions. Thousands were sold to the Royal Flying Corps and the Royal Naval Air Service but Cotton never made a cent out of his invention. The popular story is that Baron Manfred Von Richthofen, the famous Red Baron, was wearing a Sidcot suit on his last mission. Had he successfully patented it the suit could have made Sidney a tidy sum. But his father, the redoubtable A. J., had drilled it into his children that they were never to be war profiteers.

When he recovered from his illness Sid requested to be transferred to the newly formed No. 3 Naval Squadron this time based at Luxueil les Bains about fifty miles from the German and Swiss borders. The pilots were almost all Canadians and included the flying ace Raymond Collishaw from British Columbia who distinguished himself in both world wars. Sidney enjoyed the company of the easy going Canucks and felt at home with them. He did not feel so favourably inclined to some of the British officers.

No. 3 Wing was to make eighteen raids over Germany in the nine months between July 1916 and April the following year. By now Sidney was flying the more advanced Sopwith One and Half strutter which came in both fighter and bomber versions.

In 1916 dropping bombs from an aeroplane was a gift rather than a science. There was no way of accurately aiming the bombs and it would be years before they were carried internally. They were instead strung on the outside of the fuselage in a device which looked like a pipe rack. The noses of the bombs hung downwards and the stems protruded up through the holes. A pin was stuck through each stem which rested across the hole. There was a piece of string attached to it.

To launch the weapon you pulled the string. The fuses were always armed so if a bomb vibrated out of its rack while the aircraft was sitting on the ground the results could be catastrophic. Only later did bombs have to fall some distance to release the firing pin by the revolution of a vane in the tail.

Armed with this formidable armament, Sidney sallied forth to go spikebozzling the Germans. To spikebozzle was a verb coined by another pioneer flyer, and it meant to thwart and ultimately destroy. As it happened, Sidney's bombs very nearly destroyed him.

Fifty aircraft from the wing attacked the Mauser gun factory in Stuttgart. It was a long journey, deep into Germany and meant crossing the Vosges mountains which were nearly five thousand feet high in places. Sidney's engine was faltering and he found that he had to fly between the peaks rather than over the top of them. The little machine cleared the lofty Ballon de Guebwiller, but was perilously close to the dense pine forest.

As he cleared the mountains, guns opened up on him. The engine was still faltering so the only sensible thing to do was to turn back. It was just as well. A few seconds later the engine sputtered to a halt and Sidney put down in a field. The bombs, attached to their bits of string and wire were still on board. Terrified, he undid his straps and threw himself over the side of the aircraft. In thirty seconds, he had placed a good distance between himself and the aircraft but miraculously the bombs did not explode. The raid was a disaster. Fifty planes had taken part but only thirteen were to return. Most of the crews were taken prisoner.

But on a later raid Sidney was lucky to avoid being captured himself. The Saar Valley was the industrial heartland of Alsace-Lorraine which was to be the subject of a tug of war between Germany and France in two world wars. Sidney's squadron had been told to attack an industrial town called Thionville, but the weather was bad and the formation got lost in the fog. He found himself flying alone and decided to drop his bombs on a factory and head for home.

The fog got worse until Sidney was flying close to the tree tops. He kept on flying south and finally found himself over what he thought was a friendly airfield. Sideslipping the frail craft onto the grass he landed and taxied towards a couple of parked aircraft. As he got closer to them he saw that the tails bore not the red, white and blue roundel of the Royal Naval Air Service but the Iron Cross of the Imperial German Air Force. Sidney had landed behind enemy lines! Whether the Germans were on their guard or not they seemed not to notice. Sidney gunned the throttle and took off again finally landing on an airfield fifty miles south of his home base, Ochey.

Sidney was young and fit and like other pilots enjoyed the privileges of being an officer, albeit a junior one. The pilots ate good Alsace food; cabbage hotpots, liver and dumplings, and pike braised in champagne. They drank the local Alsatian wines and when they could afford it imbibed the insidiously attractive *framboise*, a brandy made from raspberries. Sidney said: 'If you have to fight a war you might as well fight it in France.'

But a gentleman's war? Not really. It was a romantic notion falling out of the sky in a machine built of rag, wires and tubing. When you hit the ground you were just as dead as those in the trenches.

When the pilots returned from their missions they went to the bar and Sidney usually joined them. But Sidney did not drink; he did not like it. He would be generous in buying a round of drinks and would sit all night with one glass of wine hoping that no one would notice he had not touched it. His fellow officers respected Cotton as a fine pilot, but they were aware he was no drinker. Surreptitiously he could be seen watering the aspidistra. 'Someone has to keep a clear head in this business,' he said, when offered another glass.

But not to drink was not to be like other pilots so Sid carried a small pewter hip flask from which he would occasionally take a swig. It was full of a brown liquid which could be mistaken for brandy but was in fact cold tea. 'Looks the same,' he said, 'and tastes just as good.'

Sidney's hip flask travelled with him in the pocket of his Sidcot suit. It had a bullet mark on it. Whether or not it saved his life is hard to say, but he never went anywhere without it.

The ceaseless raids were starting to take a physical toll on Sidney. His eyesight had never been very good; he had worn glasses ever since his teens. Now his ears were to give him trouble.

Sidney was fortunate in that he was to fly both bombers and fighters. Moving to No. 8 Naval Fighter Squadron at Couderquerque again, he transferred to the brilliant new fighter, the Sopwith Pup. This had been developed by the designer Herbert Smith from a personal aircraft flown by Sopwith's chief test pilot, the Australian Harry Hawker. The Pup was armed with a single .303 Vickers gun firing through the propeller. It was highly manoeuvrable and Sidney found it a delight to fly. He did not have to wait long to test the aircraft in combat. For some weeks the airfield had been attacked at dusk and dawn by a lone German bomber, a Taube.

'I got very tired of this so I decided to intercept him,' said Sidney.

To get in a position to attack the German he needed height so he decided to take the Pup high above the German and lie in wait. The little Pup took the best part of an hour to climb to 18 000 feet. Sidney's breathing became laboured and his fingernails turned blue. He thought that by taking it slowly like a mountain climber he would get used to the thin air but it was hard going. Today pilots would be breathing bottled oxygen from 14 000 feet.

Sidney saw the German aircraft beneath him and pulled the Pup over into a dive. Almost immediately he passed out. When he came to, the aircraft was spinning rapidly and he was only 3000 feet from the ground. He kicked the rudder bar and banged the stick hard over to the left. After what seemed an eternity the nose of the little aeroplane came up and Sidney could see the horizon. He was shaking with a combination of cold and terror, blood was pouring from his nose and ears, and the whites of his eyes were crimson with broken blood vessels. One of his ears hurt like hell. The Sopwith was a fine aircraft but it was vicious in the spin and unforgiving to novices.

The medical officer later confirmed that Sidney had perforated an eardrum and ordered him back to England. There would be no flying for a while, so Sidney was delegated to prepare a large Handley Page O/400 bomber for a secret mission to the island of

Lemnos in the Aegean. This was a long way to go for an aeroplane so the element of surprise was vital.

The mission was a success. The big bomber covered the distance in fifty-five flying hours and bombed the city of Constantinople (Istanbul) and two German warships. Sidney was flattered to learn that the crew had worn his Sidcot suits for the mission, but that they had complained that in the scorching heat of a Greek spring, they had sweated gallons!

From Hendon, Sidney was posted again, this time to Great Yarmouth in East Anglia and asked to form a special unit. Its task—to bomb Berlin.

Sidney had persuaded the Admiralty it would be possible to bomb the German capital from the base at Bacton using specially modified DH-4 bombers. Berlin was more about five hundred miles, a formidable distance in a single engined aircraft, so it was decided that after the machines had bombed their target they were to overfly Germany and land in Russia.

Sidney considered that the Rolls Royce Eagle engines that were fitted as standard were too thirsty for the Berlin flight, so he had Napier engines installed. Unfortunately the Napier was prone to overheating, so Sidney had a water tank fitted. When the level in the radiator got low he would top it up with a hand pump.

By the time Sidney's unit was operational, the Admiralty had changed its mind. The aircraft would not be going to Berlin. Instead they were to be used for photographic missions over the German naval base at Wilhelmshaven—a mission which Sidney was later to repeat in World War II.

Only one of the two aircraft had been modified with an extra water tank. But for reasons best known to themselves, the Admiralty decided to use the unmodified one—and send another pilot called Fane on a mission over the Friesian islands. Sidney thought that this was courting disaster and said so to the Top Brass. Commodore Geoffrey Paine, the chief of operations in the Royal Naval Air Service, did not like being told what to do by a junior officer.

'When senior naval officers give orders,' he barked, 'they are to be carried out.' Cotton begged Paine to let him fly the mission in his aircraft, which he was confident would get there and back. Paine refused, sacked Cotton and appointed another officer to take over the unit.

The mission was flown with the unmodifed aircraft and, as Cotton had confidently predicted, the engine overheated and it crashed in the sea. Cotton had been vindicated but Godfrey Paine was not about to admit that he had been wrong.

As far as he was concerned Cotton had disobeyed orders, but he was prepared to offer him another chance. 'I want you to go to Mudros in Greece.' Mudros was an obscure aerodrome on the east coast of the island of Lemnos in Greece which had been the staging post for the bombing mission on Constantinople. It might just as well have been Timbuktu as far as Sidney was concerned.

'No, sir,' said Sidney. 'You have my resignation here and now.' His long camel face longer than ever, Cotton gave a smart salute, turned on his heel and left the room.

He knew that after this outburst he was finished with the Royal Naval Air Service but thought there was a good chance he would be accepted in the Australian Flying Corps which was barely a year old. He had not reckoned with the power of the military and, by the time he returned to Australia, forces had already conspired against him. From the Admiralty in London came a letter which said: 'He is of a difficult temperament and unsuitable for employment in a uniformed service.'

Curiously Sidney's own service record gives no hint of his growing disillusionment with authority. Quite the reverse. His superiors speak of his ability in glowing terms. He had been in the service only nineteen months but had taken to flying like a duck to water.

On 19 February 1916 his flying instructor wrote: 'Good pilot on Maurice Farman, BE 2c cross country. Total time in the air 20 hours 24 minutes. Good mechanical knowledge. Should make a valuable officer when fully trained. Thorough in all his duties. This officer will be a credit to any commanding officer.'

By January 1917 when Sidney had converted onto the more advanced Sopwith Pup, his instructor wrote: 'Ability to command good. Clever pilot. Sound knowledge of his machine.'

And again in April at Hendon: 'Very good ability to command and take charge of men. Strongly recommended for promotion.'

Even so, on 9 September 1917 he put forward a submission for the termination of his appointment:

'He himself does not consider he is fit for flying and objects on grounds of defective eyesight.'

Sidney was short-sighted but his eyes weren't bad enough to stop him flying an aeroplane. Or for that matter, finding a wife.

Sidney had always been awkward with girls. He found it difficult to make small talk, hated socialising, did not drink and could not dance. The only song he knew was *God Save the King*. For years he had been fond of a girl called Olive Mort whose family owned a property near Hidden Vale. They corresponded regularly but while he was in England she wrote to tell him she would not be writing again.

Cooling his heels in London waiting for a boat back to Australia Sidney agreed to go to the theatre with an English friend, David Plaistowe. They went to the Golders Green Empire to see a stage play called *The Enemy Within* and among the cast was a striking Scottish actress. From his seat in the circle Sidney looked with interest not at the principal members of the cast but a quiet girl with a bit part.

She went under her stage name of Joan MacLean but her full name was Regmor Agnes Joan Morvaren MacLean. Sidney, smitten like an Edwardian stage door Johnny asked her to join him at supper, Plaistowe playing gooseberry. A month later on 16 October 1917 Sidney and Joan were married at Camberwell Register Office. She was seventeen, he was twenty-three. The marriage was to last three years. A picture taken at the time during a trip back to

Australia shows Joan and Sidney standing on the steps of their house at Mintoburn in Tasmania. She looks very young, a pretty face topped by a bob of dark hair. Sidney, handsome in his naval uniform is at least a head taller. Behind them both is Sidney's mother, a hand on his shoulder.

The relationship did not get off to good start. A great many of the troubles in Sidney Cotton's life revolved around money. Making it, losing it, spending it, or giving it away. Sid's Scots bride thought that he was rolling in it. In fact on their way back to Australia to meet the family they ran out of money in America and Sidney had to cable his father to send some more. 'She said she had understood that I had plenty of money—an innocent remark no doubt but it put the damper on things.' Whether this later placed a strain on the marriage it is hard to say but none of Sidney Cotton's three wives were ever to receive a regular income from him. Sidney was either spending money like water or flat broke.

When Sidney and his new bride returned to Australia there was no prospect of a career in aviation so he returned to the land. His father had bought a summer home, Mintoburn at Kettering near Hobart in Tasmania, which stood in an apple orchard of 200 acres. It included a factory with equipment to produce dried apples.

Sidney's father offered him the house, the factory, his yacht and a new car if he offered to stay in Australia. Sid threw himself into the job even though his heart wasn't in it and managed to pull off a few successful coups. One of them was a contract with IXL the jam manufacturer for 500 tons of dried fruit. He then devised a way of making apple jelly from the skins and cores which had previously been fed to the pigs. Sidney however could not see how the venture was worth more than £5000 a year.

'I had big ideas, and this wasn't enough for me.'

One of his get-rich-quick schemes was to buy up properties, subdivide them and mortgage them to small farmers. This inevitably was to bring Sidney into conflict with his father, who thought that the scheme would bring the Cotton name into disrepute.There were furious rows, Sidney finally threatening to return to England unless he got his own way. When he went back to Hidden Vale, Alfred Cotton hardly spoke to him. His mother took him on one side and advised him to make a life for himself elsewhere. Sidney was torn between two worlds but England offered more than Australia.

Alfred was just as obstinate as his eldest son but when he saw that Sidney's mind was made up he agreed to drive him to the railway station. Father and son sat side by side in the Cotton car as it rattled over the corrugated dirt track, Joan sitting glumly in the back with the suitcases. The train pulled slowly away from the platform but there were no tearful farewells. Alfred J. Cotton did not say goodbye. He was already on his way home. They were not to meet again for four years.

The endless squabbles and bickering had also been deeply depressing for Joan MacLean. Australia was no place to pursue a theatrical career and she was in demand on both sides of the Atlantic. Sidney and his bride were destined never to spend much time together. Sidney was still torn between a career in aviation or going back to the family property, Joan with her career on the stage. Both of them, as it happened, would have to place their careers on hold.

Joan was pregnant. Early in January 1919 they were to have a son who they called Alick John Sidney. In the years that followed Sidney was to see very little of his young son. John was not like other boys; he was a solitary introspective child who many thought was rather strange.

John spent most of his early years being shuttled around between various relatives and when the marriage failed went to live with his mother in America. Sid was not to see him again until he was fourteen when he arranged for him to go out to the family in Australia, to be looked after by Vera. For years, Sidney sent Vera £1000 a month for his upkeep.

Joan and Sidney continued to drift apart and Sidney was only to see her once more before they divorced in 1925.

The end of World War I saw the Australian Prime Minister, William Hughes, in Europe. He had been attending the peace negotiations at Versailles and when he returned to London he decided not to travel by sea but by that novel new device, the aeroplane. Hughes was enthralled by flying and readily saw that it would be a good way of bringing Australia and Europe closer together. He offered a prize of £10 000 for the first flight from England to Australia.

A number of Australian pilots announced their intention of entering the race, among them the fellow Queenslanders Sir Charles Kingsford Smith and Bert Hinkler. Sidney was keen to enter the race himself but first he had to find himself a sponsor—and an aeroplane. He had been offered a job at Napiers, who built engines for aircraft and cars. Napier, one of the greatest of the British thoroughbred engine manufacturers, said they would provide the engines and Boulton and Paul offered to build Sidney an aeroplane. It looked very promising until two other pilots were killed in an aeroplane powered by Napier engines. Napiers promptly decided to close down its aviation department so Sidney was left without a machine.

As it happened Ross and Keith Smith pipped him at the post, flying from England to Australia in twenty-eight days. But there was still South Africa. Sidney knew that an aircraft had been built for an attempt at flying the Atlantic but had not been used. It was an Airco DH-14, a big machine that could carry three passengers and had enough fuel to stay in the air for eighteen hours.

His sponsor was Sir Sefton Brancker a pioneer of early flying in England who was later killed in the crash of the R-101 airship in France. If Sidney succeeded in flying the DH-14 to Capetown, the plane, said Brancker, was his. During World War I, Sidney had become expert at landing aircraft with dead engines. It was just as well because the Cape Town flight was a succession of disasters.

In January 1920, Sidney and his engineer, a man called Townsend, took off from Hendon. They had covered no more than five miles and been in the air for only a few minutes when the oil pressure valve blew out. Sidney was forced to land at the Handley Page aerodrome at Cricklewood in North London, just south of Hendon. They fixed the trouble and started again, this time getting as far as Paris, where once again they made a forced landing with engine trouble. This time Napiers sent a mechanic over from London.

The next hop was to Rome, where once again the aircraft broke down. This time the propeller was loose. When they dismantled the engine they found that a bearing had been starved of oil. It took them two days to repair, and Sidney decided that for the next leg he would make only a short hop to Catania in Sicily, a distance of 325 miles.There was a strong headwind, and after a while it became obvious they would not reach the airfield by dark. Sidney decided to land the aircraft on a beach near Naples.

Above the roar of the engine he shouted to Townsend: 'Tighten your straps. I'm going to put her down.' He made a good landing but when the aircraft ran into soft sand it flipped over onto its back. Sidney and his engineer crawled from the aircraft unhurt. Fortunately he had the presence of mind to turn the fuel off so the aircraft did not catch fire. They made a fire from driftwood and when the local policeman arrived they were drinking tea, Sidney's favourite drink.

The machine was repairable, so they boxed it up in a crate and arranged to have it shipped back to England. Brancker was very sporting about the whole affair and sold Sidney the damaged machine for £500. He even agreed to repair it for nothing. It seemed that Sidney was not cut out for long distance flying. But by the time he returned to England he at least owned an aeroplane.

The DH-14 was to fly again. This was the heyday of air racing in Britain and later that year Sidney entered the aircraft in the Hendon Air Pageant.

## Chapter 4

# Over the Ice

At the conclusion of the Great War, London was full of pilots looking for work. The aeroplane had been an amusing novelty at the onset of the war, but by 1918 aeroplanes were going faster, further and higher than ever before and their commercial potential was not lost on many entrepreneurs. One of them was a Canadian called Major Trevor Clayton Kennedy.

In June 1920 he placed an advertisement in *The Aeroplane* magazine. It read: 'Pilots wanted, plenty of risk, good pay'. To a man like Cotton, it was the words 'plenty of risk' that leapt from the page. In 1920, flying was dangerous enough. Aviation it was said was not itself inherently dangerous but was terribly unforgiving of any carelessness. The graveyards were full of careless aviators.

Clayton Kennedy wanted a special breed of pilot to fly in one of the most hostile countries in the world: Newfoundland.

Aviation had arrived in Newfoundland only the year before.

As the nearest jumping off point to cross the Atlantic it had attracted numerous flyers: John Alcock and Arthur Whitten Brown, both British, in their Vickers Vimy bomber; Harry Hawker, the Australian and his Canadian navigator Kenneth Mackenzie Grieve; Raynham and Morgan in their Martinsyde. All were competing for the $10 000 prize offered by the British *Daily Mail* for the first crossing of the Atlantic.

Newfoundland is fog, cod and fornication, a big empty windswept place, lashed by gales in summer and snowbound in winter. It is often wreathed in mist, caused by the mingling of the warm waters of the Gulf Stream and the cold waters of the Labrador current. Great forests of spruce and pine cover the inland which are full of wandering caribou and moose. Its rivers are teeming with salmon. The communities have strange names—Quidi Vidi (which locals called Kitty Vitty), Conception, Paradise, Botwood.

But one of Newfoundland's best commercial enterprises lay offshore on the winter ice—the scores of seals which could be easily harvested by men with harpoons or guns or clubs. They made no attempt to flee and lolled around on the ice. They were butchered in their thousands and their pelts turned into coats, gloves and shoes.

Post war, Sidney's flying activities had been comfortable, puttering in and out of green English meadows, socialising at the flying club and drinking tea. Nothing was to prepare him for the privation that was Newfoundland. Now he was being asked to fly from frozen lakes and snow-covered fields. Sid met Clayton Kennedy in London who said that he had a contract to organise and operate a seal-spotting service in Newfoundland. This involved long flights over the freezing ocean in an aircraft with only one engine. The winters would be harsh, the flying dangerous, the pay erratic.

Lounging at the bar of the Royal Aero Club in Piccadilly, Sidney's fellow pilots told him it was madness. Why go to this colonial hell-hole when he could stay in England and get a comfortable job flying for one of the newly formed airline companies? But Sidney could not resist the challenge. He would even, he said, provide his own aircraft. Clayton Kennedy already had access to two De Havilland 9 biplanes but Cotton thought they would be unsuitable for long-range work over the sea. The DH-9 had been originally designed as a day bomber. More than four thousand had been built but its performance was at best mediocre and the aircraft suffered from constant engine failures. In fact many bombing raids using these aircraft had had to be aborted. An engine failure over water could not be countenanced. Also the De Havilland had an open cockpit so the pilot stood the risk of freezing to death before he could accomplish his mission.

Sidney instead had his eyes set on the Westland Limousine III, a bigger aeroplane than the De Havilland. The pilot was still exposed to the elements but was better shielded from the icy wind and there was an enclosed cabin seating another five people. The aircraft was powered by a Napier Lion engine. Westlands was a relatively small aircraft manufacturer but Sidney was confident that the big cabin biplane would prove suitable for the job and carry its passengers in a reasonable degree of comfort.

Sidney planned to leave for Newfoundland at the end of 1920 to be operational for the seal hunt in the spring of 1921. Accompanied by his second pilot David Plaistowe and two rigger-cum-mechanics named Wallace and Cleaver, Sidney left Liverpool on 5 November for St Johns on board the SS *Digby*.

Cotton chose the port of Botwood as the base for his operations. It was north-west of St Johns near the towns of Grand Falls and Bishops Falls and used by the ships of the Anglo Development Company.

Botwood was ideal for air operations both winter and summer and was within an hour's flying time to where the seals were usually found. The flights would take him over New World and Fogo islands and out into the Atlantic beyond Brenton Rock.

During the summer the aircraft would operate on floats and take off from the water; in winter when the water froze they would use skis. Sidney was to get used to hearing a new sound—clink clink clink. It was so cold that even walking in rubber-soled boots on the snow sounded as if someone was walking on steel sheets with boots shod in steel. The snow deadened everything but you could hear people walking from a long way away.

Seal spotting from the air was a visionary scheme but dogged from the outset by lack of funds. Clayton Kennedy, who Sid described as 'small, neat, well dressed, quick witted and a fast talker' had managed to talk his bank into an overdraft but this was dependent on him getting an up-front payment of £25 000 from the sealing companies at the start of the season.

Sidney's enthusiasm for the scheme was not shared by the captains of the sealing ships who regarded aeroplanes with suspicion. Sidney felt that if he could prove to the sealing companies in the first year that seal spotting could be done successfully, contracts in future years would be assured. He finally succeeded in getting a contract but at a reduced price. The companies were still sceptical and drove a hard bargain. They also took over Clayton Kennedy's bank overdraft.

When the seal spotting venture had first been mooted it had been suggested that airships were used instead of aeroplanes.

The Newfoundland government had been given two airships by the British government at the end of the war and a huge amount of equipment languished at Botwood; there were four airship cars, five airship envelopes, two travelling hydrogen plants, one stationary hydrogen plant, two large motor lorries, one travelling workshop, one large airship hangar frame with sufficient corrugated iron to cover it, a motor-driven hydrogen-compressing outfit and an assortment of other items all valued at £70 000.

Sidney wanted none of it. Airships performed best in still air. They were severely disadvantaged by strong winds, and Newfoundland was notorious for its gales.

The days of hydrogen-filled airships were in any case numbered. The R-101 disaster and the crash of the Hindenburg were to pave the way for heavier-than-air machines.

As soon as he took over the enterprise Sidney dispensed with the airship group except for one man: the radio operator, Bill Heath.

The sealing ships were due to sail within three weeks so time was of the essence. The Westland needed special benzole-petrol fuel which had to be brought by rail from St Johns, but a snowstorm blocked the track. Sidney decided to fuel the aircraft with motor spirit instead and lived to regret it. On a test flight, the engine failed and Sidney had to force land on the ice. It was to be the first of many engine failures. The Westland's engine had been damaged by using the low octane fuel, so new engine parts were ordered from England.

In the meantime, Sidney reluctantly decided to use the DH-9 which was fitted with home-made skis. The plane was of World War I vintage, and had a low powered 240 horse power Armstrong Siddeley Puma engine and in Sidney's opinion it was quite unsuitable for seal spotting.

It was however suitable for delivering mail. While awaiting his spares, Sid won a small contract with the Post Office to deliver mail from Botwood to the islands in Notre Dame Bay. He would fly over the islands and drop the mail without landing. So even though the seal spotting operation had not yet returned a profit Sidney had the distinction of flying the first airmail in Newfoundland.

The sealing ships meanwhile were already in the icefields and preparing to sail home. The spares for the Westland's engine arrived and were hastily installed. Sidney took off with a veteran sealing captain on board but had to turn back with radiator trouble. Repairs were made and he took off again, this time with only Bill Heath on board. Once again the engine failed six miles out and Sidney force-landed on the ice. David Plaistowe, Cotton's second pilot, flew after them in the DH-9 and towed the Westland back across the ice. This time the engine was damaged beyond repair so Sidney's first year of seal spotting came to a dismal end.

In May, Sidney returned to England to get the damaged engine overhauled. Before he left he went to St John's to see the owners of the sealing ships. They were not convinced that aeroplanes could do the job but were impressed with Sidney's drive and enthusiasm and agreed that he should try again in the next season.

The seal spotting operation was short of cash but Cotton's luck was about to change. In England he met a wealthy private pilot called Alan Butler who agreed to invest up to £100 000 in the venture.

Cotton's ambition was not limited to the seal operation. He proposed airmail and passenger flights and aerial surveys. He bought another aircraft a Martinsyde Type A which like the Westland had an open cockpit for the pilot and an enclosed cabin seating four passengers.

He hired a new engineer, J. R. Stannard, and a former RFC pilot, Sydney Bennett, as co-pilot. Bennett was the son of Sir John Bennett, the Colonial Secretary, who had acted as adviser to the sealing companies. Cotton sought and received support and encouragement from the Air Ministry and major players in the aviation business like Rolls Royce and Vickers. In November 1921, he shipped $30 000 worth of equipment from England to Botwood.

He set up his own company, the Aerial Survey Company with a capital of $100 000. He then asked the Newfoundland government to sell him selected items from the airship material at Botwood. He bought quantities of rubberised airship fabric and used it to make engine covers for his aircraft so the engines did not freeze in winter.

In a letter to the Prime Minister of Newfoundland on 12 October 1921 Sidney laid out his plans for the future and detailed the equipment the company owned: 'At Botwood one six seater Westland aeroplane; one three seater DH-9 aeroplane with Siddeley Puma engine plus spare engine, spares and tools; one large wooden shed which was being altered to take two more planes. Being shipped from England: One Martinsyde four seater enclosed cabin aeroplane with Rolls Royce engine fitted with skis and floats; one rebuilt Napier engine for the Westland; six sets of skis; large supply of spare parts.'

Despite the fact that Sidney was better prepared than the year before, the sealing companies were still lukewarm about using aircraft. They did not turn him down but said they would wait and see what he could report in the 1922 season and then discuss the contract. Cotton accepted this decision reluctantly. The sealing season was months away and he had aircraft sitting idle on the ground. It was clear that he needed to earn some money.

He got some more contracts to fly mail from St John's to Halifax, Nova Scotia, a distance of about five hundredf miles. They had planned to use the Martinsyde but the ski broke through the ice and the undercarriage was damaged. Sid decided to use the DH-9, and so on 10 December 1921 he and Syd Bennett took off on another first . . . the first airmail run from Newfoundland to Nova Scotia.

'We soon ran into bad weather but were coming through it well enough and had covered about a hundred miles when suddenly we saw water seeping from the cylinder head of the engine,' wrote Sid.

They landed near Deer Lake in western Newfoundland and found that the water-retaining ring in the top of the cylinder head had perished. A new part was sent out from Botwood, but after they had fitted it, the engine refused to start. The two pilots spent all day pulling the propeller through against compression. Late in the afternoon they were still at it with Bennett sitting in the cockpit and Sidney standing in front of the engine.

Sidney was on the point of giving up when the engine fired. He fell into the propeller and was thrown to the ground. The propeller hit Sidney on both elbows, causing excruciating pain. He found that he had lost the use of his arms. On examination he was found to have extensive bruising, but he had got off lightly. Not too many pilots had been struck by a revolving propeller and lived to tell the tale. He was taken to the hospital in St. John's for treatment and was laid up for several weeks. The accident was not enough to stop Sidney conducting business from his hospital bed. He tried to renew negotiations with the sealing companies but was once again rejected, although he did manage to get another contract to fly mail.

Meanwhile Bennett waited to fly the aircraft back from Deer Lake. The sacks of mail were unloaded from the aircraft and taken to the nearby railway station. Depressingly for Sid, the letters the aircraft was carrying reached their final destination by rail and steamer and not by air.

The de Havilland was doomed never to return to Botwood in one piece. Flying the aircraft back the engine failed again and Bennett had to force land it on soft snow. Bennett and his mechanic were flung into a snowdrift and escaped unhurt, but the aircraft was a write-off.

In Newfoundland in 1921 it was impossible to insure aircraft for this type of flying so there was no insurance to collect. Sidney had never thought much of the DH-9 but even so it was another setback that he could have well have done without. A black and white newsreel film taken in 1923 gives no clue as to how difficult the Newfoundland days were. Sidney's little fleet of aircraft are seen wobbling uncertainly across the ice, the crude skis attached to the spoked wheels. Sidney in a dark suit and tie with calf length flying boots strides from the aircraft and shakes hands with Stannard then stands there looking boyish and full of energy.

It was the new year when Sidney finally left hospital. By this time the Martinsyde had been repaired and Sidney flew it to St John's to the new hangar at Quidi Vidi Lake. But the sealing companies were still not persuaded that aeroplanes had any practical value.

In desperation, Sidney offered to do the job on the basis that they would pay him a dollar a seal over an eighty per cent shipload. For less than that they would pay nothing. The answer came back: Still No Deal.

Sidney realised that in order to make his sales pitch he had to find the seals from the air and guide the ships to find them. A show was required. Traditionally, when the sealing ships ventured out to sea they would sail as far as they could to the seal packs before being immobilised by ice. Then the sealers would go by foot across the ice floes armed with harpoons and clubs.

In the first week of March 1923 he decided to take his message to the seal captains—that aeroplanes were not flimsy inefficient machines but a practical tool.

Cotton decided to do something that no one had ever done before: land an aeroplane alongside one of the sealing ships as it lay entrapped in the ice. The vessel was the SS *Sagona*. This was dangerous flying. From the air a pilot had to judge the surface of the ice. If it was frozen solid and not covered in snow it was perfectly possible to land an aircraft with wheels so long as some air was let out of the tyres. If, however, the aircraft was fitted with skis it was necessary to establish the depth of the snow—a light covering of snow on top of the ice floes was dangerous in the extreme. An aircraft encountering crosswinds could skid and ground loop.

Cotton made a perfect landing alongside the ship and then delivered the crew's mail and discussed the position of the seals with the captain. This was the first time that anyone had done this. The captains were impressed and they radioed the owners asking for regular mail deliveries. The owners were still evasive. It seemed the information that Cotton could provide might not be valuable in a good season when the ships made good catches anyway, but in a bad season it might be very valuable indeed.

A week before the sealing season ended Cotton flew out in the Martinsyde with Stannard, located the fleet and ten miles north-east of the ships found a big herd of seals. He flew back to St Johns and said he had found the main herd but even then the companies would not offer him a contract! They wanted corroboration from the seal ships. If the information was correct only then would they discuss a contract.

Cotton's information was no good to him unless he could sell it, so he took the chance and revealed it to the companies, together with the ice conditions and the route the ships would have to take to get through the gaps in the pack ice. The ships were informed but they ignored Cotton's advice. They became trapped in the ice and could not reach the seals.

Cotton made a claim against the sealing companies for his services. Finally in May 1922 they grudgingly paid him $2000—ten cents for every seal sighted.

It was reckoned that 20 000 seals were taken as a result of that flight. But overall Sidney's relations with the sealing companies had not been good and he hoped for better in the 1923 season. In the meantime, summer was coming and he had idle aeroplanes.

In May Sidney sailed again for England and signed a contract with a mapmaking firm that was to prove a turning point in his career. He was engaged to take a series of aerial photographs of parts of Newfoundland so that they could revise their maps. He already had two other contracts: one with a Welsh coal mining company for a large quantity of timber pit props, the other with the Anglo Newfoundland Development Company for an aerial survey of their timber holdings in Newfoundland.

Cotton had realised that when you took pictures from the air it wasn't easy to hide things. There were no roads into the forests and travel overland was difficult and time consuming. Aerial pictures could show you where new sources of timber were. They could also show you troop movements, airfields and munitions factories.

Sidney became adept at flying the aircraft and taking photographs at the same time. He would hold the stick in between his legs and then hoist the big plate camera over the side of the cockpit and click away. Once the aircraft struck a violent updraft and the camera went over the side.

He had already taken pictures of his first military target. In 1921, the British cruiser HMS *Raleigh* had run aground off Belle Isle with its full complement of men and guns. Most of the six hundred crew were saved but Cotton circling overhead had taken pictures from the DH-4. Mountainous waves were crashing over the superstructure and the cruiser's fifteen-inch guns. The pictures were excellent quality and Sidney could have probably got a good price from the newspapers and the Admiralty. However, when he had flown some of the officers who had escaped from the stricken vessel down to St Johns he mentioned that he had the photographs. They were immediately confiscated by the Navy. Sidney was furious.

During the winter of 1921, Cotton had become interested in the west coast of Newfoundland. Now that he had the pit prop contract he decided to set up an operation at Hawkes Bay, which was within easy reach of Labrador. He and Alan Butler formed the Hawkes Bay Trading Company. The idea was to establish an aeroplane base for handling mail and supplies during the winter, and cut and transport timber during the summer.

They engaged timber experts from Canada and felling began in May 1922. Hawkes Bay became a hive of industry and at summer's end the pit props were being loaded on two ships bound for Wales. Cotton and Butler now had five aeroplanes based at Botwood. During the winter of 1922–23 Cotton and Syd Bennett flew the mail run from Botwood using the original Westland Limousine. But relations were souring between him and Butler.

Butler was independently wealthy and was only interested in the flying side of the business. Cotton was keen to make money. In the end they decided to go their separate ways. Butler took Hawkes Bay and the timber business while Sidney took up the aerial survey and communications side.

Sidney was not keen to dissolve the partnership; he always believed that there was a great future in Newfoundland for both sides of the business.

But the indifference of the Newfoundland government to Sidney's initiative was heartbreaking. Realistically, there was a lot of money tied up in the mail business, using traditional methods like steamers and dog teams. Many businessmen were not keen to let the young Australian get part of the action.

The Newfoundland government was spending nearly a million dollars a year distributing the mails by steamer in summer and dog teams in winter. Sidney offered to do the job for half the cost. The offer was rejected. 'Their objection, I discovered, was political,' he wrote. 'If they took the business away from the steamers and dog teams they might lose votes.'

In secret, Sidney had discussions with a high profile government official. 'This exalted public servant offered to get me the exclusive flying rights to Newfoundland for twenty-five years if I would give him ten per cent interest in my company.'

Sidney was not yet thirty years of age and had accomplished more in his life than men twice as old. The new lesson was a hard one to learn. 'This incensed me. I was young, and I hadn't yet heard of baksheesh,' he wrote.

Early in 1923, Sidney made one last attempt to get a sealing contract. He suggested that a small aeroplane could be carried on board one of the ships and used for local searches by operating off the ice close to the ships. Sidney meanwhile would continue to make long range flights from the land using one of the Martinsydes. He persuaded the government to meet half the cost and bought a small Avro 554. It was called the *Atlantic Baby* and had been built for Sir Ernest Shackleton's last Antarctic expedition two years earlier. Shackleton had died in Georgia, the expedition had returned and the Avro was for sale. Sidney purchased the aeroplane in England and brought over a pilot and an engineer to operate it. But the antagonism of the skipper and the crew had not diminished, and although the aircraft was carried on the ship, it was not used. To Cotton's disbelief, the pilot he had hired did no flying at all and worked as an ordinary sealer during the voyage! It was the last straw.

Sidney's morale was at its lowest ebb but he decided to make one more flight. It nearly cost him his life.

Sidney was alone in the freezing cockpit of the Martinsyde two hundred miles from land when the engine began to run rough. He was losing height and it seemed inevitable that once again he would have to force land on the ice. This time it was serious. No one knew where he was or what route he had taken and he was carrying no radio. The prospect of freezing to death on the ice floes stared him in the face. The big Napier engine coughed and spluttered and Sidney gloomily considered his fate.

Sidney vowed that if he got back alive he would give up the seal spotting and if he still could not get support from the goverment he would leave Newfoundland for good. Sidney made it back safely to Botwood. He went to Canada and sold his five aircraft. By August 1923 he had moved anything that was transportable out of Newfoundland.

The rest he turned over to his old business partner Alan Butler. The wooden hangars which they had spent so much time and energy in assembling were left behind to rot, the tarpaper roofs flapping in the cold wind. Sidney had been three years in Newfoundland and it had all come to nothing.

Perhaps Newfoundland was not quite ready for the aeroplane after all.

When Sidney's spirits had been at their lowest ebb he had failed to recognise a business opportunity that could have made him millions—and it was nothing to do with flying.

On one of his frequent trips into the interior he had made friends with an eccentric fur trapper who had asked him to stay for dinner. It was in the depths of winter and the snow was piled high against the slab walls of the log cabin. The meal was modest; steak and potatoes, and beer, which Sidney accepted and when his host's back was turned poured down a crack in the floorboards.

Sidney was astonished when his host filled his plate with fresh peas. How, he asked, was it possible to provide fresh vegetables in winter? He explained that he filled his baby's washbasin with salted water, put the peas in it and exposed it to the Arctic wind and even months later they tasted as good as when they were picked. The man's name was Clarence Birdseye. Later on, he moved back to the United States and sold his business to the Postum company for $US22 million. It became known as General Foods.

Sidney's aerial survey company was worth more as a going

concern than in liquidation. After he had paid his debts he was left with $US25 000. So in the summer of 1923, Sidney found himself strolling the streets of New York, and looking for a new adventure. It would be two years before he would set foot again in the cockpit of a plane. He had proved that he could fly a plane in Newfoundland, and if you could fly there you could probably fly anywhere.

But one other major event had happened in Newfoundland. Sidney had fallen in love again. Her name was Millicent Joan Henry and she was the daughter of a geologist.

It is half past ten in Perth, Ontario, and Millicent Joan Henry, once Joan Cotton and now Joan Hopkinson, is having a gin and tonic.

A bullfinch flies around the flower baskets on the balcony. Below, the churchgoers wave to her as they park their cars and and invite them to join her later at the afternoon service. She declines. At ninety-four she is closer to God than they are and was never much of a churchgoer anyway. She is reliving the first meeting with Sidney Cotton in 1923 at Hawkes Bay in Newfoundland. She was fifteen, he was twenty-eight. He was tall and handsome, the intrepid aviator.

She had pale blue eyes and long blonde hair down to her waist, a tomboy who loved the hills and rivers of this wild and empty island. She was a natural with animals; she would catch salmon using the feathers from her mother's hat for flies. At dusk she would sit by the lake and mimic the sad haunting cry of the loon.

'I was a young silly thing. I ran around in the backwoods wearing moccasins and a pair of my father's linen trousers.' The family, says Joan, was broke. 'We had nothing to eat apart from the rabbits I trapped and the fish I caught.'

Joan had no formal education and the only schooling she received was from her mother. 'So Sidney bought me for $2000 because Mum and Dad were broke. They had to go back to England somehow and the whole idea was that I had to go too.' Sidney's version is more altruistic than calculating. 'I thought it a great shame that such an attractive and intelligent girl should not have a better opportunity for education,' he wrote.

But there was no doubt that at the back of his mind he planned to marry her when she was old enough. Sidney placed her in a private school in Bournemouth on the south coast of England. Joan hated it. Bournemouth was a gentile seaside resort which made its money from the newly wed or the nearly dead.

It was a good place to die, full of retirement homes and old soldiers in wheelchairs. This was no place for a girl who could tame huskies and mimic the cry of the loon. Joan felt awkward in her blue tunic and sensible shoes and loathed and detested her rigid English school. At night in the dormitory she dreamed of the time when she could return to Newfoundland.

Sidney threw her a lifeline. It was called marriage. In 1926, when she was eighteen, they married at the Hanover Square registry office in London. This marriage was to last until 1944, but Joan was to see very little of Sidney for most of that time.

She takes a sip of her drink and twirls the ice in her glass. 'I was a silly little thing, but then you don't know anything when you are eighteen. A stronger woman would have sunk him.'

Now married, Sidney might have invested the money left from the Newfoundland adventure in a house or some other sort of security but seemed averse to any sort of permanent home.

He was always quick to recognise a good idea when he saw one so he decided to invest in the patents market. He now toured cities in America picking up inventions which might be developed in Britain. One of these was a snow tractor built by a company in Detroit. Instead of caterpillar tracks it was fitted with two rotating drums with blades attached to them. As it moved forwards it screwed itself through the snow.

Sidney had one of the machines shipped to Newfoundland so he could take it on a test drive in the snow. Joan went with him, and they drove it from Deer Lake to Bonne Bay on the west coast dragging a sled behind them with their tents and equipment. Every time they stopped at a lumber camp they would put on a sales demonstration. The drive took them a down a rough track covered in deep snow. At one point the track gave way and the tractor tilted over, dragging Sidney's foot into the revolving drum. Fortunately the rotating knives had missed his foot but it was crushed between the drum and the chassis.

Sidney was in incredible pain. Joan cut away his trousers and sealskin boot and wrapped the foot in a blanket. 'He stood it for about fifteen minutes then he fainted with the pain.' Fortunately for them both the mailman came by on the dog sled. Joan persuaded him to take Sidney into Lomond, the nearest lumber camp. When they unwrapped the foot they found it to be so swollen they could not see his toes. He was ten days at the lumber camp before they dared move him down to St Johns, and then by ship to New York. The foot healed of its own accord. When it was X-rayed it was discovered that the bones had knit by themselves. Sidney however had to wear a metal brace for a while afterwards. It was only when he started flying aeroplanes again that he took the brace off.

In 1926, Sidney went back to Australia to show his new wife off to the family. Annie, Sidney's mother, had been paralysed by a stroke and had been moved to the family's summer home at Mintoburn in Tasmania. At one time she had not been expected to live but she rallied at the prospect of Sidney coming home.

Alfred had tried to persuade Sidney to come back to live in Australia to help run the Brunette Downs project. With the scheme collapsed there was nothing to keep Sidney in Australia. Relations between father and son had always been strained and Sidney knew it would never work. When Sidney and Joan left to go back to Canada he knew he would probably never see his mother again. She could not speak or move her limbs but as the couple drove away she lifted herself up on the verandah rail for one last look.

She died less than a year later.

In 1919 the Atlantic had been successfully flown from west to east. The Englishmen, Alcock and Brown had flown the Vickers Vimy from Newfoundland and crash-landed in a bog on the west coast of Ireland. But no one had yet flown it the other way—let alone between Paris and New York. Two Frenchmen, Charles Nungesser and Francois Coli were to try.

Nungesser was a handsome muscular youth who loved boxing, swimming and racing motorbikes. He had a distinguished career as a pilot in World War I and had won a chestful of medals. Four years before he had starred in a silent film in Hollwyood called the *Sky Raider*. Coli, who had lost an eye flying in the Great War was a capable navigator who had already made the first non-stop flight from Paris to Casablanca.

Together they supervised the building of their aircraft, a handsome white biplane called *L'Oiseau Blanc* (*The White Bird*). The plane was designed to drop its wheels on take off to save weight and increase the speed, then land on the water on its watertight fuselage made of sealed plywood.

The aircraft was to fly from Paris to New York where it would land in New York harbour. On the morning of 8 May 1927, the aircraft wobbled into the air from Le Bourget aerodrome. An hour and a half later it crossed the French coastline and disappeared into the clouds over the Channel. It was last seen off Ireland by which time it was making slow progress against the twenty-five miles an hour head winds.

It was estimated to take at least thirty hours to make the crossing. *L'Oiseau Blanc* had enough fuel for more than forty hours. But a day and a half later they had still not arrived. Breakfasting at a diner in New York Sidney had picked up a newspaper and read about the disappearance of Nungesser and Coli. He was at the time trying to clinch a deal with an American automobile manufacturer, Paul Dupont, who made a particularly exotic brand of straight eight cars.

Du Pont was a prominent French-American and he wanted to engage the services of Mr Cotton to find the two fliers. Du Pont had heard of the extensive flying which Sidney had done in Newfoundland and considered him the man for the job. Sidney said he would be happy to go if he was given a free hand and Du Pont met all expenses. Later Harry Guggenheim the copper magnate agreed to bankroll the rescue mission as well and put up $25 000. Sidney himself was to receive $5000.

Cotton was confident he could find the missing flyers but there was a catch.

His name was Cyrus Caldwell and he was a journalist and a drunk. He was to join the mission as co-pilot and to send regular reports back to the newspapers and an aviation magazine called *Aero Digest*. If they found the missing fliers it would be a great scoop but he was to become a constant source of irritation to Sidney.

Sidney did not want to take a journalist. He wanted to take Joan. The couple had only been been married a year and she was his constant companion. She also knew the country well and would be invaluable if the aircraft was forced down in the backwoods. However Guggenheim had refused to allow Joan to join him arguing that the tabloid press would make fun of the expedition.

Joan, or as Sidney called her, 'Joey', was bitterly disappointed that she could not fly with him but she resolved to follow her new husband around Newfoundland by road and train.

The editor of *Aero Digest* was Frank Tichenor who had also set himself up as trustee of the funds for the expedition. It was at his insistence that Caldwell joined the team so Sidney was suspicious of his motives. He thought that Mr Tichenor was more interested in the circulation of his magazine than the safety of the flyers.

Everybody it seemed was preparing to fly the Atlantic except Sidney. Looking for the lost fliers was a humanitarian misson but there was much more prestige—and money—to be made by flying the Atlantic.

Three rival groups of flyers were in New York preparing for the flight: Clarence Chamberlin, Richard Byrd and Charles Lindbergh.

Commander Richard Byrd had been one of the first to set off but his Fokker Trimotor had crashed during a test flight. Anthony Fokker, the Dutch aircraft designer had been piloting the aircraft himself. He was thrown clear but Byrd had broken his arm and his navigator Floyd Bennett had a broken leg.

Sidney visited Bennett in hospital telling him of his plans to look for the missing Frenchmen. Bennett wished him luck and gave him a present of twenty pounds of pemmican (dried meat) which they had intended to take on their Atlantic flight. It could prove useful if they came down in the middle of nowhere. The interior of Newfoundland was dotted with lakes so Sidney decided he needed a floatplane rather than a landplane—this would give them a greater margin of safety if they got into trouble.

With the money from Guggenheim Sidney bought a single engined Universal floatplane from Fokker, the same company which had built Byrd's Trimotor. This was flown from Little Ferry on the Hackensack River to Port Washington and moored to a buoy. The plane was originally fitted with a metal propeller which turned at 1900 revolutions a minute and consumed too much fuel. Sidney asked that a lighter wooden propeller be fitted, and a spare carried on board for emergency use. He also insisted that an earth induction compass be installed.

Sidney obligingly demonstrated the aircraft for the waiting press and newsreel photographers. The aircraft handled well and lifted easily from the water after a run of just a few hundred metres. He now made arrangements with an oil company to lay down fuel supplies at various points along the Newfoundland coastline. A third man was also to join the team—a Fokker aircraft engineer called MacPhail. Sidney did not like him either.

Sidney knew that the search for the two fliers would be almost as dangerous as the Atlantic crossing itself. Once again he would be flying in erratic weather with the constant risk of a forced landing in inhospitable terrain.

'No one knows what rotten flying country it is excepting myself, and I am wondering why I ever thought of going on this expedition, knowing what was ahead of me.'

Tichenor thought it would be good publicity if the Fokker was flown from New York to Newfoundland. Sidney disagreed. There would be enough dangerous flying without risking the rescue aircraft on a ferry flight. The weather was bad, and Sidney insisted that the floatplane be taken by ship. The aeroplane now called the *Jeanne d'Arc* was taken by ship from Halifax in Nova Scotia to St Johns Newfoundland, then lowered into the water by crane. Barely had the team arrived in St Johns however when the Newfoundland government demanded a $34 000 bond before the aircraft was allowed to land.

After Sidney had attempted to sort this out with the Premier, the Fokker made its first search flight along the south coast. There was an enormous amount of coastline to cover and no way of knowing where Nungesser and Coli had crashed even if they had made it as far as Newfoundland. 'The country is devoid of settlements and there are thousands of miles that are not even visited by trappers.' If Nungesser and Coli were still alive, reasoned Sidney, they would be in the interior surviving on their emergency rations, supplemented by whatever fish and game they could catch and whatever lichen and edible green stuff they could collect.

For the next few weeks the three fliers combed Newfoundland but found no sign of the missing aircraft. There were rumours of wreckage and flares. One witness claimed to have seen the aircraft on fire on a local headland; another said they had been found in dense forest owned by the Quebec Lumber Company; another report was that the aircraft had come down on an iceberg. All proved to be groundless. Sidney did not want to give up and still had a strange feeling that the missing fliers were out there somewhere. And he felt that if they had more than one aircraft it would double their chances.

He was reluctant to take the aircraft back to New York and hoped that Caldwell would take the hint and go back to New York by train. But Tichenor had cabled Caldwell and told him to stay with the aircraft until they came back together.

They had left St Johns at 5 a.m. for the long flight back to New York with refuelling stops at Portland West, Rockland in Maine and Newport, Rhode Island. They left Newport in the afternoon and immediately flew into thunderstorms and torrential rain. The weather was so bad that at times Sidney was flying only twenty feet above the waves and salt water spray lashed the cockpit.

Cyrus Caldwell was sitting behind Sidney in the cabin. He now certainly realised that Sidney Cotton was a very good pilot. Sidney felt a tap on his shoulder and Caldwell passed him a note. Sidney gave a grim smile as the waves flicked by only feet beneath them.

Caldwell had written: 'At last we look like finding Nungesser and Coli.'

Harry Guggenheim was pleased to see Sidney back in one piece and was also pleased with the search even though it had not yielded any results. He gave Sidney all the remaining equipment from the flight as a souvenir.

A reporter from the *Sunday Times* telephoned Sidney for his story but he said he did not want any publicity. When he went to his bank he found that he was overdrawn by $3000, so he was out of pocket on the expedition.

All Sidney's efforts to find the Frenchmen had been eclipsed by the joyous news that an American called Charles Lindbergh had successfully flown from New York to Paris. Cotton claims in his book he had met Charles Lindbergh before he had set off on the flight. However there is no mention of this in Sidney's diary. When Sidney lunched with the Guggenheims, the butler and maid produced brand new autograph books and asked for his signature.

The only other signature in the books was that of Lindbergh.

'So I am in good company,' wrote Sidney.

The search for Nungesser and Coli had been in many ways more dangerous than flying the Atlantic but he sorely wished that it had been him and not Lindbergh in the *Spirit of St. Louis*.

Sidney however still had an uncanny feeling that the Frenchmen had landed in Newfoundland: 'It was the last stage of a fruitless effort, and even though I've searched almost all the possible spots in the island, I still have that feeling and would like to have completely satisfied myself that they did not land there.'

He could after all have been right. In 1961, thirty-four years after the *White Bird* had disappeared, the instrument panel from an aircraft was trawled up by fishermen 120 miles off the coast of Maine. Then in the 1970s a piece of blue painted aluminium was found on a rock—this it was felt could have been part of the red, white and blue French markings which adorned the wings and tail of L'Oiseau Blanc.

Perhaps Nungesser and Coli had made it after all.

At the beginning of the search expedition Joan Henry had travelled with Sidney from New York to St Johns where he had to leave her. For a time she returned to Hawkes Bay on the west coast, where she had grown up. The search took two months and she saw little of him during that time, although he tried to keep in touch by telegram. He was not with her on 17 June, his thirty-third birthday.

His diary reads: 'Telegraphed Joey. I hate being away from my darling Joey on my birthday but it cannot be helped.' Tichenor was however in some ways justified in wanting the aircraft to return to New York. Joan said: 'Although Sidney was only loaned the aircraft he used to act as if it was his. He would use it for his private business or to see friends or to take photographs. He would fly across Newfoundland to see me.'

Joan too believed that the two Frenchmen had made it across the Atlantic and were almost certainly planning to land the aircraft off the French islands of St Pierre et Miquelon.

'The sea was so rough that day that they would have been looking for smooth water.' She thinks they might have tried to land on an inland lake somewhere on the Burin peninsula.

'But the lakes are full of peat moss. The plane would have been swallowed up.'

## Chapter 5

# Colour by Dufay

Sidney Cotton made more money out of the stock market than he ever did out of aviation. But the late 1920s were not a time to be playing the markets. On 24 October 1929 a wave of panic selling hit the New York stock exchange. Thirteen million shares changed hands, banks and businesses failed and the world was plunged into economic crisis. Sidney was not in New York to see the investors jumping from skyscrapers; he was in London. Like everybody else he ordered his stockbroker to sell all his shares, ending up with £10 000 in cash.

'I got rid of my three telephones, seeing them, at last, for the snare and delusion they were, and went on holiday to calm down.'

He was intrigued by colour photography and put a small amount of capital with an optical engineer to conduct some experiments.

Now he was to be asked once again to look for an explorer who had gone missing. His name was Augustine Courtauld, and he was the only son of Samuel Courtauld, the millionaire founder of the company that had pioneered man-made fibres. Courtauld had been a member of a team of Cambridge University students who had set out overland to explore the possibility of setting up an air service, using the Great Circle route to fly over the North Pole to Canada.

The expedition had set up its base camp near Angmagsalik on the coast of Greenland then had struck out across the ice using dog sleds. They had established a meteorological station 120 miles north-west of Angmagsalik. It had enough food to support one person but not two so Courtauld had stoically volunteered to stay behind there when the rest of the team pulled out.

Courtauld was a young fit man but he had little idea of what he was letting himself in for. He had set up his tent on the ice cap but gradually it became buried in snow until only the ventilator was exposed. Above it was a flagpole with a tattered Union Jack that had been almost shredded in the high winds.

The ordeal lasted three months. Courtauld was trapped under the snow in almost complete darkness, freezing temperatures and blizzards. Unknown to his companions he was already low on food and water and was down to his last candle. He was too weak to dig himself out of the buried tent and had no means of communication with the outside world. The radio at base camp had in any event broken down. From the air, the ventilator shaft was difficult to see so a previous air search had found nothing. A rescue team that had set off across the ice had been forced back by bad weather.

Sidney had developed aircraft with skis in Newfoundland and was experienced in flying them from ice and snow. He reasoned that the chances of finding Courtauld would be improved if more than one aircraft were used. A Swedish pilot would fly the first machine, the second by Sidney and a relief party would set off overland as soon as the weather improved. Reykjavik in Iceland was chosen as the base.

Samuel Courtauld gave Sidney a free hand to organise the expedition and told him to spare no expense to find his son and heir. It was the sort of assignment that Sidney liked. He shopped around for a suitable aircraft and decided on an American aircraft, a Bellanca Pacemaker that he had flown over from Italy. The wheels were removed and skis fitted in their place. The plane carried a dismantled sled that could be dropped by parachute onto the ice. The Bellanca was also equipped with supplies of food, silk tents and flares.

Joan Henry had not been allowed to join Sidney on the Newfoundland mission. This time she was to be part of the great adventure. She stood next to him on the Icelandic steamer *Dettifoss* when they sailed out of Hull harbour on their way to Reykjavik. Also with them was John Stannard who had flown with Sidney during his days in the Royal Naval Air Service. 'It was all very exciting. Sidney was in his element, giving orders, pacing backwards and forwards about the ship. This time there was no one to tell him what to do,' said Joan.

It took them four days to reach Reykjavik and the Bellanca was lifted off the ship and assembled on the dockside. The next day, 10 May they were ready to go. By this time the Swedish pilot Captain Ahrenberg had already left Reykjavik in his aircraft but was forced back by bad weather. Sidney knew that the time was running out for Courtauld. 'I was hoping to be in on the search and yet I knew it would be a serious matter if Courtauld had not yet been located.'

They were just about to set off when they received a cable from Samuel Courtauld in London. Augustine Courtauld had been found. The overland rescue party led by Gino Watkins had located the tent and Ahrenberg had flown over and dropped supplies to them from the plane. By the time they found him, Courtauld had run out of food and candles and was burning ski-wax to make a light. He was melting some ice with his primus stove when he heard a muffled shout from the ventilator above his head. The rescue team smashed a hole into the roof and Courtauld saw blue sky and sunshine again for the first time in three months. He was emaciated and exhausted but quickly recovered.

Sidney was relieved that Courtauld had been found. Now there was nothing to do except dismantle the big Bellanca and return to England. He decided to keep the aircraft. Later he was to nearly kill himself in it.

Joan Henry did not share Sidney's passion for flying despite the fact he had bought her an aeroplane. It was an Avro Avian biplane G-ABWE which Sidney kept at Hanworth aerodrome south of London. She took lessons with Sidney as her instructor and although she could fly straight and level she never really mastered take-offs or landings.

'I hadn't got the education to be a pilot,' she said. 'I've never been to school in my life. I could fly all right but when it came to having a licence I would have been turned down.'

After the rescue mission to find Augustine Courtauld, Sidney had brought the American Bellanca back from Iceland. He had the floats removed and the wheels refitted and then used it for weekend flying and the occasional trip to Europe. One weekend he was to fly it from Hanworth to Woodley aerodrome near Reading with five passengers on board.

There was much excitement at the Reading Flying Club about the performance of the powerful American machine, and how it could climb very steeply out of the smallest field. Sidney opened the throttle and roared across the airfield, holding the machine down until the last moment to get up some speed. The plane climbed steeply but at two hundred feet the engine cut dead and black smoke poured from the exhaust. An engine failure, with a full load of passengers on take-off is the nightmare that most pilots dread. If that happens you do not have enough altitude to turn. The textbook lesson is to push the stick hard forward and land ahead on what is left of the runway.

Sidney did nothing of the sort. Unfortunately he had run out of runway and only a quarry lay ahead. 'There was a sickening feeling and dead silence,' said Joan. 'A man called Jimmy Rarnell was in the co-pilot's seat. He was scrabbling at Sidney's right shoulder and whimpering. Sidney said in his perfectly quiet voice: 'It's all right, Jimmy, I've got her.' Using his dwindling speed he pulled the aircraft up into steep climb then kicked on full left rudder. The aircraft was now facing back down the airfield but Sidney was too high to land inside it. He banked hard to the left and side-slipped until he was in a position to land downwind. He realised, however, that he had so little runway left he would probably end up going through the fence and crashing down the steep embankment to the road below.

Watching from the clubhouse, the chief flying instructor cried: 'My God, they haven't a chance,' at which point the mother of one Sidney's passengers fainted. At the last minute Sidney pressed down on the left hand brake pedal and ground looped the aircraft hard. It swung round and stopped just a few feet from the fence.

Joan was furious with him 'You're a nice one,' she said. 'You always said that if your engine cuts, keep straight ahead.'

'Yes I know,' said Sidney, 'But there are some times when you have to do that.' Joan thumped him on the back: 'Practise what you preach!' she said.

Joan was more interested in cars than aeroplanes and Sidney was to indulge her with all manner of exotic machines. 'I desperately wanted to go back to Newfoundland but he bribed me to stay in England by buying me an Aston Martin.'

Joan took part in four Monte Carlo rallies, driving first the Aston Martin, then an MG, a Lancia and a Humber which she entered for Lord Rootes. In the thirties the Monte Carlo Rally attracted few women drivers.

It was no mean feat to negotiate the poor roads of the time especially the infamous section from Monte Carlo to Grenoble with its icy mountain passes, which had to be driven at night. A picture at the time shows Joan in a convertible Delage accompanied by Tommy Rose, her co-driver in one of the British rallies.

Chartres Cathedral in France stands out from the surrounding flat farmland like an index finger. The spire of the great Gothic church can be seen for thirty miles.

In May 1932 Sidney Cotton, his voice even more hushed than usual, stood in the aisle of the great cathedral with a woman called Madame Durand. Sidney was not religious but this was as good a place as any to conduct a business deal. Shafts of sunlight streamed into the nave through the magnificent stained glass windows, gilding the altar and throwing a rainbow onto statues and paintings. Madame Durand told Cotton that she could create the same colours artificially, and that she owned the secret to a new type of colour film. Dufaycolor could exactly reproduce the colours created by the Almighty.

In 1932 most people took photographs in black-and-white. Very few owned anything more than a Box Brownie let alone a roll of colour film. It would be seven years before cinemagoers would see a feature film in Technicolor. The movie was *Gone with the Wind.*

Dufaycolor had been invented by a Frenchman called Louis Dufay. The technique was to put the dots of the three primary colours—red, blue and green—in a very fine pattern on the film base itself, then cover the dye with photographic emulsion to protect it. Dufay had earlier offered to sell the process to the English Ilford film company for £25 000. They had turned it down.

Sidney Cotton had been interested in colour photography since his days in Canada. In 1931 he had befriended an optical engineer called Chapman and they had experimented with a similar technique. The colours of the spectrum would be split on the negative and brought together on the positive.

'We got some nice results before I discovered that it didn't work commercially,' he wrote.

A year was to pass before Sidney got interested again. Madame Durand, a shrewd businesswoman with a ready grasp of technical processes, was Dufay's principal backer. Sitting next to Sidney in a pew in the great cathedral she explained to him how the process would work. The main obstacle to overcome, she explained, was to find a suitable transparent film base on which to put the three primary colours.

Seen through a microscope the colours appeared as a pattern of alternating blue and green squares and red lines, known as a reseau (network). The grid of colours was reproduced up to 600 times per inch. The film was exposed through the base and the light passed through the reseau before reaching the emulsion. The advantage of Dufaycolor was that incorrect exposures could be corrected during processing, and either intensified or reduced.

Sidney, stooped like a tired butterfly over the petite Englishwoman, tried hard to conceal his enthusiasm. Giving the man in the street the ability to take happy snaps in colour was potentially worth a fortune. 'Dufaycolor was a negative that anyone could put into any camera and develop in the same way as black-and-white film,' he said.

Madame Durand had already acquired the overseas rights to the new film base. Sidney meanwhile had formed his own company, Colortone, but wanted to acquire the Dufay patents and the Spicer contract. They agreed on a figure of £5000. Madame Durand extended a small gloved hand and they shook on it. Dufaycolor was registered as a limited company in January 1933 with Sidney holding 52 per cent of the shares.

Sidney Cotton did not know it at the time, but the clinching of this deal was to be his passport to Nazi Germany. Sidney had already visited the Agfa company in Germany when he was investigating the manufacture of his own film. Now he went to Kassel to talk to a German company who made stainless steel rollers.

The rollers were engraved with lines, too small to be seen with the naked eye which made up the network of three primary colours. This mosaic was designed so that dots of red, green and blue were regularly spaced alongside each other. When light shone through them they looked as if they were joined together. The film that Spicers were making had 350 000 squares of colour to the square inch but Sid wanted better definition. The British could not do it so he bullied the Germans into it.

Sidney liked to compare Dufaycolor to a cork which could float behind and be sucked along in the wake of the big photographic companies. He had to persuade companies like Kodak in America, Ilford in England and Agfa in Germany to use the Dufay negative to produce their own colour results.

There was no doubt that Dufaycolor was a viable process but there was one problem; in 1933 there was no successful process available for producing colour prints, although a number of companies were developing them.

Sidney was only too aware that 80 per cent of the world's photographic business was in America. The great movie studios in Hollywood chewed up miles of film each year. If he could get a piece of the action he could make a substantial killing. He decided to establish Dufay companies in both the United States and England and to get Ilford to handle the rights for the British Empire.

Ilford was the English company which had been offered the rights to Dufaycolor and turned them down. But now they had seen the results using the stainless steel rollers which Sidney had acquired in Germany. They liked the quality of the roll film and 35 mm film for movies but thought the 16 mm stock was slightly distorted.

In 1934 a new company was formed to take over the British Empire rights. It was to be called Spicer-Dufay-British. Spicers were to make the transparent film, and Dufay the colour process. Ilford would have fifty-one per cent of the new company giving them a controlling interest and they were prepared to put up £250 000 to develop the new company.

Sidney now set his sights on the United States. This time there was a rival product, Kodachrome, but on the face of it Dufaycolor had a distinct advantage. Photographers who used Kodachrome film had to return the film to the Kodak company in Rochester to have it developed.

With Dufaycolor the negative could be developed on the spot in an ordinary photographic developer so a photographer's pictures could be seen immediately. This had particular advantages for professional photographers who needed instantaneous results. This was not lost on *National Geographic* magazine who made Dufaycolor their preferred format.

In 1937 news of Dufaycolor had come to the ears of the art

director of the *New York Mirror* magazine, Vic Guinness. Curiously his interest eventually brought together two technologies, the colour film itself and the aeroplane which Cotton was later to use on his spy flights.

In 1937 television was in its infancy and to see moving images of recent events people went to the cinema to watch newsreels. Newsreel films had to be taken by ship across the Atlantic so it would be at least a week before audiences in England would see events that had happened in America.

Two airline pilots H. T. 'Dick' Merrill and John S. Lambie had a different idea. The German airship the Hindenburg had just crashed in New Jersey but the spectacular film of the accident had not yet been seen at cinemas in England. The two pilots decided to fly a Lockheed 10 across the Atlantic to take film of the Hindenburg disaster and on the return flight bring back film of the coronation of King George VI. It had only been ten years since Lindbergh had flown the Atlantic and as yet there were no scheduled air services.

Merrill and Lambie did not bring back movie film but colour pictures taken in Dufaycolor.

Vic Guinness was quite excited and wrote: 'Dear Major Cotton. Colour film is ideal for news photography. A very important item is the fact that we can develop and see the results in seven minutes thus saving the cost of film and model's time. Our world scoop of the 1937 Coronation was taken in London with Dufaycolor and flown across the Atlantic, developed and ready for press 24 hours later.'

The previous year, 1936, Sidney had crossed the Atlantic twenty times to promote the new format. Dufaycolor Inc had been formed in May 1934. But Sidney's team was playing away from home and the opposition was prepared to play dirty. In Florida, Sidney persuaded three photographic agents to put on a window display of Dufaycolor film. Within days Kodak salesmen had visited the shop demanding an equal display for Kodachrome. It was tough going, and it was wearing Sidney down. The technical experts had said that Dufaycolor was a superior format to Kodachrome, but it was obvious that the American company would stop at nothing to suffocate it.

Sidney went to see George Eastman, the elderly founder of Kodak and suggested the formation of a separate company to handle Dufaycolor outside the British Empire. Eastman agreed to put the proposal to his board of directors. He was frail and was recovering from a serious illness, but he seemed receptive to Sidney's proposal. Two days after Sidney had seen him he took out a revolver and shot himself. In a suicide note he said that his life's work was done and he did not want to become a burden to his family.

As if the negotiations in America were not difficult enough, Sidney now faced a claim from the Official Receiver in England for £13 800 owed to a firm of stockbrokers, who had gone into liquidation, followed by a demand for £18 000 in back taxes from the Inland Revenue.

The Official Receiver agreed to settle for £5000 but Sidney was not in England to pay the money into court. A receiving order was made against him which automatically stripped him of all his directorships. So by the time he got back to England he was no longer a director of any of the Dufaycolor companies he had created! These were Dufaycolor Ltd, Spicer Dufay British and Dufay Chromex Ltd. It took him years to get his money back but Dufaycolor as a film format was left to wither on the vine. Dufaycolor Inc ceased trading in the United States in September 1939.

Paul Lamboit had been based in New York as technical sales representative and had worked on the Dufaycolor project since 1928. 'It was not really a process that could stand up competitively to other colour methods being developed simultaneously. As an additive process, with tricolor lines printed on the film base, too much light was absorbed when the result was viewed either as a transparency or as a motion picture. Even when Dufaycolor prints were made from the film, processed either to a negative or a positive, the results were never very satisfactory.' Its main advantage was that the processing could be done by amateur photographers in the home instead of the film being sent to the laboratory.

Ilford tried to popularise the roll film by selling it for 3s 6d a roll, unaware of the fact that it cost more than that to produce. It survived until the 1950s then disappeared. It was a pity; a great many experts had testified that the film was superior to Kodachrome but in the end it was Kodachrome that killed it off. Joan Henry had had fun with it. She had borrowed a wind-up movie camera from Sidney and gone into the backwoods of Newfoundland to film caribou.

Dufaycolor had shown promise but had ended up another costly failure just like the earlier Newfoundland adventures. So by 1938 Sidney was in London, broke and miserable. All that was about to change.

It is said that if you've got it, you flaunt it. Sidney's extravagance when he was trying to pull off the Dufaycolor deal in America, knew no bounds. He would travel by liner to New York—usually the *Queen Mary* or the *Queen Elizabeth* and take his beige drophead Rolls Royce with him.

These days, with the advent of car rental companies, one wonders why anyone would go to the trouble, but Sidney was showing the flag. True there were Rolls Royces in America but not one like his. 'Sidney adored his Rolls Royce coupe. Wherever we went in America it was always ooh and ahh—a nine day wonder,' said Pat Martin. Occasionally he would let her drive it.

Pat Martin preferred travelling on the German liner the *Bremen*. 'It had a wonderful restaurant with a domed glass roof. Sidney loved that restaurant. He had lots of money and I never asked where it came from. I just assumed that everyone had money in those days.'

Wherever he went, Cyril Kelson accompanied him. Cyril Kelson was twenty-five, the son of a man who ran a public house with the curious name of the Gate Hangs Well in Leicestershire.

Kelson had been in service since he was fourteen, he was a qualified motor engineer and had a Rolls Royce certificate.

He was Sidney's Jeeves, or more correctly his Honourable Crichton. Jeeves only knew about protocol and manners; a screwdriver to him was a type of cocktail. Crichton could turn a coconut husk into part of a gramophone. Kelson was intensely practical; he could fix cars but also had a working knowledge of most things. He would advise Sidney about his clothes, and he would be discreet about his women. Kelson had a way of including himself in the conversation. He would say to Sidney: 'Perhaps we should wear our brown suit today, sir.'

In 1938, according to Sidney it cost him only £40 to take the Rolls Royce and Kelson to the United States on board the *Queen Elizabeth*. There he would repair to his rented thirteenth floor apartment in Park Avenue. There was business to attend to but there was also pleasure. During the day Pat would go riding in Central Park, joining him in the evenings for dinner, usually with business clients.

Two Mexicans, Albert and Iggy Miranda were very much part of Sidney's set, and at one of their cocktail parties Sidney met a racing driver called George H. Robertson. Robertson had won the Vanderbilt Cup race in 1908 but since then the race had all but disappeared. Now it was due to be revived. He had created a four mile racing circuit near Westbury on Long Island.

The Vanderbilt Cup race was an international event which brought together both American and European drivers. All the big European names were there: Tazio Nuvolari in the Alfa Romeo, the German, Bernd Rosemeyer in the rear-engined Auto Union and Jean Pierre Wimille from France in a Type 59 Bugatti. Alongside them were big American cars like the Duesenberg,the Miller and the Offenhauser. Sidney had bought an English racing car, the ERA (English Racing Automobiles). These had a small one and half litre supercharged engine and had been built for the voiturette class in Europe.

Joan Henry was not interested in aeroplanes but she liked the cars. Whether or not Sidney had any money, they would occasionally go window shopping to all the car showrooms in Portland Street London.

On this occasion Sidney had telephoned and said: 'Joey—can you buy me an ERA?'

Sidney had intended to drive the car himself and but he finally allowed it to be driven by the Honourable Brian Lewis after Lewis's Type 59 Bugatti was damaged during a practice lap. Sidney's car was one of five ERAs entered but although it performed well in the trials it did not win a place. The only ERA to do well was the one driven by Pat Fairfield which was placed fifth overall. The Germans swept the field and tried to turn the race into a propaganda exercise for the Third Reich. Swastikas adorned the sides of Rosemeyer's Auto Union and the supercharged Mercedes Benz driven by Dick Seaman. This was unusual, as it was otherwise only carried on races held within the borders of Germany.

Rosemeyer completed the picture by wearing the traditional German lederhosen—presumably to elicit the support of the large German community living in the New York area. Over the loudspeakers came the strains of the *Horst Wessel* song. All the members of both German teams raised their arms in the Nazi salute.

Among the pit crews, engineers and hangers-on in the Auto Union team, Sidney spotted the corpulent glaring figure of Dr Ferdinand Porsche, the designer of the Volkswagen. Two years later Porsche would start work on developing tanks for the Wehrmacht and building the prototype People's Car.

Sidney probably had no idea that only three years later he would be spying on the German military machine that created it.

We are back in Perth, Ontario, and Joan Henry is in her wheelchair chuckling about her meeting with royalty.

After the first few years of their marriage in 1926 she had seen very little of Sidney. They had been married for ten years and although at first she had been constantly at his side she had tired of the endless travelling. She hated high heels and silk stockings and people talking over her head.

Sidney had taken her to meet Ramsay MacDonald, Britain's first Labour Prime Minister. 'I was shy. People knew that I had no education,' she said. 'I could not understand what they were talking about and found myself making small talk with his boring little wife.'

Joan had been taken reluctantly to the high society life, and pined for the backwoods. But barely had they arrived in London when Sidney announced that she was to be presented at the court of King George V. Sidney had booked them into the Dorchester Hotel. Joan possessed only a handful of dresses and none of them were suitable for an audience with royalty.

Together they toured the gown shops in Mayfair. Sidney announced: 'You have forty-eight hours to design a dress.'

When the dress arrived Joan locked herself in the hotel room and spent hours practising how to curtsey. Finally she felt confident enough to curtsey before Sidney. 'All right,' he said, 'let's see it.'

As she bent her knees two little lumps appeared on each side of her hips.

'What are those?' said Sidney. Joan explained that they were embroidered roses which were attached to the sides of her satin pants. 'Well, you can't curtsey like that,' said Sidney. 'You'll have to go to court without your pants on.'

She did. The reception at Buckingham Palace was a glittering affair in front of King George V, Queen Mary and Edward the Prince of Wales. Also to be presented was the Maharani of Johore, who wore a sensational diamond tiara. 'It made Queen Mary's diamonds look like Woolworths,' said Joan.

Finally it came Joan's turn to curtsey before the royal party. She chuckles.

'I think the King was aware I was wearing no pants because he gave me a sweet smile' she said. 'Queen Mary looked daggers at me, but the Prince of Wales gave me a knowing wink.'

Sidney had no way of knowing it then but twenty years later he would be entertaining Edward Windsor on board his yacht.

In 1936 Joan Henry told Sidney she was leaving him. Sidney was never around when she needed him and had been away from the marital bed for too long. Joan had taken counsel from her gynaecologist. 'It was a miracle to me that we ever had even one child,' she told me. 'But then we never had much sex anyway. He was as dull as dishwater. That's why I kicked over the traces.'

The child that Joan talked about was Jill who was born in 1930. She was to spend the greater part of her childhood with nannies and in boarding schools and it was not until after the war that she got to know her father.

Today Jill Cotton, now Jill Seaton, lives in Jasper in the Canadian Rockies. Like her mother she is a keen naturalist and actively concerned in conservation. She loves hiking and the solitude of the forests and the lakes. 'We were a most dysfunctional family. My father flitted in and out of my life. He was one of those people who was simply never there. Eighty per cent of his life I knew nothing about.'

She was only ten days old when her mother left her to go on a motor rally in the South of France.

In England she lived in Old Oak Cottage near Datchet with her Nanny Edith and the admirable Cyril Kelson, chauffeur, valet and odd job man.

'My father was away so Kelson used to take me to school in the Rolls Royce. He wasn't just a chauffeur, he did everything. He would fix things around the house. He was invaluable. Once he had fixed the toilet seat and he used to say "if you wriggle around on that seat, Miss Jill, something will come up and bite you". It terrified me.'

In the first year of the war Jill was evacuated to the United States to stay with some family friends. For the next three years she went to an American high school, but she heard very little from either of her parents during that time.

In 1944, when she was fourteen, she flew back to England. 'I arrived back in London flying from Philadelphia to Lisbon in 1944 then flying in a blacked out Dutch aircraft to Bristol.' When she arrived back in England she was sent off to a new school in Dorset. 'I was going out of Paddington on the train to go to school in Dorset and this weird thing flew over.' It was a V-1 flying bomb.

Sidney was surprised to hear that his daughter was back in England and going to school in Dorset. 'But my school fees were rarely if ever paid on time. He either had so much money he was rolling in money or he had none. I always thought he was much better company when he had none. He was a driven man. He was driven by the desire to make money. Once he'd got it he was always onto something else to make more. He was very generous to his friends but he never gave me an allowance.'

Jill's mother Joan meanwhile had found a new man, a sea captain in the Royal Navy called Peter Hopkinson. Sidney had set her up in a farm at Checkendon on the River Thames. She was still on good terms with Sidney and had met Pat his new mistress. Sidney took an instant liking to Hopkinson and they even went out on the town together. Once the three of them walked into Quaglinos the expensive West End restaurant .

'I think most people watching would have wondered who was married to whom, but the truth was that we all got on well together,' she said.

She had broached the question of a divorce but Sidney would have none of it. He had told Joan. 'What's the good of having a divorce? If you divorce me now you'll get nothing.'

Sidney said pointedly he was now a wing commander in the RAF doing dangerous work. 'If I get killed at least you'll get a pension.' As it happened they were not to get divorced until 1944.

# Chapter 6

# Cloak and Dagger Fred

According to Frederick Winterbotham, Sidney Cotton was bankrupt when he discovered him, and looking for a new challenge.

In September 1938 Sidney was sitting in his office in St James Square when he received a telephone call from a man with a 'superbly anonymous' voice. The voice was that of Winterbotham.

'Major Cotton?'

'Speaking.' (For some reason people addressed Cotton as Major although he had never been in the army. It was the equivalent to his retiring rank in the Royal Naval Air Service.)

'I understand that you have just returned from Paris, where you met my friend Paul?'

'Yes,' said Sidney, 'that is so.'

Winterbotham said that he would like to come and see Sidney straight away. It was but a brisk walk from No. 10 Broadway to Sidney's office.

There was quiet look of discretion about Mr Winterbotham. 'I am Paul's friend,' he said. 'I want you to take some pictures from the air. We will provide you with an aircraft.'

Fred Winterbotham was no James Bond but he was a spy. His official title was Chief of Air Intelligence of the Secret Intelligence Service or MI6. Unlike its sister bureau MI5 (whose responsibility was espionage, sabotage and subversion directed against the UK), MI6 was responsible for intelligence-gathering overseas.

Tall, patrician with grey eyes and greying hair he was indistinguishable from any other of the bowler hatted civil servants trotting around Whitehall. His colleagues called him 'Cloak and Dagger Fred'.

Winterbotham wrote: 'Cotton was a good pilot with a considerable knowledge of photography; more useful even than that, he was connected with a firm which was trying to expand the development of colour photography in England and Germany, so he was not only well versed in the whole subject but he had good commercial connections which would enable him to fly into Germany without arousing suspicion.'

Winterbotham was also aware that Cotton had previous experience in aerial photography. During his time in Canada had he not undertaken aerial mapping for a logging company? 'I gathered that his firm was not doing too well and that the extra sum of money I could offer him would be very welcome. He was paid a very generous allowance which covered his luxury flat in London, living expenses, the salaries of his co-pilot and mechanic and all maintenance, fuel and aerodrome costs.' The generous allowance was £200 a month plus expenses.

Cotton and Winterbotham talked easily together. They had a number of things in common. They had both flown as fighter pilots against the Germans in World War I. Winterbotham had been shot down and spent eighteen months in a prisoner of war camp. They had both been jackaroos on outback properties in Australia. Winterbotham had come to Australia as a teenager and fallen in love with the country. Cotton meanwhile had become an accomplished horseman on his father's properties in Queensland.

Cotton had gone to school in England spending two years at Cheltenham College. Winterbotham went to Oxford University. Where they differed was Winterbotham's ability as a linguist. Eighteen months in a German prison had not all been in vain. By the time he had been released at the end of World War I he spoke fluent hoch-deutsch with a good accent. Cotton could speak only basic German.

Winterbotham was a regular visitor to Germany during the 1930s, a time when intelligence about what was happening in Germany was becoming increasingly difficult to obtain. Rather than run a spy network he decided to do the job himself. 'I found it necessary and stimulating to operate in Germany myself in order to keep up a running commentary on the progress of German re-armament,' he wrote in his book *Secret and Personal*. But rather than attracting suspicion Winterbotham appeared to be genuinely welcomed.

The Germans were stifled by the terms of the Versailles Treaty under which they were not allowed to have an air force. The main purpose of Winterbotham's visits was to discover to what extent they were breaking that treaty by training pilots and building new aircraft. He had a number of meetings with some of Hitler's deputies, among them Alfred Rosenberg, the architect of the German policy of Lebensraum and Rudolf Hess, Hitler's deputy. In 1934 he had an audience with Hitler himself. The meeting, according to Winterbotham, was both comic and sinister. He walked the length of the Chancellery, heels clicking on the marble floor, to find a short man wearing a brown shirt sitting behind an enormous desk.

The Führer liked the tall Englishman with his grey hair, Aryan good looks and fluent German. Winterbotham was similarly fascinated and amused by the little Austrian corporal with his pasty complexion and bulging eyes. Hitler told him quite frankly that whether the British liked it or not the Luftwaffe would have five hundred aircraft in front line service by the end of 1934. They had already been secretly training pilots in Russia.

This was an open challenge to the Versailles Treaty. But Hitler did not wish to make war against Great Britain. To him, the British Empire was a stabilising influence throughout the world and the common enemy were the Bolsheviks. The British were after all Anglo-Saxon cousins and he had enormous respect for their ability to control the numerically superior races of the world with relatively small forces. His intention was to persuade the British government to join the Germans in the fight against Communism.

In World War I aerial photographic intelligence was in its infancy. Aeroplanes were still a novelty—dangerous and unreliable. Reluctantly the army and the navy had to rely upon this most junior service, the fledgling Royal Flying Corps, to get its pictures.

It would have been an understatement to say it was an inexact science. The photographic aircraft were slow and vulnerable. They had to fly so low to get their pictures that they became easy meat for the fighters. The observer manhandled a large plate camera over the side of the aircraft and clicked away.

Winterbotham knew from his own experience the value of aerial photography.

He had been taking part in a photographic mission over the trenches of Flanders when he had been shot down. His job had been as a scout pilot protecting the plane taking pictures. It had cost him a broken nose and eighteen months of liberty, but during his imprisonment in Germany as well as learning to speak German fluently, he studied at close quarters the Prussian psyche.

Even twenty years later it was still not possible to take pictures above 8000 feet because the lenses of the cameras fogged up with condensation. And at 8000 feet the photographic aircraft would be just as vulnerable as the primitive biplanes of World War I. At this height the aircraft would be a prime target for anti-aircraft fire

Fred Winterbotham's opposite number in the Deuxième Bureau was Georges Ronin. Ronin was as keenly aware as Winterbotham of the German build-up on the other side of the Rhine; moreover if war came to France it would come from the east. Ronin had engaged a Parisian portrait photographer to fly up and down the Rhine in a very old aeroplane with an ancient wooden camera. The idea was to photograph the German fortifications on the other side of the river.

'What to do?' asked Winterbotham. 'One could obviously not cruise around over Germany at eight thousand feet and above taking pictures from a civil aeroplane, so Georges and I decided that we each ask our bosses for a new fast, high flying commercial aeroplane on which we could try to develop a technique to get what we required.' Two aircraft were needed, one for the French and one for the British.

In 1939, you could buy a very nice aeroplane for £12 500. Fred Winterbotham bought two. He chose the new American Lockheed 12A a twin engined aircraft with a heated cabin which could seat six people. The Lockheed 12A was a slightly smaller version of the earlier Lockheed 10 Electra and had been developed for feeder-liner work in the United States. It was powered by two Pratt and Whitney Wasp nine cylinder engines and had a range of more than a thousand miles. To avoid suspicion, the order for the aeroplanes was to be placed by Imperial Airways (the forerunner of British Airways) and the bill paid by the Air Ministry.

'We were advised by Lockheed that they could ship one aircraft to be assembled in England within two or three weeks but the second aircraft would not be available for several months. So the French Lockheed was not delivered until October 1939.'

The Deuxième Bureau paid for it with a large sackful of high denomination French banknotes instead of a cheque. 'The French Secret Service were cautious,' wrote Winterbotham.

The aircraft for MI6 arrived at the docks and Winterbotham rushed down there with a note from the Treasury so that the aircraft could be imported duty free. Winterbotham had arranged with a friend to hire an isolated hangar at Heston aerodrome and in conditions of the greatest secrecy the Lockheed was assembled.

The plane was registered in the name of the Aeronautical

Research and Sales Corporation of 3, St James Square, Piccadilly, London SW 1.

As the French had put up most of the money for the first aircraft, Sidney was given the job of teaching them how to fly it. Sidney had not flown an aircraft for two years, but he quickly fell in love with the Lockheed. It was a small modern airliner. Moreover it was all metal, not like some of the wood, stick and string machines they were still building in England. The interior was luxurious. In many ways it was the executive jet of its day. Sidney found it a delight to fly but unfortunately he could not keep it for himself.

A French pilot arrived at Heston, but Sidney very quickly found his flying ability left much to be desired. At 10 000 feet he handed over the controls to the Frenchman who had no feel for the aircraft and wandered all over the sky. His landings were even worse; on the fourth try Sidney had to take over and land the plane himself. Sidney's French was poor and the Frenchman knew no English.

Eventually an interpreter accompanied them on each flight. He carried a large French–English dictionary from which he translated while the hapless pilot was under instruction. Sidney refused to fly with the Frenchman again and insisted that he do the flying alone. Now it was time to try the cameras. If the flying lessons had been a joke, the early photographic missions were also verging on the absurd.

The aircraft was flown across the Channel to France and then down to the Franco–German border. The Deuxième Bureau were keen to see what fortifications the Germans were building on their side of the Rhine and they had brought their own photographer who sat glumly in the back of the aircraft nursing an enormous camera more than four feet in length. The photographer had attached two long pieces of string to Sidney's elbows that snaked back along the fuselage. When he wanted him to turn right he pulled the right string; to go left he pulled the left one. It was like something out of a comic opera.

The French were so sensitive about the pictures that at first they refused to show them to Sidney, so he had no way of knowing how well he was doing the job. When finally they relented he understood why. They were hopeless. There were huge gaps in the coverage so some of the most important targets had been missed altogether.

'We would have to improve our methods which were crude in the extreme,' wrote Sidney. He was also worried that anyone who observed the erratic track of the aircraft would guess what they were up to. 'It was clear that any further cooperation with the Deuxième Bureau on this project was impossible. If worthwhile results were to be obtained I must have my own aircraft and operate it in my own way.'

The French were not bold enough to make flights very deep into Germany. Sidney Cotton and Fred Winterbotham believed they could do better. The first Lockheed G-AFKR was handed over to the French. By now MI 6 and Sidney had its own machine. The second Lockheed G-AFTL is probably one of the most significant aircraft in the history of aerial espionage. Moreover Fred was well pleased with the man who was going to fly it for him. It was a secondhand plane which had previously been owned by an American oil company and had been acquired by Mr Alfred J. Miranda who took a small commission.

'He (Cotton) flew the Lockheed around as if he had been piloting it all his life.' It was certainly a very smooth aircraft. We tried it out for height and obtained a ceiling of 22 000 feet. Fortunately it was fitted with oxygen. We realised that if we were ever to get the cameras to operate at high altitude this would make a wonderful flying laboratory.'

The team was now in place: Winterbotham the spymaster, Cotton the pilot. They needed a skilled navigator. Winterbotham suggested Robert Niven, a Canadian. Good-looking and quietly spoken, Bob Niven was born in Calgary where he had once driven buses for a living. The Lockheed needed two people to fly it—Sidney in the left-hand seat and Bob Niven in the right. The only other seat in the aeroplane was reserved for the woman Sidney

Cotton called Mata Hari. Her real name was Patricia Lucillia Martin and she was his mistress.

A few years before he died the Australian National Library negotiated at length with Sidney Cotton to donate his personal papers to them or the Australian War Memorial. Sidney took some time to painstakingly prepare and annotate many folders. Only these were sent to Australia after his death and all other papers were destroyed. Even though telling only part of his story they make fascinating reading.

There are the black-and-white photographs taken from the air; documents and letters marked 'Secret', 'Confidential' and 'For your eyes only'; letters, and hand-drawn maps showing the borders between Germany and France. There is an avalanche of correspondence between Sidney and various government departments. Tucked away in a plain brown envelope is a small colour picture of an attractive woman in a low cut dress. The hairstyle and fashion are umistakably 1940s. On the back of the envelope Sidney Cotton has written simply 'Pat Martin—Mata Hari'.

In his book Sidney had briefly mentioned Pat Martin as an aquaintance who once went on a flight with Sidney and Bob Niven to help them with the photography. In a collection that chronicles Sidney's war years it is extraordinary to find a personal photograph. There is no other clue as to who she is. None of Sidney's surviving relatives had ever heard of the mystery woman. It was as if Sidney had left a hint to a parcel of information that sooner or later he wanted someone to unravel.

Kauai is one of the quietest of the Hawaiian Islands. There is none of the unashamed hedonism of Waikiki with its surfers, skyscrapers and syrupy Hawaiian ballads.

If it were not for the coconut palms you could almost imagine that this was England; it is greener and less mountainous than Maui or Oahu and the little fields are dotted with cattle and horses. Pat

Martin spent eight years of her life as Sidney Cotton's mistress and is the only survivor of the spy flights over Germany. Today she lives on top of a hill in Kauai in the company of two dogs, a cat and a horse.

An elegant woman in her eighties, she greets me in Hawaiian dress, a blue and white checked mu-mu. Patricia Lucillia Martin Conan Beck is still unmistakably an Englishwoman although her accent has been subtly modified by forty years of living with Americans.

In the paddock beneath the balcony of her house a chestnut horse called Carla crops the grass, a horse which to her regret she no longer rides. It was, after all, horses that first brought Sidney and Pat together in 1933. Patricia Martin felt more comfortable on a horse than anywhere else. She had been born with club feet, and for most of her youth she had worn metal braces on both legs. Walking was difficult and she felt humiliated by the attention it drew to her. If she was riding or swimming she could conceal her deformity. When Sidney met her she was working as a stablemaid. She loved the company of horses rather than people; they at least were indifferent to the way she walked.

It was a summer day in July 1933 and Patricia had been working at the Aldershot Tattoo, one of the prime equestrian events in England. Her job was to groom and prepare the horses for the riders. She was seated on her favourite mare when she first sighted Sidney Cotton.

'There was a touch on my knee. I looked down and was aware of a tall powerfully built man,' she said. Patricia Martin was not hard up for suitors but this was not one of the handsome young horsemen who followed her about the stables getting in her way.

'This was a man probably in his forties, and with deepset blue eyes. He was tanned and healthy looking and dressed with infinite care. "Are you in charge?," he said. "You seem a little young to be handling all this."'

Patricia was impressed. He was kind and attentive and seemed genuinely interested in everything she had to say. As with all of

Sidney's women there was a great disparity in ages. She was eighteen, he was nearly forty. What followed was a classic seduction; the innocent stablemaid and the man of the world.

Sidney was a capable horseman. His father Alfred had, after all, made money from selling Australian wild horses to South Africa during the Boer War. The reason he was at Aldershot was that three of the horses were his. They chatted about horses. Could she join him for dinner after the horses had been bedded down for the night?

'I was always uncertain of myself in the social arena. But Sidney seemed unaware of the braces on my legs.'

He took her arm and walked her slowly to the car park where he opened the door to a beige drophead Rolls Royce. The horses, his clothes and the car all spoke of money. It was a heady cocktail for a young girl but somehow he made her feel safe. He drove her to a pub, and as they sat in the booth with her twisted legs out of sight under the table she regained her confidence. He told her that he had been married but had been divorced for five years. (This was not true. He was separated from Joan Henry but would not divorce her for another eleven years.) He said that the horses had belonged to his wife, but that now he enjoyed them and rode most days.

He told her of his flying career in the war and his time in Canada. That he was a businessman with interests in the city and in the United States. That he was in the middle of launching a new colour film, Dufaycolor, and expected to make a lot of money out of it. In fact that was the reason he was at Aldershot—he was making a film about the Tattoo shot in Dufaycolor.

Sidney drove her home and holding her hand a moment at the door said: 'We must do this again. I have been happy with you this evening.' He left her without another look and she did not expect to see him again.

But two days later he asked her out to dinner. This led inevitably to coffee at Sidney's country house Old Oak Cottage at Stanwell Moor in Buckinghamshire. That night they became lovers and Pat moved in with him not even bothering to go home to collect her own things. 'He was a hell of a good lover, and kind and sweet and gentle. I think I had the best years of his life. He was at the peak of achieving things and he hadn't been slapped down yet. We lived right on the crest,' said Pat.

Sidney was appalled by the fact that Pat could not walk properly and decided to do something about it. He scoured Europe for the best orthopaedic surgeon and paid for the operation at a London hospital. It was a long and painful process and she spent three months with plaster casts on her legs. Sidney bought her an electric wheelchair and she trundled around London in it.

In 1933 Sidney was dividing his time between his flat in London and a house in the country. But he was rarely in one place for very long. The next few years were to be like something out of a fairy story. The girl who loved horses was growing up fast. Pat had hardly travelled abroad before but now she was constantly on the move. Sidney seemed to have an entrée to the cream of society. There were the five star hotels in Cannes and Paris, the receptions and dinners, the cruise boats and luxury yachts, the elegant motor cars, the race meetings, the regattas, the motor rallies and above all, the aeroplanes. Where, she wondered, did he get the money for this sybaritic existence? She wasn't the only one to wonder.

Sidney owned a number of private planes before the Secret Intelligence Service had bought him the Lockheed. He still had the Bellanca Pacemaker from the Courtauld expedition and it was in this aircraft G-ABNW that he and Pat regularly flew to Europe.

Sidney tended to keep Pat in the background. Many of Sidney's friends were aware that he was still married to Joan Henry, even though they had not lived together for years. She was usually introduced as Sidney's girlfriend. These were less liberal times and the term 'kept woman' was spoken under the breath.

By the late thirties Joan and Sidney were living separate lives, even though still fond of one another and in frequent contact. Joan was aware that Sidney had a mistress although he tended to keep them apart. Sidney,' said Pat Martin 'had a very sophisticated arrangement with his women.'

One occasion when the two women met was when Joan was taking part in a rally in Monte Carlo. Sidney decided to take an aeroplane down to the south of France to meet her and Pat Martin was in the passenger seat. Now it was *her* moment to see just how good a flier Sidney was.

The twin-engined aircraft (Pat cannot remember what type it was) had just crossed the English Channel and was still within sight of the sea. 'We were first going to an air rally then flying on to Monte Carlo to see Joan,' she said. Suddenly the starboard engine caught fire. Sidney said: 'We're not staying here. Put this parachute on.'

'It was a man's parachute and it was a bit big, so I was half standing and I wiggled into it. Then he put his parachute on and opened the side door. It was my side of the plane that was giving trouble and the engine was well on fire.'

They stood on the wing for a minute. Sidney held her right hand and put her left hand on the parachute ring. He shouted: 'When I tell you, jump and count to five thousand before you pull the ring.'

They jumped together hand in hand but as soon as they hit the slipstream their hands were torn apart. 'I lost touch with him. All I could hear him yelling was "wait until you pull" and then I lost sight of him.' Pat was terrifed: 'ONE thousand, TWO thousand, THREE thousand . . . ' On three thousand she panicked and pulled the ring.

Fortunately they were both well clear of the spiralling aircraft. As the parachute opened, the harness cut into the tops of her legs. But she got down safely: 'I was very athletic and I rolled when I landed. Sidney came down hard and was scratched and bruised'.

The couple were not sure where they were. In fact they had landed next to a country house in the Belgian countryside. 'The people came out of the house and took us in. They were very nice to us. We had lost all our clothes in the plane so Sidney hired a car and we drove to a town and bought some more. Then we carried on with our journey to Monte Carlo. Mundane things like that Sidney took care of. I never concerned myself with the details.'

'I loved him dearly for seven years. He didn't use me; I was a willing tool,' she said. 'I know now that he was a great con man, although he never conned me. He took you along and you didn't question it. He was quiet and convincing and intense and people got picked up and carried along with him.'

Patricia was, by her own admission, young, naive and in love. She never enquired about Sidney's business dealings or the constant stream of mysterious visitors who came to the flat at Arlington House. Increasingly, they were men wearing uniforms.

'I always had plenty of money. I only had to go into his office in St James' Square and see his secretary. She would say "Yes, Miss Martin, how much do you want?" I didn't want to know what he was doing.'

It is difficult for me to imagine that this articulate grey-haired lady sitting across the table is the same woman who took part in espionage operations against a foreign power.

The Lockheed always offered the means of escape should they be sprung but the harsh reality was that Cotton, Niven and Martin were spies. Had the Nazis really known the purpose of their mission their would have been put against a wall and shot. Unbeknown to Pat, she had already taken part in some of the clandestine flights over Germany. Only a handful of people knew the real purpose of Sidney's flights. Now it was time for him to bring her in out of the cold.

One day in 1937, Sidney sat her down and told her about the secret work he was engaged in. In his paternalistic way he said: 'You are old enough now, Pat; you might as well know what is going on.'

He explained that she fulfilled an important role. She was part of the cover and that her glamorous looks were an integral part of the masquerade. That because of the nature of the work she would now have to go to the headquarters of the Secret Intelligence Service (SIS) in London and sign the Official Secrets Act.

Sidney Cotton needed a little holiday. Somewhere warm perhaps, like Italy or Greece or even the Middle East. This time he would not be posing as the boss of a photographic company but as an eccentric archaeologist interested in the local ruins. Or an executive of Imperial Airways surveying a new air route. Or if the mood took him he would claim to be a movie director looking for locations.

The Lockheed would certainly be looking for locations but they would be of a military nature. Having made some trial flights over Germany Winterbotham now needed to know what preparations the Italians were making for war.

So in June 1939 the Lockheed was to make its longest flight yet: 15 000 mile round trip from England to Djibouti in French Somalia. The Lockheed was extensively modified for the journey. The two long-range tanks which were fitted would more than double the aircraft's still air range from 700 to 1600 miles, made it very heavy. The authorities granted Sidney a temporary permit so long as the long-range tanks weren't used. If someone accidentally filled them both up to the brim, it was scarcely Sidney's fault!

The aircraft was bristling with cameras. Sidney had simple fittings made up to take three F 24 cameras in line ahead. The cameras were attached by cables to electric control boxes which could be operated from the cockpit so Sidney could fly the aircraft and work the cameras at the same time. They needed to take lots of other equipment—spare cameras, film stock and lenses. These Sidney stuffed into ordinary suitcases and covered them with old travel labels.

For the Middle East trip the aeroplane was to be painted in the pale blue-green called Camotint. Sidney claims to have got the idea for this colour from that of an aeroplane owned by the Maharajah of Jodphur. Curiously both Sidney's wife and his mistress claim to have had a hand in its invention. Pat Martin says she got the idea while observing the undersides of fish in a bowl. Joan Henry said that the colour closely resembled the colour of the egg of a type of duck called Khaki Campbells.

The word had gone around at Heston that the Lockheed was carrying so much extra weight that it would not get off the ground. Sidney noticed that an ambulance and fire truck moved into position as they lined up to take off. Surprisingly the aircraft used only half the length of the runway to get airborne. Sidney waited until the speed built up to 130 mph then threw the aircraft around in a climbing turn past the control tower. It was typical Sidney to have the last word.

They flew to Malta in a single day. There Sidney was to meet another man who was to become an integral part of the unit, Flying Officer Maurice Longbottom. Longbottom had served with a flying boat squadron and was passionate about aerial photography. Before leaving England Cotton had tried to get permission for a photographer to join the team. 'Shorty' Longbottom fitted the bill. Sidney called him: 'A young man with a slide rule mind.'

'Within ten days a single aircraft piloted by a supposedly wealthy man with a taste for desert ruins was able to secure photographs of most of the areas of the Italian Empire which during the past few years had been exercising the British and French naval and air staffs,' Winterbotham wrote in *The Nazi Connection*. 'These were Sicily and the Dodecanese, Eritrea, the Red Sea Islands, Italian Somalia and Cyrenaica.

'It is a striking fact that in nearly every case the Secret Intelligence Service was rephotographing vertically localities previously covered obliquely by Royal Air Force machines flying discreetly beyond the six mile limit; only the angle of photography was modified as the need for information grew more insistent'.

They were photographing anything of interest; gun emplacements, new airfields, a floating dock, bases for submarines or flying boats. When war came, these pictures would be invaluable.

The biggest coup was when they headed back to Malta. This time they flew over Libya and places that four years later would become very famous—El Adem, Tobruk, Derna, Bernice and Benghazi. They had been told of the existence of a secret arms and fuel dump. By following the railway line near Bernice they found it. It held two years' supplies for the Italian army in North Africa. Clearly Mussolini was preparing for the long haul.

When the Lockheed returned to Heston the films were unloaded from the cameras and quickly taken to the laboratories for processing. The aircraft would be in the air at first light and would not return until dusk but by suppertime the pictures would be on someone's desk in Whitehall. Usually when the aircraft returned Sidney and Pat would go home exhausted, their work done. Someone else would see that the pictures were delivered.

But on two occasions Pat was delegated by Sidney to take the pictures to Churchill herself. She was told not to go to No. 10 Downing Street or even to the Cabinet War Rooms but to a nondescript row house in Whitehall.

From the outside the house looked unoccupied. The brown paint was peeling off the front door. Inside the house had been gutted and was a labyrinth of dark corridors, one of which ran through into the house next door. People in uniform came and went carrying manila files; the place was a beehive of activity. Inside it was very dark and windows had been blacked out. The lights were on despite the fact that it was a summer evening and the sun would not set for another two hours.

'They were probably all Foreign Office but from the outside they looked like nondescript villas. I got the impression that here was a network of passages between the various departments because people suddenly appeared without having stepped out onto the street.'

Pat was apprehensive about meeting the great man. As she stopped in the outer office to show her papers, a secretary said: 'Good luck, girl.' In the afternoons, Winston would take a nap. Nobody was ever quite sure what sort of mood he would be in when he woke up. She was shown down a corridor to a big room which was obviously two rooms which had been knocked into one.

Winston in his blue suit, waistcoat and blue and white spotted bow tie had pulled his chair around to the end of the table and was sitting drinking a brandy and smoking a cigar.

The familiar rumbling voice asked her if she would like a brandy. Pat said she didn't drink. 'You will one day girl, you will,' he said, gesturing for her to sit down. The pictures they had taken that day were of great interest to Churchill. They showed the German battleship the *Bismarck* and its cruiser escort the *Prinz Eugen* in dock. Churchill knew that when these two ships put to sea the Royal Navy was in trouble.

There was a sheaf of black-and-white prints. Churchill took a magnifying glass from a drawer and squinted through it. Some of the pictures showed trains pulled up alongside the ships unloading supplies. 'He said "What's this? And what's this?".' Pat showed him that by the length of the shadows one could tell the size of buildings. Churchill grunted.

He asked her about her work. She told him about the long flights in the Lockheed and mentioned that it was cold and uncomfortable. He was impressed. Certainly Sidney Cotton had a powerful ally in Winston Churchill. Later on in his service career he would need all the friends he could get.

Sidney Cotton had many addresses in England although he never spent much time in any of them. But his flat at Arlington House at No. 3 Curzon Place was his busiest residence. It was strategically positioned behind Park Lane in Mayfair but within strolling distance of Whitehall and close to two of his favourite haunts, the Dorchester Hotel and the RAF Club in Piccadilly.

As the war escalated, the flat very quickly became a rendezvous for aviators, politicians, scientists and spies. The floor strewn with blueprints, diagrams and empty coffee cups; the air thick with excited chatter. In fact Sidney had been instrumental in naming it Curzon Place. It had originally been known as Seymour Place. Close by was Seamore Place. He was missing some mail so he went round to the other Seamore Place and found all the mail which had been intended for him inside the door of a bombed out building.

'So he went to the Post Office and raised hell and got the name changed,' said Jill Cotton. 'It is a good story but then father was prone to exaggerate. A good story got better.'

The flat extended over three floors. Visitors went up in the elevator and got out at a hallway leading to a kitchen and a bedroom. The second floor had another two bedrooms and a magnificent sitting room with plate glass windows overlooking Hyde Park. Sidney's bedroom had a separate bathroom with a black bathtub. On the third floor there was a balcony with an even better view of Hyde Park and the London skyline. During an air raid while everybody else would dash to the air raid shelters, Sidney would dash up the stairs to the balcony 'to see the fireworks'.

'One felt,' said Joan Astley, a family friend, 'that if Sidney announced he was going to put on a parachute and jump off the balcony into Hyde Park he could probably do it. With him, anything was possible.'

Winterbotham needed the answers to two questions. Could the Lockheed be fitted with hidden cameras which could operate at altitude without the lenses freezing over? And could the cameras be installed in such a way as to be invisible? Sometimes Cotton and Winterbotham stayed up all night working on the details. How for example to provide suitable frames on which to mount the cameras? Cameras which needed to be discreet and small.

Winterbotham had decided not to use any of the bulky cameras used by the RAF. From Germany he had acquired some of the new Leica Reporters, an expensive 35 mm camera favoured by ornithologists, press photographers and anyone else who needed a lot of shots of the same subject. For its day the camera was very advanced. In addition to being able to carry ten metres of film in its enlarged film chambers it was fitted with an electric motor drive which made it ideal for Cotton's purpose.

The three cameras were mounted in a frame, one pointing

straight down and the other two at an angle of forty degrees. They were synchronised to fire simultaneously and the timing had to be just right to give the correct overlap at heights of 20 000 feet or more. From that height Cotton could photograph an area ten and a half miles wide. This was much higher than the RAF had ever taken pictures before. A hole was cut in the belly of the Lockheed and the three cameras mounted above it on a triple frame. A sliding panel was then installed over the hole, which when closed looked like part of the skin of the aircraft.

Winterbotham wrote, 'This was not an easy job because it affected the stress of the fuselage itself and I had to have the job specially done by an aircraft factory with the utmost secrecy, since it was essential that as few people as possible knew of our efforts.'

Cotton and the team of engineers had been looking for a suitable mechanism to operate the sliding panel. Driving his car to the airfield one wet day, Cotton had noticed the action of the windscreen wipers. It was his suggestion that an ordinary car windscreen wiper be adapted to open and close the secret panel, the device operated by a button under the pilot's seat.

The sliding panel had another unexpected benefit. When it was opened to the slipstream it drew warm air from the heated cabin to flow over the lenses so even at a height of 20 000 feet the lenses did not fog up.

'I suggested to Cotton that he should start off at 8000 feet, take a series of pictures and then climb 1000 feet at a time until he reached the Lockheed's ceiling. When we developed the first three rolls of Leica film we found that we had been taking perfectly clear pictures to nearly 20 000 feet. Just how we had accomplished it we did not realise, but it was exciting to say the least.'

It was only when they crawled under the belly of the plane to check on the operation of the sliding panel that they discovered why the lenses remained free from condensation. 'The engines had been running for about ten minutes and had nicely warmed the cabin. It was then we discovered that, with the engines running, warm air was coming out of the cabin and flowing beneath the camera lenses.'

Winterbotham realised that he had stumbled on a secret that must be kept. 'I decided there and then,' he said, 'that I would tell no one until we had carried out full scale experiments with RAF camera equipment. So off they went and his secretary—who was also his mistress—lay in the bottom of the Lockheed and worked these three Leicas. Click click click turn turn turn. And then for about half a dozen up they went again. And they took photographs from 15 000 to 17 000 feet. And of course they all came out perfectly.'

Pat Martin knew why. It was she who had diverted the warm cabin air over the lenses using bookends! The first results were surprisingly good but when the prints were blown up the detail was indecipherable. Winterbotham now decided to ask the RAF if he could borrow some of their cameras. They acquired two of the large F 24 cameras which had been introduced in the interwar years. The F 24 was 5 x 5 inch format, fully automated with interchangeable magazines and able to be fitted with a range of different focal length lenses. As these were military cameras to be fitted to a civilian aircraft Winterbotham spent a busy evening filing off all the RAF numbers in case they got caught.

Cotton fitted one of the large F 24 cameras into the hole facing straight down. He regulated the timing gear for the exposures to allow for the greater area of ground covered at high altitude. The camera was boxed in below the cabin floor and camouflaged to look like a spare fuel tank so that anyone looking under the floorboards of the plane would have no reason to suspect what was going on.

Once again the sliding panel was operated from the cockpit and could not be opened from outside. The cameras were coupled to a device for automatically timing the taking of the pictures according to the height and speed of the aircraft.

'Now that we had the technique,' said Winterbotham, 'I had to organise the method.'

To see if the cameras were undetectable Cotton flew the aircraft into Berlin seven times on spurious business trips to see if the Germans would search the aircraft. On these trips he never took any photographs so that even if they had found the cameras there would have been nothing on the films.

Sidney was still trying to get Dufaycolor established in Germany and the word was out that he was looking to franchise the format. Now the Germans came to him. At the end of June 1939, a man called Schoene came to see Cotton at his London office. He too had been an aviator and had flown with Goering in the Richthofen Geschwader.

Between the wars he had been a flying instructor in Brazil. Now his interests were in the film business. He explained that Tobis, the big German film company, was keen to buy Dufaycolor so long as Agfa provided the base and the emulsion coating it.

Both the two major German film companies Tobis-Tonbild-Syndikat AG and Ufa (Universum Film AG) had been forcibly acquired by the Nazis and were now making propaganda films extolling the virtues of racial purity, anti-semitism and compulsory euthanasia. But most of these films were still in black-and-white, not colour. Agfa had their own colour technique. Why would they be interested in Dufaycolor? But here, for the first time, was an open invitation by the Nazis to visit Germany. Could it be a trap?

Sidney visited Winterbotham at his 'cover' address—a house in Wimbledon. He was keen to fly to Berlin at once but Winterbotham was opposed to the idea. Already Sidney had made many flights into Germany. This could be one too many. Sidney, as usual, disagreed. 'It was a risk I felt we would have to accept. If anything went wrong of course it would be no good asking for any help.'

Pat Martin was not on board when Cotton and Niven flew from Heston to Berlin on 28 July 1939. Cotton thought that this was too dangerous a mission even for her. They carried no cameras either—that would have been asking for trouble. The four-hour flight to Germany was uneventful but both men were uneasy. This time, would they get sprung? When they arrived, the terminal at

Tempelhof was bedecked with black and crimson Nazi banners. As Sidney taxied in he could not help but notice that the airfield was now surrounded by anti-aircraft guns. The propellers were freewheeling to a a stop when he saw a dozen soldiers armed with Mauser rifles running across the tarmac towards them.

'Look what's coming,' he said to Bob. 'Christ, we've had it,' said Niven.

The Lockheed was what is today known as a tail dragger—it had its main wheels under the wings and a small wheel in the tail. To exit the aircraft you had to walk downhill to the door at the rear. This they did slowly. It gave them time to think what they were going to do next. As the door opened the soldiers formed a guard of honour either side of the door. Sidney could hardly conceal his amusement. Schoene lifted his arm in the Nazi salute. 'You see how close I am to Goering,' he said.

Quick to grasp the situation, Sidney returned the Nazi salute and then strolled confidently down the line of soldiers. There was no point in upsetting people. Besides, England and Germany weren't at war just yet. The big black Mercedes cars with flags on the wings were waiting to take them to the hotel. But who would look after the Lockheed? Herr Schoene flapped his arms. 'Do not worry about the aircraft, it will be looked after.'

'But looked after by whom?' mused Sidney.

As Niven cast an eye over his shoulder he saw the Lockheed being pushed into a hangar. It was certain that the aircraft would be searched. There were no cameras on board but would the Gestapo find the sliding panels that concealed them in the wings?

'All we could do,' said Sidney, 'was keep our fingers crossed.'

That night as they were entertained at dinner, Schoene sounded out Sidney on whether the British would be drawn into the war if Germany invaded Poland. Sidney was suitably vague. He said that as an Australian he was not very interested in British politics. 'But if you are asking my opinion I think the British will fight.'

At the Tobis laboratories, a trial run of Dufaycolor was carried out using the Agfa base. The next day Sidney and Bob Niven flew back to London to have it developed and printed at the Dufaycolor Laboratories. Despite an atmosphere of increasing tension the Germans still raised no objection to a civil aircraft flying anywhere so long as it was flying high enough . . . say 20 000 feet.

'And I think,' said Winterbotham, 'that the fact of Sidney Cotton being an Australian flying an American aircraft might have helped.'

It is interesting to speculate what sort of reception would have been afforded an Englishman flying a British aircraft.

Paul Koster, known to both Winterbotham and Cotton, was now an arms dealer. Like many of the people in the armaments business it was often difficult to determine which side Koster was on. In 1934 he had testified before an American Senate enquiry into the armaments industry that Germany was building submarines in Sweden, Switzerland and Holland in contravention of the Versailles Treaty. The same year he was identified as working for the Germans as a director of the Bergmann company in Berlin—a firm which made machine guns. Now Koster was working for the Americans—a company called the American Armaments Corporation. He also did some spying for MI6 on the side.

The American Armaments Corporation of New York was also familiar to Sidney. The company was run by two colourful Mexicans called the Miranda Brothers. Alfred J. Miranda Jnr and Ignacio Miranda had been trading in weapons for years and their friendship with Sidney went back to the Newfoundland days. The Mirandas had an amazing knowledge of most new technologies. They were self-made men with a finely honed contempt for authority, which made them immediately attractive to Sidney.

After the end of World War I there was a glut of surplus weapons in Europe, especially in England. The Mirandas would buy up obsolete rifles and ammunition and sell them to anyone who wanted them. But it wasn't just guns. They dealt in tanks, military uniforms and even aircraft. In fact the Mirandas had been the middlemen in the deal to buy the Lockheeds.

In 1934, the Mirandas were the key witnesses before a US Senate committee which was investigating illegal arms dealings in South America. Through their British agent the Mirandas had access to $US30m of surplus war matériel such as Lewis and Hotchkiss machine guns, Colt pistols, light artillery and other weapons including 125 000 000 rounds of ammunition. Most of it was surplus British equipment left over from the Great War.

It was enough to start a war—in fact the war had already been started. The weapons had been ordered by Bolivia in its border dispute with Paraguay—the so-called Gran Chaco war. This contravened an arms embargo imposed by the United States. The Chaco was a desert region that bordered Paraguay and Bolivia. Bolivia had made a territorial claim to the Chaco to give it access to the ocean. The war lasted three years by which time a total of 90 000 men had been killed on the two sides. That represented a lot of guns and bullets to the Mirandas.

Alfred J. Miranda was as passionate about motor cars as he was about weapons. Sidney and Alfred had first met at the New York Motor Show in 1927. During the search for Nungesser and Coli, Miranda had arranged for Sidney to have a special DuPont car made in New York.

But for men who dealt in death the Mirandas were a surprisingly sophisticated duo. Alfred was squat and short but Ignacio—or Iggy as he was more commonly known—had the wasp waist of a Latin dancer. In fact he had taught the rhumba to both Cotton's wife and mistress. Sidney could not dance and hated it. Dancing with him, said Joan, was murder. He would sit glumly watching while Iggy strutted his stuff with Joan, placing his feet as carefully as a man laying tiles.

'He was a superb dancer,' said Pat Martin, 'Sidney did not like to dance but Iggy and I danced all night in New York.'

'They affected white fedoras,' said Joan. 'They were charming, amusing and very kind. One of them escorted me to a nightclub in Paris and I was propositioned by two lesbians who wanted to dance. I had never seen lesbians before and thought it quite interesting but there was trouble brewing so I was persuaded to leave.'

The Gran Chaco case dragged on for six years and it was not until 1940 that the Mirandas were sentenced. The brothers received prison terms of a year and a day and were fined a total of $US24 000. Alfred J. Miranda was interned at the Federal prison in Lewisburg, Pennsylvania.

So for three years British Intelligence had been doing business with two men who had criminal records. But then spying, as Sidney was wont to remark, was a dirty business. 'If they trip over you in the grass, never admit anything and never, ever explain,' he said.

Patricia Martin was cold. The plane had been in the air for three hours and her fingernails were turning blue. It had been dawn when they had left Heston and all she had had to eat was a cheese sandwich and a mug of tea.

Her seat in the back of the aircraft was not the best. It bounced around with every air pocket and the endless throbbing of the engines was giving her a headache. She had killed time by writing letters and even the odd line of poetry but her writing did not seem as neat as usual; that was the way it was when you were deprived of oxygen, you went a bit strange.

From time to time she went to one of the side windows of the aircraft and slid it back, pushing her head out into the freezing air. The rearward view from the Lockheed was poor but Sidney had told her to keep a sharp lookout for fighters. They were somewhere over Germany. Hamburg was it, or Mannheim or Kassel? Patricia had long since lost interest in exactly where.

Occasionally she picked up the oxygen bottle and pushed the rubber tube up one nostril. It hurt a bit. You would think they would have had masks. The hot pink angora sweater served two purposes, one was to keep her warm, the other as a signal to go on oxygen. Normally the sweater made her look chubbier than she really was but above 14 000 feet the hairs lay flat.

The cabin of the aircraft had heaters but if you opened the

window it very quickly went cold. Why not, she reasoned, install in its place a plastic blister into which she could put her head and look fore and aft of the aircraft. 'I thought something the shape of a washbasin would do the trick,' she said, and resolved to talk to Sidney about it later. Sidney thought it such a good idea that he arranged for Pat to explain it to some aircraft engineers at Farnborough. Later he claimed that the invention was his. The patented teardrop was licensed to the Triplex glass company and 10 000 of them were fitted to British and American aircraft during the war. Sidney said that he never made a cent out of the invention. Pat, however, recalls that he later asked her to sign a document at the Air Ministry agreeing to make no claim for payment.

'There was a moratorium on war profits. I got nothing,' she said. 'Later Sidney got me to sign a second document to give the Americans permission to use the teardrop canopy on their heavy bombers—the Liberator I think it was.' It occurred to Pat later that the allowance that his secretary paid her possibly came from the money he made by licensing the canopy to the Americans. 'But I could not be sure,' she said. 'And I did not care. I loved him and he looked after me.'

The big camera was mounted in the floor and this also drew warm air out of the cabin. Sidney had told her that the lenses needed to be kept warm if they were not to attract condensation. This would cause any photographs taken to be out of focus. She experimented by pushing bookends down into the cavity and deflecting the air over the lenses. It worked. Later the hole in the floor was modified with L-shaped aluminium baffles. Pat Martin was not an aircraft engineer but she had a fertile mind.

Sometimes the Lockheed would be in the air for eight hours. Keeping a constant lookout for fighter aircraft became very tiring, but only on one occasion were they intercepted. 'We were going to the Friesian islands when a fighter came alongside and took a look at us,' said Pat. Sidney did not wait to see what was going to happen. He pushed the control column forward and headed for the deck flat out.

'Then we roared up as high as we could go,' said Pat. Even though the Lockheed was a passenger plane it had a fair turn of speed and could outrun many aircraft.

If they were intercepted they had a plan to dump the cameras. The technique which Sidney rehearsed many times was to throw the plane into a dive them pull out just above the treetops. With the flick of a switch all the cameras would be jettisoned into the trees. Then Sidney would fly the aircraft erratically, looking as if he was out of control. He would land the plane at the first available aerodrome and then pretend to the authorities that he was lost. If the cameras were found in the woods they would deny all knowledge of them.

Sidney's luck had held so far. But there is no doubt that his frequent trips in and out of Germany were starting to arouse suspicion. On 17 August while en route to Berlin he made a diversion forty miles off his usual track to photograph airfields north of Berlin.

Among them was the highly sensitive German Air Ministry's test centre at Rechlin where new aircraft were evaluated.This time somebody saw him and telephoned airfield security at Tempelhof. What was this civilian aircraft doing nosing about over Rechlin? The eversmiling Schoene was there to greet Sidney as he landed. 'Security would like to see you,' he explained. 'They want to know why you were flying so far north.'

Cotton thought quickly. How could he justify approaching Tempelhof from due north when the airfield was south of the city? Aviators making long distance flights often take what is known as a great circle route, the shortest distance between departure point and destination. Sidney had taken a northward arc. 'I always fly on a great circle course,' he said, which would have explained him coming from the north. That seemed to keep Schoene happy.

Sidney's egotism and single-mindedness did not endear him to everyone. But his most faithful paladin was Robert Niven, his engineer, navigator and co-pilot. When he had first been looking for a co-pilot he had specified a Canadian or Australian rather than an Englishman.

'I wanted someone with initiative who wouldn't mind roughing it if necessary,' he said.

Sidney liked the look of Niven from the first time he saw him. Joan Henry thought him closer to Niven than anyone. 'Bob was very loyal to Sidney and they were a great team,' she said. 'But Sidney was always the boss.'

'When I told him I did lots of flying to various places and the flights were not altogether devoid of risk, his interest grew,' Sidney said of Niven.

During the Great Depression Niven had driven Greyhound buses in Calgary. At technical college he was in the first class of nine students registered for the Faculty of Aeronautics Technology, before he had learned to fly. He got his wings with the Calgary Aero Club but there were few opportunities for pilots either as a civilian or in the military. In the 1930s the Royal Canadian Air Force was only a small military force, whereas in England the Royal Air Force was looking for qualified students to register for short service commissions. Niven was the first Canadian to be accepted.

Niven was so keen he agreed to work his passage to England, accompanying a herd of cattle first by train to Halifax, Nova Scotia, then by ship to England. He was zestful and enthusiastic but he knew never to question Sidney's command. His strength lay in precisely navigating the aircraft on its missions over Germany. Sidney found navigation tiresome and preferred to leave it to the Canadian.

Bob Niven ended up marrying Sidney's second cousin, Andrea Johannson. She had been visiting Pat Martin at the hospital in London where she was recovering from one of the many operations on her legs. Andrea, petite and blonde had been doing photographic modelling at a department store. She had also landed a bit part in the Robert Donat movie *Goodbye Mr Chips*.

'Bob opened the door for me and I thought what a nice voice he's got.'

They rode up in the elevator to Pat Martin's room in the hospital.

'I was aware that he and Sidney were doing this secret work, but Sidney was always very much under control and I didn't ask questions. I was never quite sure where Pat Martin fitted into the picture but she used to darn Sidney's socks.'

Andrea and Bob had dinner at the RAF club in Piccadilly after the outbreak of war. They were married on 18 June 1940. At the service Sidney gave her away and Maurice 'Shorty' Longbottom was best man.

Bob Niven did some of his most dangerous flying with Sidney. But unlike his commanding officer he would not survive the war.

## Chapter 7

# The Reichmarschall

On 28 July 1939, Sidney flew back to Germany, and this time the secret cameras were in place. The event was an international air meeting for sports pilots in Frankfurt; the second Internationalen Luftrennen. The flying meeting was packed with Luftwaffe officers including Erhard Milch, deputy head of the Luftwaffe, Generalleutnant Ernst Udet, Gruppenfuhrer von Molitor, KorpsFuehrer General der Flieger Christiansen and Rudolf Bottger the commandant of Templehof airport. Two of the men in that list had something in common. Later in life both Udet and Bottger were to put a pistol to their heads and blow their brains out.

Cotton's German agent, Herr Schoene, explained that the Luftwaffe had been ordered to attend the meeting in force as a demonstration of their great friendship for England. Cotton also pointed out that this could have been an attempt to intimidate them.

But one of the most striking Nazis was Albert Kesselring. Kesselring was a Reichswehr colonel in mufti who had transferred from the artillery to become Milch's chief of administration. To his officers he was known as 'Smiling Albert' but beneath the smile there was an ambitious man. Winterbotham had met him during his intelligence gathering trips to Germany, and was impressed.

'Kesselring was very clever and very charming and we got on extremely well. We both knew that we were going to be enemies but that didn't stop him. He still thought right up to 1937 that Britain would not fight.'

Kesselring, square, swarthy, with beetling black eyebrows and a taciturn almost rude manner bluntly asked Cotton if he could go for a flight in the Lockheed. Sidney, charming as ever, said he would be delighted. Kesselring was a keen pilot. Could he take over the controls?

'Of course,' said Cotton. They took off to fly up the Rhine to Mannheim. 'Despite the presence of the great Kesselring, the opportunity was too good to be missed,' said Winterbotham. Cotton reached under the seat and activated the cameras. The only indication that the cameras were running was a green light on the control panel that started to click on and off showing the continuity of exposures.

Kesselring was intrigued. What was the flashing green light? Cotton glibly explained that the light showed the petrol flow to the engines and Kesselring seemed to accept the explanation. So below the Nazi's very jackboots the cameras snapped away! The joyflight turned spyflight and the German Leica cameras had produced some excellent pictures of new airfields on the fifty mile flight up the Rhine to Mannheim, pictures that Winterbotham desperately wanted. There was no need to fly high—the Lockheed had permission for the joyflights and rarely flew higher than two thousand feet.

Kesselring was not the only German to ride in Cotton's aircraft In fact there was a lot of competition for joyrides. Rudolph Bottger, the commandant of Templelhof airport also took a trip when Cotton said that he wanted to visit a beautiful part of the Rhine at Mannheim which was much beloved by his maiden aunt—a total fabrication. Passing over a particularly conspicuous military installation, Cotton made a show of being embarrassed. Hiding his face in his hands he said, 'I'm sure I'm not supposed to see that.'

Pat Martin did not accompany Sidney on this flight. Given the clandestine nature of the operation, it was curious that Cotton should have chosen instead two journalists, Gilruth and Grey, to accompany him. Margaret Gilruth, the strikingly beautiful daughter of James Gilruth, the administrator for the Northern Territory of Australia, was the European correspondent for the Melbourne *Herald* and was later to become secretary to Lady Casey.

Charles Grey, or C. G. Grey as he was known in his magazine *The Aeroplane*, was the one of the world's best known aviation writers. Grey's report of the Frankfurt flying meeting gave no hint of the spy flights down the Rhine. If Grey had any inkling of the real reason for Cotton's visit he was not letting on. His report waxed lyrical on the spirit of international friendship and the great hospitality of the Germans. Britain and Germany would be at war within two months but Grey was optimistic.

'I suggest seriously,' he wrote, 'that a colossal meeting on such a scale would be an excellent way of not so much promoting as celebrating the outbreak of Peace next year.' (The same time next year, July 1940, the Battle of Britain was being fought.)

Margaret Gilruth's report was similarly cheerful. Sandwiched in between the springtime fashions and and the wedding notices she wrote: 'Foreigners were to be the guests of the Aero Club of Germany and an international non-political atmosphere would prevail.'

Alex Henshaw the test pilot was one of the ninety British racing pilots who had taken a light aircraft to Frankfurt. He did not find the atmosphere quite so non-political. He had known a number of German fliers when they had visited England. Now he found they were wearing Luftwaffe uniforms.

'I do not think,' wrote Winterbotham, 'there was any Italian aerodrome, barracks, naval base or other object of military interest in southern Italy, the Eastern Mediterranean or North Africa which was not recorded in great detail by those splendid cameras.'

Cotton experimented with both the Leica and F 24 cameras and a combination of both. At one point he installed the Leicas in the leading edge of the wing. In addition they carried Leica cameras loose in the cockpit that could be hidden away should the aircraft be searched.

It was all going very smoothly and the men in Whitehall were more than happy with Sidney's pictures. Now Sidney was to undertake a mission which had the potential to blow the whole operation.

Eighty kilometres north of Berlin on the road to Bremen is a country house called the Karinhalle. To get there takes you through one of the most beautiful forests in that part of Germany: the Schorfheide.

The road to the Karinhalle stretches for eight kilometres through the woods. From his seat in the front of the black Horch limousine Sidney Cotton could just see the two swastika flags mounted on the wings and not much else. In his briefcase he had some colour photographs which demonstrated the startling trueness of the Dufaycolor format. Sidney had an appointment with another aviator, Hermann Goering.

Sidney had met Goering on a number of other occasions. Once he had taken his mistress, Pat Martin, to an air rally in Wiesbaden. Goering was guest of honour at the reception.

'There were a bunch of other aviators with their fancy planes,' said Pat. 'You got points for flying from A to B and points for how fast you had done the trip. The reception was at a magnificent house with great big halls that they had turned into dining rooms for all these aviators and their hangers on. They would take crews ahead to take care of the aircraft when it landed.'

Goering's table was on a raised dais and Pat caught his eye. What had attracted her attention was the fact that at the feet of the Deputy Führer was a leopard on leash. Goering loved big cats.

He would bring lion cubs to his house and romp with them in the living room floor. When they were mature he would donate them to the Berlin Zoo. Pat loved all animals and wanted to stroke the leopard. But Sidney had shaken his head and said no.

Hermann Wilhelm Goering, the second man of Germany, was passionate about many things: aeroplanes, art, cognac, hunting, beautiful women and of course Adolf Hitler. He counted among his triumphs the creation of the *Geheime Staatspolizei* or Gestapo and in 1933 he had placed his signature on a document setting up the first concentration camp, Oranienburg, in a suburb of Berlin.

In the early years of the NSDAP later to become known as the Nazi party, he had been one of Hitler's true believers. In 1939 he controlled the biggest air force in the world. A music hall joke of the time said that when Hermann Goering pressed a button he could put so many planes in the air even the birds had to walk.

A seemingly endless procession of luminaries were entertained at his luxury house in the Schorfheide forest—not just aviators and diplomats but art dealers, music hall stars and photographers. Goering had entertained Hitler many times at the Karinhalle and also the Duke and Duchess of Windsor, who were known to be sympathetic to Hitler. Lord Halifax, the British Foreign Secretary, and Nevile Henderson, the British Ambassador, had gone hunting there and Henderson had shot a stag through the heart. Ernst Udet and Adolf Galland had visited the Karinhalle to discuss the operations at the Luftwaffe.

Charles Lindbergh who had made the first solo crossing of the Atlantic in 1927 went there in 1936 with his wife, Anne Morrow Lindbergh. Like the Windsors, they were favourably inclined towards the Third Reich.

Hermann Goering's massive oak desk, which had once belonged to Cardinal Mazarin of France, befitted a man as substantial as the Reichsmarschall. On the desk, between the green shaded lamp and the telephone stood a dish of white pills which some might have mistaken for mints. They were in fact paracodeine pills which had a powerful narcotic effect when taken in quantity. In Goering's case they were a substitute for morphine. He gobbled them like a schoolboy with sweets.

It was from behind this desk in May 1939 that he received the tall Australian. Goering, pomaded and obese, polished a fingernail and looked at Sidney Cotton with interest. Emmy Sonnemann his second wife and former radio star hovered at his side with a pot of coffee.

The Iron Man waved her impatiently aside. He looked through a magnifying glass at half a dozen colour photographs which Cotton had spread on the desk in front of him. The colour quality was excellent. This, explained Sidney in his quiet doctor's voice, was Dufaycolor. He had found it, he had patented it and he partly owned it. The success of Dufaycolor, Cotton's new colour photographic technique had already reached Goering's ears.

The Nazis had nationalised the film industry and under the influence of Joseph Goebbels was making propaganda films or sentimental melodramas. Later in the war the German film industry was to produce the heroic epic *Pour Le Mérite*, which celebrated Goering's life as a fighter pilot in World War I. Goering was on the board of the Agfa company. In fact, Goering was on the board of many companies.

The Reichsmarschall had a passing interest in photography. During World War I Goering had taken pictures from the air himself. As an observer it had been his job to manhandle the huge plate camera over the side of the aircraft. His pictures of French artillery positions were said to have been excellent but they were in black-and-white. Cotton's were in colour.

The Deputy Führer rose to his feet. He was dressed, thought Sidney, like Robin Hood. Velvet knickerbockers, shoes with gold buckles and a sleeveless leather hunting jacket. 'These pictures are good, Herr Cotton. I would like to show you some of my pictures.'

Touching Cotton on the elbow he led him down a great gallery hung with Gobelin tapestries and paintings by the old masters. Goering had turned the Karinhalle into a private museum full of art treasures, some acquired in legimate transactions and some from enemies of the state—mostly Jews—whose possessions had been seized.

It would be a year before Goering was to go on his shopping trip to Paris and acquire even more art treasures. Then he was to drive down the Champs Elysées in a confiscated Rolls Royce, stopping off at galleries to steal everything that was not screwed to the floor: paintings by Cranach, Velásquez and Goya; oriental carpets; alabaster vases and furniture; even a huge wooden crucifix.

In halting English and occasionally assisted by Schoene, Goering took Cotton on a guided tour of the great house and explained to him the history of the Karinhalle. It was built, he said, in honour of his first wife the Swedish countess, Karin von Kantzow, who was buried there in a pewter sarcophagus. She had died in Sweden but the Swedes had defaced her grave in the Lovo cemetery in Stockholm. Perhaps it was the swastika on the headstone that had upset the cautious and conservative Swedes? It was of no consequence. After the Germans became the masters of Europe its empire would stretch from northern Norway to the coast of North Africa.

The Führer himself had attended the reinternment of the beautiful Karin in the underground mausoleum at Karinhalle. It had been a grand ceremony. The orchestra played Wagner. The soldiers carried the huge bier. A fine tribute to a woman that the Führer had called the noblest in all Germany. Would Mr Cotton like to visit the tomb—down by the lake?

The Reichsmarschall's estate was formidable and eclipsed the modest properties of some of the other Nazi leaders. In his position as Minister for Forests and Minister for Hunting Goering had acquired vast areas of the Schorfheide forest that had previously been public land. The forest was stocked with game—deer, boar, bison and even elk imported from Sweden. Did Mr Cotton like hunting? The Deputy Führer was passionate about it. Life at the Karinhalle was like the court of the Borgia's. Guests dined on game in a banqueting hall adorned with hunting trophies and tapestries, and sipped the finest wines from crystal glasses. Goering loved the good life.

'Rank has its privileges,' said the Reischsmarschall, offering Cotton a cigar. Sidney politely declined and discreetly steered the conversation towards common ground.

Had they not both been aviators in the Great War? What a pity they had been on opposing sides. The British and the Germans were cousins, argued Goering, they were Anglo-Saxons. The common enemy was the Bolsheviks. The Russians and Poles were of little consequence. Had not the Bolsheviks murdered their royal family the Czars? Had not the British attempted to stage a counter-revolution in Russia?

'Of course, Mr Cotton, I have done a little flying myself,' said Goering.

'I have been to England. I have friends there. In fact I would love to see London again.'

In World War I Goering had taken over command of the legendary Richthofen Geschwader after the Red Baron had been killed and had personally shot down twenty-two British and French aircraft. But had not Mr Cotton also flown in combat?

Sidney made the grand tour to the Gasteflugel guest wing, the Bibliotheksflugel library wing and the Wirtschaftsflufgel kitchen wing past the elaborate dining hall. Goering proudly showed him his enormous model railway layout which occupied a room of its own. Cotton noticed it even had small aeroplanes which at the touch of an electric switch could be made to drop bombs.

Sidney waited until the Deputy Führer drew breath. It was indeed a splendid house. Would it be appropriate to have photographs taken in Dufaycolor? Of course, beamed Goering. But, he said, his smile congealing, it might not be appropriate to film the air raid shelters which were under construction, or the flak towers with their 88 millimetre anti-aircraft guns. The fat man was shrewd enough to realise that his house could become a prime target for bombers. Goering was as concerned about his personal safety as he was about his collection of fine wines. 'And I am sure there would be people in London who would like to know where to find me.'

Just above the tall pine trees Sidney could see the flakturm (flak towers). At the rear of the house, builders were excavating Goering's private air raid shelter, the *unteridischer bunkern*. There were mounds of earth, piles of cement, scaffolding and steel girders.The underground bunker complex was enormous with reinforced concrete a metre thick in places. The entrance was at the base of the house facing out over the lake known as the Grosser Dollnsee.

The two Dufaycolor photographers, whom Cotton had recruited from the Tobis plant, had been cooling their heels in the reception hall of the great house. Now Sidney told them to go for a stroll and get whatever pictures they could. In addition to shots of the house and the gardens with its bronze stags, Sidney made it clear what he wanted.

'Get the travel brochure stuff,' he said, and then, more quietly, 'and anything else of interest.' The photographers snapped away at the entrances to the bunkers.

When Cotton flew out of Tempelhof a few days later he carried a briefcase full of colour pictures of Goering's Waldhof. Goering's house was now a target on many maps, but curiously, it was never bombed by the Allies. Only by the man who owned it.

In the last days of peace, Cotton's Lockheed had achieved almost ambassadorial status in Germany. Sidney made regular trips to Berlin to see Herr Schoene and another man called Traeder. Both of them professed not to be members of the Nazi party. Winterbotham thought otherwise. And both had a place at Goering's table.

For the early flights, the hatch in the belly of the aircraft was kept closed and no cameras were installed. Winterbotham was convinced that the Germans had made a close inspection of the aircraft at night the first time it was parked at Tempelhof. Having found nothing suspicious, the Lockheed was no longer of any interest.

The cameras were then reinstalled and the Lockheed became operational for espionage. Cotton varied his flight plan into Berlin, sometimes refuelling at Hamburg or Frankfurt which would give him a 'run' over new aerodromes, factories or military establishments that the Secret Intelligence Service wanted photographed.

On one of his Berlin trips, Cotton sounded out Schoene on the prospects of war. 'Goering is wavering,' said Schoene. 'He used to think that England would not fight over Poland but now he's not so sure.'

The last week of August was hot and sultry in Berlin and to avoid the humidity Berliners sat in the shade of the chestnut trees dotted around the Wannsee. Most British and French civilians had closed down their houses, packed up their belongings picked up their families and shipped out. Hitler had planned a big rally at Tannenberg on 27 August but it was cancelled as was the annual party convention in Nuremberg. That same day, the government announced that rationing would be introduced on food, soap, shoes, textiles and coal.

Most Germans thought that an attack on Poland was justified, having been sold a line by that brilliant propagandist Joseph Goebbels. For the previous six years, the free press in Germany had been stifled by the Nazis. While the rest of the world believed that peace was about to be broken by Germany, the Germans believed it was Poland threatening Germany with invasion. The *Bild Zeitung* headline screamed:

'POLISH SOLDIERS PUSH TO EDGE OF GERMAN BORDER.'

In fact, one and half million German soldiers stood on the border between Germany and Poland. Germany wanted Britain to keep out of the conflict with Poland; it wanted a pact or alliance and the return of its overseas colonies. In return Germany would pledge itself to defend the British Empire, which Hitler considered a stabilising influence throughout the world. Like many others in England, Cotton was dissatisfied with the conciliatory way in which negotiations with the Germans had been handled. A firmer hand was needed.

Neville Chamberlain had been to Germany several times for talks with Hitler and was anxious to avoid war at any cost. But Hitler had never been to England and was not likely to. Goering, however, had Hitler's ear. If Goering could be persuaded to come to England on an informal visit perhaps he in turn could be persuaded that Britain would fight. There is certainly no doubt that Goering was receptive to the idea.

He had been to England once before in 1925.

During the Great War he had made friends with Captain Frank Beaumont, a British pilot in the Royal Flying Corps. Frank Beaumont had crashed behind enemy lines injuring his foot. Goering, himself a fighter pilot, had refused to allow Beaumont to be imprisoned and brought him chocolates and brandy. At the end of the war the two gentleman fliers met again in Munich. When Goering travelled to London in 1925 Beaumont repaid Goering's earlier kindness by being a lavish host. They remained friends until the outbreak of World War II.

Cotton was not the only peacebroker coming and going from Heston. The Swedish businessman Birger Dahlerus had high connections in Berlin and London. Like Cotton he had contact with Lord Halifax but he was also friends with Goering. Unlike Cotton he went to considerable lengths to conceal his movements in both Whitehall and the Wilhelmstrasse.

Goering was certainly planning to go to London. He did not want war. He believed that if only the British would bring pressure on the Poles to talk, the conflict could be avoided. On 19 August he saw Hitler and received permission to fly to London, providing Chamberlain agreed, for talks with the Prime Minister and other members of the cabinet. On 21 August he phoned Dahlerus in Stockholm and said: 'I am going to try something radically different. It's the only way to break the deadlock I think.'

At the same time the British Ambassador in Berlin, Sir Nevile Henderson (who always believed that Goering was the only reasonable man in the Nazi party) sent a cipher telegram to London saying that Goering was prepared to fly to Britain on 23 August.

'This seemed the best remaining hope of averting war,' wrote Cotton.

Goering's visit was to be made in the greatest secrecy. Chamberlain's staff at his country residence, Chequers, would be given leave of absence and their chores done by the Secret Service. 'All telephones are to be disconnected,' Lord Halifax reported. 'It looks as if it is going to be a dramatic interlude, and having laid the plans we await confirmation from Germany.' That confirmation never came.

On 21 August German radio announced that the Greater German Reich and the People's Republic of the Soviet Union had agreed to a mutual non-aggression pact.

Cotton asked Schoene if he would ask Goering to fly with him to England for talks with Neville Chamberlain and Lord Halifax the British foreign secretary (who had already met Goering and even visited the fabulous Karinhalle), Sir Alexander Cadogan and others. The Lockheed, which had been such a hit in Frankfurt, was to be placed at the Deputy Führer's disposal. The scheme was entirely of Cotton's doing.

To Cotton's astonishment, the invitation was accepted. Goering was to fly to England with Cotton on 24 August arriving not at Heston but at White Waltham aerodrome which was close to the Prime Minister's country seat of Chequers. Cotton passed the offer on to Lord Halifax and a day later a letter arrived from No. 10 Downing Street. It read:

> Dear Mr Cotton,
> I write this note to say that if your friend comes over soon, the Prime Minister and I who have both already met him shall be glad to see him. Yours Sincerely, Halifax.

It was not his place to do so but Cotton tried to stage manage the whole visit. As Goering was flying to England in his aeroplane, should he not be picked up at the airfield in Cotton's red Hotchkiss and not a government car? Would this not be less formal? The visit should be as informal as possible.

'We do not want a battery of impeccable politicians and civil servants with black coats, striped trousers and long faces, all sitting around ready to pounce.' Perhaps Sidney Cotton had already had enough of British protocol. He was after all an Australian who called a spade a bloody shovel!

Fred Winterbotham did not approve. Cotton was not a diplomat, he was an aviator and a businessman. Winterbotham thought that Cotton was suffering from delusions of grandeur to think he could broker peace between Britain and Germany.

'Cotton was riding high on the success of his photographic missions,' said Winterbotham. 'He was impatient to cash in his new image. Apparently encouraged by his friends in Berlin he produced a hare-brained scheme to fly Goering from Berlin to London to meet Halifax in an effort to avert war. In his new found glory he took his idea over my head to Stewart Menzies, who in turn was always prepared to try to get a bit of kudos from Downing Street. Presumably not understanding what it was all about, Chamberlain gave permission for the flight, and unknown to myself Cotton set off for Berlin'.

Sir Stewart Menzies was boss of MI6 from 1939 to 1952. He was considered to be no great intellect but to have exceptionally good social connections and did not disguise the fact that he was an illegitimate son of Edward VII. He had a passion for fox hunting and a taste for the smartest London clubs like Whites and Boodles—traditional recruiting grounds for MI6. Menzies' speciality was to take the credit for work done by his officers by turning up at 10 Downing Street, presenting little parcels of intelligence to the Prime Minister and passing them off as his own work.

Cotton had been introduced to Stewart Menzies on 19 August and told him that he felt that Goering had more influence on Hitler than anyone else. Menzies saw that the mission might be a chance to make a name for himself, hopeless though it was. He told Cotton: 'Well done, this might change everything.'

In Cotton's presence he called the Prime Minister, Neville Chamberlain, and within minutes Lord Halifax the foreign secretary told him: 'The Prime Minister has agreed to your proposal. You will receive a letter saying your friend will be welcome.'

Winterbotham was scathing of Cotton's 'hair-brained crackpot scheme'.

'He could never resist playing politics and getting mixed up in situations he did not understand.'

And since the records of MI6 remain closed to historians there is no way of knowing for certain how or by whom this approach was made. However, Winterbotham was justifiably concerned. If the Germans had found out what Cotton was up to he would almost certainly have faced a firing squad. By this time he had installed various combinations of cameras in the Lockheed. But when he and Niven flew back to Berlin on 22 August they were careful to leave the wing Leicas behind and take only two cameras loose in the cabin.

In 1939 the best place to stay in Berlin was the Hotel Adlon at 77 Unter den Linden. Since it had opened in 1907 it had become the most fashionable meeting place in Berlin. It was the favourite hotel of Kaiser Wilhelm II who treated it as one of his palaces. Greta Garbo, Charlie Chaplin, the tenor Enrico Caruso and Franklin D. Roosevelt had all stayed there. Albert Einstein, whom Hitler despised for practising what he called Jewish physics, used to wave to crowds from his corner window on the Pariser Platz overlooking the Brandenburg Gate.

Sidney Cotton, as usual, was doing things in style. As he strolled through the lobby past the elegant black marble fountain with its carved elephant heads the faint sounds of a waltz were drifting from the ballroom. The war was only days away but it was business as usual at the Adlon. As he stepped onto the balcony of his room overlooking the Unter den Linden, a different kind of music was coming from the street: the sound of jackboots and the coming and going of staff cars. The Wehrmacht was on the move that day.

Cotton slipped a deutschmark into the hand of the waiting porter who thanked him and murmured, 'Der beginn eines wunderbaren Aufenthalts,' (the start of a wonderful day).

As it happened it was to be anything but.

Cotton was to stay at the Adlon and await further instruction. His *carnet de passage* was the Halifax letter which he had entrusted to Traeder to show to Goering's chief of staff.

The tentative arrangement was that Cotton was to fly to Munich, land at Hitler's private aerodrome, pick up Goering and return to England via Berlin. Even Sidney was starting to have second thoughts. Did he seriously think that he could broker a peace agreement between the two superpowers simply because he had a tenuous business agreement with the Deputy Führer and had taken some flattering pictures of his house?

Winterbotham had thought the whole affair extremely dangerous and warned Sidney: 'I don't want you to get caught in Berlin when the balloon goes up. If the situation looks really desperate I'll cable you saying Mother is ill and sign it "Mary". If you get a cable like that come back at once.'

In an atmosphere of increasing tension, Sidney waited by the telephone in his hotel room for the call that never came.

On 23 August, Hitler signed a non-aggression pact with Stalin—a pact that was to last just ten months. Cotton was one of the first foreigners to be told. Schoene and Traeder rushed round to the Adlon Hotel to tell Cotton that the pact with Stalin might alter everything. A short time later word came that Goering's trip to England was off. The trip had been dismissed out of hand by the German Under Secretary Ernst Woermann, head of the political department and, by coincidence, also the Foreign Ministry's liaison officer with the various German clandestine services. He dismissed it as 'amateur diplomacy'.

Cotton went back to his room to find a telegram from Fred

Winterbotham. 'Mother is ill,' it said and was signed 'Mary', Schoene and Traeder also implored Cotton to get out while he still could. 'I was determined not to leave until I had done everything I could to convince the Germans that Britain would fight.'

While Cotton was with the distraught Germans, another cable arrived from 'Mary'. It read: 'Mother very low and asking for you.'

'I admired Winterbotham's phraseology; undoubtedly it was time to go,' said Cotton.

He screwed up the telegram and tossed it into the wastepaper basket. His suitcase was open on the bed. He threw the rest of his clothes into it, slammed it shut and headed for the lobby.

'I was an Australian and Bob Niven was a Canadian but if England went to war I had no doubt that our countries would follow suit at once and we would both be interned. Undoubtedly, it was time to go.'

He got into the car and threaded his way through the southern suburbs of Berlin towards Tempelhof.

In 1939, Tempelhof was Berlin's main civilian airport and the airliners of many nations were usually lined up in front of the terminal building. Now the departure hall was eerily silent and the tarmac packed with row after row of freshly camouflaged fighter aircraft. The tourists and businessmen had all departed. Tempelhof was at war.

In the air movements section, Sidney tried to persuade the Germans to let them go, but his control of the language was barely adequate. Sidney was used to talking his way out of things but this time he was up against a brick wall. It was *verboten*. All flying had ceased. Nothing was flying in or out of the airport.

'Even the birds are walking,' said one official in a rare flash of German humour.

Cotton decided to make a dash for it. Bob Niven, fortunately, had remained behind at the airport to prepare the Lockheed for flight.

The engines were cold so before starting Niven had to pull the propellers manually around until the blades had passed him nine times. This was to clear any oil that might have been in the cylinders. In the cockpit Sidney Cotton's heart was pounding. He tried to look calm as he switched the master switch to 'FLIGHT'.

He had started the Lockheed a million times but now he was all fingers and thumbs. Prime left engine—ignition switch ON—mixture fully rich—crack throttle. He pushed the BOOST and START buttons. The left engine coughed and the propeller turned, the exhaust blowing black smoke. Sidney waited for the oil pressure to come up before starting the right engine. The propeller turned but it would not start. Finally after what seemed an eternity it fired and blew smoke. They were on their way.

They taxied out slowly to the holding area just off the runway and Sidney ran up the engines to check for magneto drop. All they needed now was a green light. But as he turned the plane into the wind to start his take-off run a steady red light shone from the tower. While they sat waiting, Cotton wondered about the best escape route. The shortest way out of Germany was via Poland, but that was the way the troops were heading. Then he thought of heading to Italy at treetop height but that made them vulnerable to anti aircraft fire and fighters.

After waiting in the plane for an hour, Cotton and Niven saw a car driving towards them across the airfield. Could this be trouble? Were the airfield guards coming to arrest them? The engines were still warm and Cotton prepared to restart them, his hands moving towards the throttles.

But the car contained Schoene, Traeder and the airport commandant Rudolf Bottger. Sidney stood at the door in the rear of the plane and Schoene handed him a slip of paper with the flight instructions clearly marked. Schoene was agitated.

Their flight out of Germany had been approved, and the anti-aircraft batteries had been advised of their route. So long as they flew at a height of nine hundred feet they could leave German airspace unmolested. Cotton liked Schoene; he had been a genuine friend but despite the warmth of his handshake he knew that soon they would be on opposing sides.

The Lockheed roared down the runway and lifted off. Even the normally insouciant Sidney looked ruffled under his white cotton shirt. Bob Niven sat red faced and silent over the map. It had been a close call, and there were still 250 miles to go to the border. They flew over Rathenow, Salzwedal, and Soltau, striking the border between Holland and Germany near Oldenburg.

During the earlier spy flights they had rarely encountered enemy aircraft. Now beneath them they saw bombers heading east towards Poland. They were painted dark green and it was not easy to see them against the tops of the trees.

But there was work to be done. Looking back over their shoulders towards Germany they could see an amazing sight; the autumn sunlight glinting on hundreds of ships. It was the German naval base at Wilhelmshaven and it was just waiting to be photographed.

There was the cruiser *Emden*, a ship of the Scharnhorst class, an armoured ship—probably the *Scheer*—and two destroyers.

Also at anchor was the slim outline of Hitler's personal yacht the *Grille*.

Niven and Cotton retrieved the handheld Leicas from their hiding places and clicked away excitedly. Here was something that would interest the Admiralty. Sidney was exhausted so he asked Niven to take over the controls for most of the return trip.

Three hours and fifty five minutes after they had taken off from Tempelhof, Sidney lowered the wheels and the Lockheed sighed onto the tarmac at Heston. 'Where have you come from, Mr Cotton?' asked the customs official.

'Berlin,' said Sidney.

'Left it a bit late, haven't you?'

So the famous Lockheed achieved the distinction of being the last civilian aircraft to leave Berlin before the outbreak of World War II.

A week later Hitler marched into Poland.

Cotton's 'amateur diplomacy' in the Lockheed had infuriated Winterbotham so much that they were barely on speaking terms. He felt that if the Lockheed had been detained in Germany it would have blown the whole aerial spying operation.

In his book Winterbotham even disputes the fact that Cotton took the Wilhelmshaven pictures. 'I dared not try to contact Cotton personally but I managed to get a signal to the Air Attaché in Berlin asking him to send Cotton back if things looked like getting too hot. I knew quite well it was a hopeless mission from the start but of course it had got Cotton once again closer to Downing Street. 'There is no truth in Cotton's story that he took the pictures on the way back from Berlin. He had only been allowed to leave Berlin if he agreed to fly at five hundred feet on a given course to London, nowhere near the Elbe and certainly not high enough to see it.'

Winterbotham claimed that the pictures of Wilhelmshaven were taken not from the Lockheed but by a small Beechcraft piloted by Niven the following day. This was a Beechcraft Staggerwing registered G-AESJ which was used as a communications aircraft by the unit.

The cameras had been operated by a 'very gallant passport photographer who normally supplied us with both real and false passport photos'. As the Beechcraft flew nearer to the mouth of the River Elbe two German fighter aircraft came up and started firing shots across the nose of the little biplane. They turned but at that moment the sun shone and the photographer took five long range oblique pictures. It was touch and go.'

Winterbotham was so annoyed about Cotton's unauthorised mission to Berlin that he told him he was now going to ask the Air Ministry to ground the Lockheed. 'The Air Ministry were already asking me to pass over to them the whole outfit so that they could adopt the technique for the air force who were proposing to start it up as a proper RAF unit. I was glad to do this for I felt that Cotton in uniform would have to do as he was told.'

Pat Martin now became a permanent member of Sidney's team. But being Sidney's kept woman she scarcely gets a mention in his own memoirs. 'She lacked neither courage or looks and was an expert photographer,' wrote Cotton.

One evening she had called at Cotton's flat in Arlington House while he and Niven were planning a mission to photograph Heligoland, the Danish island of Sylt and airfields in the Friesian islands. Sidney had asked her out to dinner but she arrived to find the two aviators sprawled on the floor studying maps. Dinner, said Cotton, rather curtly, was off. Pat pestered Cotton to take her on the mission. The two pilots were hungry. She would cook them dinner at home but only if they agreed to take her on the flight. Cotton agreed.

On this mission the aircraft was loaded with cameras. The remotely operated F 24 cameras installed in the holes in the fuselage could be operated from the cockpit but a spare hand was needed to operate the handheld Leicas. The aircraft took off from Heston on a flight plan which would take them towards Copenhagen. Cotton's cover, as ever, was that he was flying to Copenhagen on Dufaycolor business.

This time Pat sat up the front taking pictures with handheld cameras.

The best photographic results, said Pat, were always taken in early morning or late afternoon. 'If you were directly overhead the target at noon it was no good. You have to have slanting shadows to compare the size of things.'

Cotton had one more mission to France before the outbreak of war. It was to take the Lockheed to France, pick up Winterbotham's children and fly them back to England. They were staying in Dinard. Tony Winterbotham was eight and having a pleasant summer holiday with his sister Susan. 'Sidney arrived in the middle of the night and we were told to pack our clothes in a hurry. We were very frightened.'

The Lockheed droned through the night back to England where the children were offloaded into Sidney's car and driven home. It was an enormous Plymouth, another of Sidney's fleet. She had never been in a car with leather seats before, let alone in one with

Sidney Cotton in 1941—with his immaculate suit, piercing blue eyes, and an expression that gave nothing away.

Air Vice-Marshal Sir Cyril Newall. It was Newall who gave Cotton his own photographic unit.

Air Chief Marshal Sir Richard Peirse, head of RAF Bomber Command. A career officer, he loathed Cotton, and conducted a lifelong vendetta against him.

'The girl in the red dress.' Pat Martin was Sidney's mistress for seven years, and was with him on the secret flights over Germany.

Sidney Cotton at the controls of his famous Lockheed 12 Junior Electra —the aircraft he used for his spy flights.

Crown Prince Faisal being entertained on board the *Amazone*. Just before the photograph was taken, he asked for his glass of whisky to be moved out of the picture.

Cotton's Lockheed—it is still flying in America today.

The *Amazone*, Sidney's 250-ton luxury motor yacht. It is still afloat in Rotterdam.

*Above*
Sidney with his first wife, Agnes Joan Regmor McLean, and his mother, Annie.

*Right*
This was taken on the steps of Mintoburn, the family home in Tasmania.

Air Marshal Sir Geoffrey Tuttle, the 'less controversial officer' who took over the Photographic Development Unit when Cotton was sacked.

Sidney Cotton in RAF uniform with Air Marshal 'Ugly' Barratt, commander of the RAF in France. They are examining some of the pictures taken by the PRU Spitfires.

The car which Cotton built in 1914 at Cassilis in New South Wales. Belt-driven and powered by a single cylinder engine, it had an infinite range of gears.

Sidney at the controls of the big Westland Limousine in Newfoundland.

The Westland, operating on skis from the ice.

A meeting of the Air Council in 1940. In the centre is Sir Kingsley Wood, and to the right, Sir Cyril Newall.

The man and his mission: Sidney Cotton farewells 'Shorty' Longbottom on the first photographic sortie in a PRU Spitfire, Lille 18 November 1939.

a cocktail cabinet and a radio with a speaker in the back. The radio was playing softly: *South of the Border Down Mexico Way*. To this day the song still triggers off memories.

Pat Martin, meanwhile, was to go on a solo espionage mission not to Germany but to Italy. For years she had been friends with an English family in Rome whose father was well connected with Mussolini. Pat was sent out to Rome as a listening post. Her task was to do the round of the cocktail parties to see what she could find out.

Germany was in the war but nobody was quite sure about Italy. Pat's assignment was to find out what the military were doing. She spoke good French and passable Italian. 'I would hear that a certain army officer was "moving south to Sicily with his troops", that "My son has taken his company north".'

She learned to listen and to converse but never to ask direct questions. The task involved a round of dreary cocktail parties which she hated. She wore her prettiest frock, smiled a lot and moved easily among the guests. At one function she was propositioned by one of Mussolini's sons, Carolino.

'He was charming as he was fun and no doubt it was prestigious to be seen with a blonde, blue-eyed Englishwoman. The Italians thought that Englishwomen were easy. This one wasn't.'

When she got back to England she filed her report. Her conclusion was that Italians would come into the war on the side of the Germans. In 1940 they did.

Cotton's spy flights in the Lockheed were not confined to Germany. They were to include a number of reconnaissance flights over neutral Ireland.

On 10 September 1940, Sidney Cotton opened the door of his flat in Mayfair to a debonair man in the uniform of a lieutenant commander in the Royal Navy. The man inserted a hand-made cigarette into an ivory holder and introduced himself as Ian Fleming of British Naval Intelligence. Fleming, who before the war had been a stockbroker, was later to achieve fame as the creator of the James Bond books. In many ways, Fleming was James Bond.

Fleming was personal assistant to the Director of Naval Intelligence, Rear Admiral John Godfrey. He drank martinis played roulette, drove fast cars, and chased the girls.

It would be fourteen years before Ian Fleming wrote the first James Bond book. But even in 1940 he acted the part. His office, in the headquarters of the Admiralty in the Mall, was number 39. It was popularly referred to as the 'Dirty Tricks Department'.

Fleming was interested in dirty tricks. He had suggested capturing a German bomber and crashing it in the English Channel so that the crew—posing as Germans—could capture a German rescue boat and its code books. He cultivated a man called Fraser Smith who specialised in fountain pens which could fire tear gas across a crowded room. Cotton liked that sort of stuff—now Fleming was to make use of him.

It was Fleming who had taken Sidney's pictures of the German fleet at Wilhelmshaven to the First Sea Lord Admiral, Sir Dudley Pound. On examining them Pound called for a magnifying glass but his secretary was unable to find one. Fleming had only been in the job a few weeks and was anxious to please. He picked up a glass bottle and suggested that it would do the trick. Pound said: 'Ah, I see you're one of those chaps who can see in the dark.'

Cotton liked Fleming right from the start. In fact Fleming had entertained Pat Martin and Sidney at his flat in Pimlico. Pat Martin however wasn't very keen on Fleming and found him remote and supercilious. 'He was out to make an impression but I was not impressed,' she said. 'He was very full of his own importance but did not come across to me as a virile man. If anything he was rather invisible. It is the same with lots of men. If they have a great talent they become completely isolated from reality.'

Some might have dismissed Fleming as an effete womaniser who lived out his fantasies through the handsome, ruthless character of James Bond. But Fleming was no coward.

He had organised the escape of British nationals from Bordeaux after the fall of France and was later to take part in the ill-fated Dieppe raid. Fleming made little effort to hide the fact that he found most women inferior and in conversation immediately set out to provoke them. He was gaunt and slightly effeminate. Some women might be attracted by his good looks but did not necessarily care for his manner.

Although Sidney didn't share Fleming's capacity for alcohol he admired his 'restless fantastic mind'. They were both enthusiastic about machines, weapons and gadgets.

His Majesty's Government, said Fleming, was worried about the back door. By this he meant the Irish Free State. At the outbreak of World War II Britain had the most powerful navy in world. But Germany had the means to sink it—the U-boat. Hitler had accelerated the production of submarines to a point where they threatened to outnumber those of the Royal Navy. A U-boat blockade of the British Isles would be a disaster. Moreover, His Majesty's Government were concerned that the Nazis might try to set up refuelling bases in the remote west coast of Ireland. There were scores of bays and inlets in the counties of Kerry and Cork where submarines could be hidden. Even before the war the German Intelligence Service, the Abwehr, had established links with the IRA and was poised to introduce German agents into Ireland.

There were good reasons to be concerned about the Irish back door. In 1939 the IRA had launched a bombing campaign in London and provincial cities such as Birmingham and Coventry. While preparing itself for an inevitable war with Germany the British people now had also to face an enemy from within.

At the outbreak of war, Ireland had declared itself neutral. The German Embassy operated openly from a house at 58 Northumberland Rd, Dublin, and was equipped with a powerful short wave transmitter.

As Fleming explained this to Cotton he asked whether the Australian could use the Lockheed to take pictures of the Irish coastline. In some ways this could be as dangerous as flying over

Germany. But Cotton did not seem unduly concerned about flying a spy mission over a neutral country.

'But it could be embarrassing if you were shot down?' said Fleming.

'I think that's unlikely,' said Cotton. 'The Irish only have one anti-aircraft gun. It was sold to them by an arms dealer friend of mine.'

The arms dealer was the Mexican Alfred J. Miranda who conducted all his European business through Cotton's London office.

Cotton and Niven took off from Heston, refuelling at Speke airport in Liverpool, then set a course for the west coast of Ireland. At a height of 10 000 feet they comfortably photographed the coastline without interference. But if the Irish were unconcerned about the spy flight, the Royal Air Force was decidedly peeved. Cotton and Niven were running low on fuel so they landed unannounced at the RAF base at West Freugh on the west coast of Scotland.

Both were arrested as spies and placed under close guard by the infuriated station commander Group Captain Smith Piggott. They were only released two hours later after a telephone call was made to Heston confirming who they were. Smith Piggott had taken a dim view of two civilians swanning about in a private plane.

Two weeks later the officer in charge of air traffic control at Heston gave Cotton a letter of passage addressed to the commanding officer of the RAF base at Aldergrove in Northern Ireland.

The letter read: 'Sir, will you please give all facilities to the pilot of G-AFTL (Lockheed Electra) who is proceeding on a special flight authorised by Fighter Command headquarters.'

When Cotton next met Fleming he had to report that the Irish flights had yielded nothing. But Fleming thought that the 'amazing Mr Cotton', as he called him, would prove an important asset to the navy. Fleming promised him the rank of captain if he switched his allegiance from the air force to the navy. It was, after all, the

Royal Naval Air Service that Cotton had served in during World War I, even if he had resigned his commission.

Once again Winterbotham was furious with Cotton. 'Cotton casually told me he thought of taking the job, despite the fact that he was still on my payroll and the aircraft and all the equipment belonged to the Secret Intelligence Service.'

The chief of staff took the matter to the Prime Minister and Churchill rightly ruled in favour of the RAF. But the relationship between Winterbotham and Cotton was irreparably damaged. Cotton had been a valuable ally. Now he was turning into a maverick. 'The affair was too much for Cotton's ego and he now declared that he would work on his own directly with the various directors of intelligence.'

Winterbotham threatened once again to ground the Lockheed. It was after all the SIS's aeroplane not Cotton's. Not only was this a breach of faith with Winterbotham and the Air Ministry, but random operations might cost them the secrets of the photographic operation and maybe the aircraft itself. 'I naturally advised the Air Ministry and, as a result, a violent row broke out between the Chief of Naval Staff and the Chief of Air Staff; not only because of the underhand way in which Ian Fleming had tried to entice Cotton, but also because there was a definite agreement between the services that the RAF alone was responsible for aerial photography.'

Ian Fleming enjoyed provoking the RAF. In 1939, the development of radar was still in its infancy and Cotton expressed serious doubts about the ability of the RAF to detect an enemy aircraft invading British air space. They devised a stunt whereby Cotton would fly the Lockheed from Heston to Portsmouth to Weymouth and back to Heston.

Fleming then contacted the Air Ministry saying that an enemy aircraft had been seen over Weymouth. Had the RAF seen it? The Air Ministry said that no plane had flown there, either friend or foe, which made a mockery of the RAF's primitive early warning system. The Irish flights were unproductive but Cotton was laying down a bedrock of intelligence with his flights over France.

## Chapter 8

# Cotton's Crooks

When Chamberlain reluctantly declared war on Germany on 3 September he offered Winston Churchill the post of First Lord of the Admiralty. The new War Cabinet was announced the following day and the message flashed to the fleet 'Winston is Back'. Churchill liked the navy and the navy liked him.

Churchill was more than impressed with Cotton's unit. 'When the Admiralty asked the RAF for photographs they couldn't get a single picture,' wrote Sidney. 'When they asked me for photographs I brought them an album.'

The RAF were now under pressure to take over Cotton's unit. Churchill, meanwhile, who had to depend upon the RAF for his pictures, said that if the air force didn't take it over the Admiralty would. Sidney was now to become acquainted with a man who was to make his life a misery. Air Marshal Sir Richard Peirse, the Vice Chief of Air Staff, thoroughly disapproved of Cotton and his unit. This was a job for professionals. What would Cotton know about it?

'Peirse was tall and with a proud carriage, hair greying at the temples but well brilliantined,' said Sidney.

'His manner seemed to dare anyone to oppose his ideas.'

German naval movements had been reported off the coast of Holland. The Admiralty urgently wanted pictures and Churchill was very disturbed about it. Could Cotton help?

'Lend me a Blenheim,' said Sidney. 'And I'll get the pictures straightaway.' The idea of lending a military aircraft to a civilian was unthinkable but the Air Force would be grateful for any suggestions he could make. The meeting ended in impasse. Sidney went back to his office in St James Square and gazed out across the rooftops. It was a perfect day for flying—a blue September sky with a few bits of fleecy cumulus.

If the air force wouldn't lend him a Blenheim perhaps it was time for the Lockheed to make just one more trip to Germany. Sidney called Heston and told the faithful Niven to prepare the Electra for the flight. Sidney told his secretary he would be out for the rest of the afternoon. Less than an hour after the meeting with Peirse, Cotton was rolling down the runway at Heston towards the gasworks at the end of the strip.

The war was two weeks old and movements by civilian aircraft were restricted. They had to have a cover story. Sidney radioed Heston control and said he was taking the aircraft on a test flight over the Channel just off the coast of Kent. In fact they headed out towards the Dutch coast.

They dodged in and out of the clouds to avoid any fighters that might be nosing around, but saw no other aircraft. They flew over Flushing at the entrance to the River Scheldt and set the cameras running. The weather conditions were ideal for photography. Having seen all they needed, Sidney turned the Lockheed back across the North Sea and headed for home.

The photographs were printed overnight. Cotton snatched a few hours sleep and then turned up at the office of the Director-

General of Operations, Air Vice Marshal Richard Peck, with an album containing the pictures taken at Flushing.

Cotton was a master of theatrical timing. He let the meeting run for half an hour before dropping the bombshell. Producing the album from his briefcase he set it on the table. Peck assumed that the pictures had been taken before the outbreak of war. 'These are first class,' he said. 'But we wouldn't expect this sort of quality in wartime.'

There was a pause then someone asked when the pictures had been taken.

Cotton said: 'At three fifteen yesterday afternoon.'

The room was in uproar. Peirse and some of the other officers thought it was scandalous that Cotton had deliberately flaunted authority by taking pictures of military targets while on an unauthorised civilian flight. One officer said that Cotton should be arrested. It was nothing that Sidney hadn't heard before: 'I could stand such nonsense no longer and I decided to get out of the room before I told them what I thought of them.'

Sidney turned on his heel and slammed the door as he went out.

Sir Richard Peirse was not a popular officer. As its commander in chief he achieved a reputation for an arrogant overconfidence in the work of Bomber Command. One associate said: 'He seemed to have little grasp of operational realities and was a most convenient scapegoat. He inspired little sympathy or affection among his subordinates at Bomber Command and little faith in his judgment in high places. He also paid the price for being the man in command at the lowest ebb of Bomber Command's fortunes.'

Churchill would not tolerate failure and by 1942 Peirse was gone, to be replaced by a man whose very name would symbolise terror in Germany. Arthur 'Bomber' Harris.

All this was cold comfort to Sidney.

Churchill, however, was excited by the work of Sidney's little team. On 13 February 1940 he wrote to Sir Kingsley Wood, the Secretary of State for Air, that he was more than impressed with the aerial photographs taken of the Ems River. Moreover he wanted to meet Cotton. Meetings of the chiefs of staff of the army, navy and air force were usually held in the evening so Cotton had already dined by the time he mounted the steps to the War Room at the Admiralty.

Sir Richard Peirse was there. As soon as Cotton entered the room he tracked up to him like a movie camera and confronted him with a baleful eye. 'What are you doing here, Cotton?' What, in other words, was a civilian doing in the presence of such greatness? Admiral Sir Dudley Pound, the First Sea Lord, apologised to Peirse and told him that Cotton was there at the invitation of Churchill.

Churchill was in a meeting with the king, so they started the discussions without him. Meanwhile Pound asked the officers to come to the table. Pound always sat in a high-backed armchair with the senior air force officer one side and the senior army officer on the other. While Cotton was waiting to see where Pound wanted him to sit, he saw Peirse moving towards one of the seats closest to Pound.

'I'd like Cotton to sit there, Peirse,' said Pound. 'Would you mind moving down one.'

Peirse glowered at Cotton. It was going to be a bumpy ride.

The main topic of discussion was once again which ships of the German navy had put to sea. Cotton presented some of the photographs which had been taken of the German battleship the *Tirpitz* in its graving dock at Wilhelmshaven two days earlier. There was a murmur of approval.

For some time Cotton had been using two civilian companies, the Aircraft Operating Company and Aerofilms, both of which possessed sophisticated equipment for interpreting photographs. The equipment included one of the specialised *Wild* machines which could make measurements using aerial photographs. Peirse had never heard of the machine and asked why it had not been requisitioned. The truth was the Air Ministry had already been offered the equipment and refused it! Peirse hadn't know this.

Peirse was not at all keen to see the work of his RAF photographers pre-empted by Cotton's upstart unit. 'I thought we had made it clear that this is a most difficult task, and that some of the best brains in the air force are working on it,' he said.

The First Sea Lord interjected: 'Perhaps you might get better results, if you tried some of the lesser brains for a while.'

Peirse turned puce. At the best of times there was no love lost between the Senior Service and the RAF. Clearly Pound was using Cotton as a stick with which to beat him around the ears.

Churchill, meanwhile, was in no doubt what he wanted to do about the Aircraft Operating Company. 'It is most desirable that the organisation, including the expert personnel, should be taken over by one of the Service Departments without delay. I imagine the Air Ministry would be the most suitable department for them to come under, but if for any reason the Air Ministry do not wish to take it over we should be quite prepared to do so.'

Cotton had an enemy in Peirse but found a powerful ally in Sir Cyril Newall, Chief of Air Staff. Newall had heard that Cotton was getting good pictures whereas the RAF were not. He asked Winterbotham if he would be willing to hand over Cotton's outfit to the RAF if they could find some way of accommodating it. Winterbotham agreed and thought that Cotton's techniques of high altitude photography should replace those being used by the air force.

Cotton walked from Piccadilly down to the Air Ministry office in Whitehall. At twelve-thirty he was joined by Newall.

The Chief of Air Staff was characteristically blunt.

'So you are the person who is giving us all this trouble,' said Newall.

'No, sir,' said Cotton evenly, 'his name is Hitler.'

Quite suddenly Newall asked, 'What's wrong with the air force's photography?'

'Do you really want the truth, sir? If so you must remember that I'm an Australian, and someone once said that an Englishman calls a spade a spade but an Australian calls it a bloody shovel.'

Over lunch Newall asked Cotton if he would be prepared to join the RAF. Cotton exploded with laughter. Why, he protested, he had just been asked by Ian Fleming if he wanted to join the navy! Grasping his opportunity Cotton took advantage of Newall's good humour to tell him what he really wanted: his own civilian photographic unit and a free hand to hire both military and civilian personnel who could do the job, and to choose his own machines and equipment. To Cotton's astonishment Newall agreed. But military aircraft and personnel could scarcely be handed over to a civilian. Cotton would have to join the air force. Cotton reluctantly agreed to be commissioned as a squadron leader with the acting rank of wing commander.

So Sidney Cotton, businessman, was now acting wing commander RAF, service number 75444. 'Now that he was part of the military machine, which RAF base would Cotton be operating from?' enquired Newall.

Cotton said: 'That's just what we don't want, a military base. It will give the game away. I suggest we use Heston. No one would suspect that secret work would be done from there.'

Sidney's unit was now a military one but he was keen to keep the old team together. He asked Pat Martin to join the unit as a flight lieutenant in the Women's Auxiliary Air Force. He said: 'I want you to stay with the team.'

Pat was resolutely civilian. She did not like the idea of being in uniform. Sidney pointed out: 'Then you can't fly with us. Because if we get shot down you will not be in uniform and you will not be a prisoner of war. As a civilian you will be shot as a spy.'

Pat Martin spent the rest of the war as a volunteer ambulance driver. From then on she was to see less of Sidney. They were starting to drift apart. He bought her a flat in Dolphin Square in Pimlico. 'There was a swimming pool and a dance floor and the square was full of young people in uniform.'

By 1941 the affair was over. Sidney was now forty-seven and Pat was twenty-five.

He encouraged her to find someone else. She did. She started dating again. She did not smoke or drink, which made her popular with the boys. 'In the war you could only get one packet of cigarettes and one drink. With me they got two.

'When I saw Sidney again he suddenly looked terribly old. He sat me down and said, "I'm too old for you, Pat. Now is the time for you to go off and find someone your own age". Looking back his life was dominated by what he could get from people, and how he could use them. He had a complete disregard for whatever the order was. He thought he was better than most people and I thought so too.'

She pauses; 'I wonder if I would think so today?'

Heston was the smallest and least important of the three aerodromes serving London, and lies just off what is today the M4 in West London.

In the 1930s it was owned and operated by Sir Nigel Norman, a member of Winterbotham's Old Boys network. Nigel Norman was an RAF reserve officer who had close ties with the Air Ministry. It was Norman who provided the discreet hangar for the Lockheed. 'I knew him well as a personal friend and I knew that I could trust him,' said Winterbotham.

He almost certainly agreed that operating the spy flights from a small airfield mostly used for private flying would attract less attention than one of the bigger aerodromes like Croydon or Northolt. Heston is where Neville Chamberlain waved his famous piece of paper during the Munich crisis in 1938. Curiously Chamberlain had never flown before and his first flight was also in a Lockheed 12a of British Airways.

Sergeant Jim Muncie who had joined the RAF School of Photography at Farnborough was posted to the No. 1 Camouflage Unit at Heston early in 1940.

'I was informed it was a highly secret unit experimenting in high altitude aerial photography,' he said, 'hence the reason for a civilian airport. No one would suspect anything. We were allocated a hangar for the aircraft and space to build photographic darkrooms, away from the passenger terminal area.'

Newall promised Cotton aircraft to do the job. Cotton wanted Supermarine Spitfires, which were in short supply and also desperately needed for Fighter Command. Spitfires were being made at the Supermarine works in Southampton and the giant shadow factory at Castle Bromwich near Birmingham. The Birmingham factory had only just started to produce them in quantity and every one was needed for the front line squadrons.

Newall could only offer Cotton Bristol Blenheims which were precisely the aircraft he did not want and had proved virtually useless as reconnaissance aircraft. The Blenheim had first flown in 1936 and was used by the RAF as both a light bomber and a long-range fighter. It was capable of 260 mph at 12 000 feet which was far too slow for what Cotton had in mind. 'I said I would accept the Blenheim for the time being but I flew back to Heston that night with a feeling of deep frustration,' wrote Cotton.

'I appreciated that I had to be realistic about the choice of planes but I knew the Blenheim wouldn't do.'

Taking photographs from a Blenheim was like a suicide mission. The nose of the aircraft had been extended and the camera operator manhandled a huge camera through the perspex nose of the aircraft. The pilot sat behind him. At a given signal the aircraft would dive towards the target and the photographer would try to take pictures from the nose. Small wonder that so many Blenheims had been shot down.

On 21 September, two Blenheims flew into Heston and Cotton set about making them go faster. First he had all the thick dope removed and replaced by a hard semi-gloss paint with a smooth surface. All the holes were filled with plaster of Paris and sanded smooth. A retractable tailwheel was added and the propellers were both fitted with spinners.

But the process of Cottonising, as it came to be known, added only eighteen miles an hour to the top speed. Cotton was hoping to achieve at least an extra hundred miles an hour. But if it had not been for the modification of the Blenheims, Cotton would not have got his precious Spitfires. Cotton's version of the story is that Air Chief Marshall Sir Hugh Dowding, the Commander in Chief of Fighter Command, paid a visit to Heston to observe the modifications to the Blenheims.

The RAF was desperately short of front line fighters and, to make up the shortfall in high performance Spitfires and Hurricanes, Dowding wanted to bring the Blenheims into play as long-range fighters. The Blenheims might not have the speed or the manoeuvrability but they did have the range. The Blenheim could fly 1500 miles, three times the distance of the Spitfire or Hurricane. Dowding was curious as to how Cotton had extracted extra performance out of Bristol's dated design—so intrigued that he agreed to let Cotton have two Spitfires.

'What do you want them for?' he asked. Cotton explained.

'When do you want them?' asked Dowding.

'Yesterday,' said Cotton.

But if Cotton had struck up such a rapport with this serious and private man, why did Dowding send the following signal to the Air Ministry?: 'Earnestly request that my Spitfire resources may not be trenched upon for any purpose whatever than home fighting.'

To get his hands on more Spitfires, Sidney went directly to the people who were building them: 'The natural anxiety of the commanding officer of the Photographic Development Unit sometimes led him to adopt a course of action which in practice may have retarded rather than accelerated the delivery of successive types,' wrote Air Vice Marshal Peck. 'By treating direct with the manufacturers as with Supermarine at Southampton and short circuiting the usual channels he not only caused irritation in the quarters best placed to help him but endangered the even flow of production.' On the other hand it may be argued that unorthodox methods did in fact gain time for the Photographic Development Unit and that since it was high policy to have this ready for operations in the spring the irritation caused in official circles, and even some dislocation in general production may not have been an extravagant price to pay. It was Peck's thankless task to placate everybody. He wrote: 'The difficulties we have constantly to smooth out. The ideas have been good but to get the benefit of them we have suffered great inconvenience. The first and fundamental question is whether to go on with Cotton enduring much tribulation for the value of what further ideas there may be—and I think there will be good ideas—or whether we regularise everything and *dispense with Cotton.*'

The RAF persisted in using the low flying Blenheims in photo-reconnaissance missions, with disastrous results. Less than an hour after the declaration of war, a Blenheim had been despatched on the first official photographic mission from Britain to photograph the German fleet at Wilhelmshaven. From 24 000 feet the pilot had seen and identified many of the German ships. The weather was perfect for a high altitude bombing raid but the camera in the Blenheim could not provide the evidence because the lenses of his cameras frosted over. An immediate raid was required but there were no pictures. Bomber Command vacillated and by the time the bombers returned to the target the weather had deteriorated.

Blenheims were again used in the bombing raid which was disastrous. There was a 500 foot cloud base and flying under the clouds the Blenheims were sitting ducks for the German anti-aircraft guns. Of the twenty-nine aircraft sent on the mission, seven failed to return. The bombers hit their targets but the bombs used were delayed action which meant they bounced off the steel decks and into the water.

The lesson of this disastrous raid was not lost on Cotton. He pointed out that if the bombing had been in good weather from high altitude, it might have been more successful. And he had already proved with the Lockheed that his camera lenses did not freeze over.

It was Joan Henry who gave the name to duck egg blue—the colour scheme that Sidney used to paint his Spitfires. By 1939 Sidney had been estranged from Joan for six years but they remained on reasonably good terms. Sidney was living in London but had bought Joan a farm at Checkendon near Henley-on-Thames. Joan had always been more interested in animals than aeroplanes.

Sidney was still either flush with money or down on his luck, and although he never provided her with a regular income he would occasionally splash out on extravagant gifts. Once she casually mentioned that she needed a tractor. He bought her one.

Her little farm had sheep, a few cattle, some chickens and ducks. One day Sidney walked into the kitchen with a piece of aircraft aluminium painted a pale bluey green. 'What colour would you call that, Joey?' he asked.

Joan pointed to a bowl of duck eggs on the kitchen table. 'Its like my Khaki Campbells,' she said.

'What are Khaki Campbells?' asked Sidney without much interest.

'They are ducks, of course,' retorted Joan.

'And the colour is the same as my duck eggs—duck egg blue,' she said.

The duck egg blue was to later achieve lasting fame as the colour of Sidney's Spitfires.

It was Maurice 'Shorty' Longbottom who had first conceived the idea of the stripped down high speed Spitfires. Sidney picked the idea up and ran with it. After the conversation with Dowding, Cotton got his Spitfires, although not before Richard Peck had him on the carpet. What did Cotton mean by getting new aircraft without reference to the Air Ministry; did he know that Fighter Command were desperately short of these planes? How did he intend to fly and service them without trained staff? But Sidney was getting used to being hauled over the coals. He was not worried about treading on toes so long as he got the job done.

As soon as they arrived at Heston, Cotton and his engineers set about the process of Cottonising the Spitfires. The eight machine guns were removed as was the ¼ inch armour plating behind the pilot's seat, and the gun ports blanked off with metal plates. All

The spy who hired Cotton: Frederick Winterbotham, the head of Air Intelligence for MI-6. They were good friends at the beginning, but the relationship soured when Cotton was given his own unit.

Sidney with his third wife, Thelma 'Bunty' Brooke-Smith. They were married in 1951, and she was thirty years his junior.

Sidney (second from left) in the Royal Naval Air Service in 1917, with fellow officers E.C.B. Betts, G.S. Trewin and A.H.B. Gilligan. The Admiralty thought that Sidney was 'unsuitable for employment in a uniformed service'.

Sidney as a travelling salesman in Newfoundland. He was selling a new type of snow tractor, but had an accident and had to be taken to hospital by dog sled.

One of the Avro Lancastrian used by Cotton for gun running to Hyderabad.

A programme for the Frankfurt Flying Meeting in July 1939. It was here that Cotton took a number of Nazi officials for joy flights while secretly taking photographs from the air.

Tel. No. : HOUNSLOW 2345.
Telegraphic Address : " AIRCONTROL, HOUNSLOW."

AIR MINISTRY CONTROL STATION,
HESTON AIRPORT,
HESTON.

All letters on the undermentioned subject should be addressed to :—
THE AIR TRAFFIC CONTROL OFFICER-IN-CHARGE
and the following numbers quoted :—

*Your Ref.* :—

26th September 1939.

The Officer Commanding,
Royal Air Force Station,
Aldergrove. N.Ireland.

Sir,

Would you please give all facilities to the Pilot of G-AFTL (Lockheed Electra) who is proceeding on a special flight authorised by Fighter Command Hqrs.

Air Traffic Control Officer i/c.

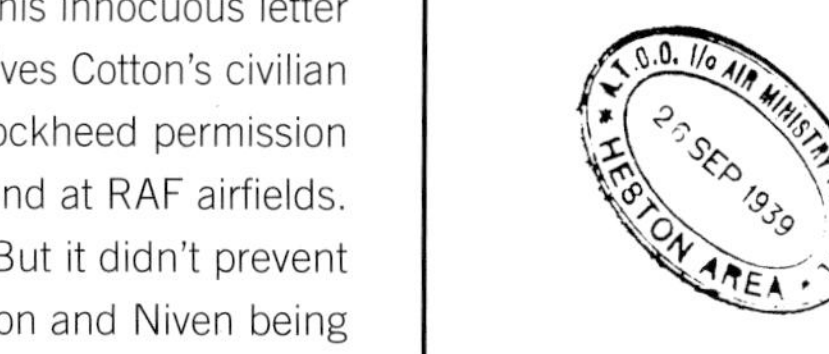


This innocuous letter gives Cotton's civilian Lockheed permission to land at RAF airfields. But it didn't prevent Cotton and Niven being arrested and locked up by the commanding officer at the RAF station at West Freugh.

10, Downing Street,
Whitehall,

Dear Mr Cotton

I write this note to say that if your friend comes over soon, the Prime Minister and I, who have both already met him, shall be very glad to see him, and will arrange a meeting under suitable conditions.

Yrs sincerely

Halifax.

Aug 21. 1939.

The letter from the British Foreign Secretary, Lord Halifax, giving approval to Cotton to bring Hermann Goering to England.

Sidney through the porthole. A picture taken by Joan Cotton on board the steamer which took them to Newfoundland.

Cotton aged 25. He had resigned his commission from the Navy, and was considering a life on the land.

The Karinhalle, Goering's opulent country mansion. Cotton was invited to the Karinhalle to show Goering his colour film, Dufaycolor. Sidney's photographers took clandestine pictures of the house and its complex of air raid shelters.

Sidney's model aeroplanes and cars—this picture was probably taken at Cheltenham College in England in 1911. Victor, Sidney's brother is on the right.

**Leica Model FF (Model 250)**
***"Reporter"***

The Leica Reporter camera used by Cotton to take spy pictures from the air. Advanced for their day, the Leicas could take 250 exposures on a single roll of film.

Cotton at the wheel of his ERA (English Racing Automobile). He entered the car in the Vanderbilt Cup Race at Roosevelt Field New York in 1936, where the Honourable Brian Lewis drove it.

A group of Cotton's pilots in France in 1940, all wearing the Sidcot flying suits invented by Cotton in World War I. Bob Niven is centre left and Maurice 'Shorty' Longbottom centre right. Niven was killed in 1941 and Longbottom in 1945.

Bob Niven—Cotton's faithful paladin, co-pilot, engineer and navigator. Before he learned to fly, he drove Greyhound buses in Calgary.

A heavily bombed airfield in southern Germany. The scorch marks on the runway (left) suggested to the Allies that for the first time the Germans were operating jet aircraft.

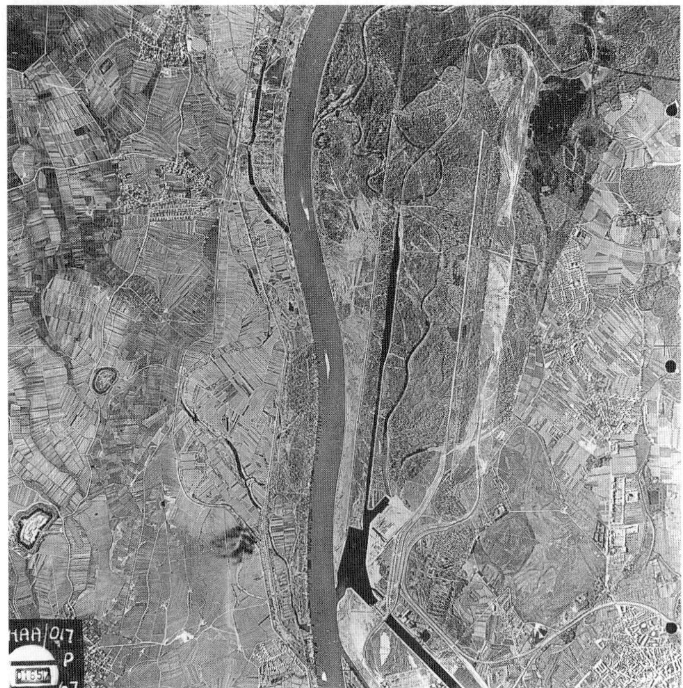

The River Rhine near Strasbourg on the French–German border. Photo interpreters could tell where the Germans were building fortifications on their side of the river.

Constance Babington Smith, one of the team of skilled photo interpreters who expertly scrutinised the photographs taken by Cotton and his pilots. She was very fond of Cotton, who she described as 'tall and wolf-like'.

cracks were filled with plaster of Paris, and fine sanded then the whole aircraft was given a coat of Cotton's Camotint duck egg blue-green. With these modifications the top speed of the Spitfires went from 360 to nearly 400 miles an hour. Having made them go faster he now had to increase their range. Spitfire pilots traditionally flew with a 37 gallon petrol tank sitting in their laps. Now Cotton wanted to put some more high octane fuel under their seats, a 30 gallon tank which would increase the range of the aircraft to 1250 miles at 30 000 feet.

Cotton could not initially get permission to modify the aircraft to carry more fuel. The Spitfire had a range of only 650 miles. Precious fuel could not be wasted in flying the Channel so it was necessary to deploy the aircraft to forward airfields in France.

In the beginning it was decided to fit the cameras in the wings rather than the fuselage. Each F 24 camera with its five inch focal length lens was fitted in the place formerly occupied by the ammunition boxes for the inner machine guns. They both pointed directly downwards with a slight overlap to give stereoscopic vision. So that the pilot could see downwards without banking the aircraft, two teardrop canopies were installed on either side of the Perspex hood.

The only problem with the five inch focal length cameras was that they gave too little detail on objects of less than thirty feet in diameter, taken from the operational altitude of 30 000 feet. Sidney thought that they might supplement the coverage they were getting with the five inch camera by using a camera with a 20 inch focal length which gave a scale of 1:18 000 as against 1:72 000 for the five inch.

Later Sidney also wanted to fit two cameras behind the pilot's seat, but the boffins at the Royal Aeronautical Establishment at Farnborough thought that two might affect the centre of gravity and make the aircraft tail heavy. One camera, however, was acceptable. Sidney had to accept their ruling on the matter, and had one of the aircraft taken down to Farnborough to be test flown.

After the flight Sidney asked whether during the test flight the centre of gravity had been all right. They said it had.

Sidney then asked for a screwdriver and unscrewed a panel in the rear of the aircraft. Inside he showed them the 32 pounds of lead weight he had secretly installed as a substitute for the second camera! 'There were some red faces at Farnborough but they now agreed to the installation of the second camera,' he said. Sidney still had the infuriating habit of being right.

Modifications to the Spitfires continued throughout the war. By October the unit was flying the Spitfire PR 1D which, in addition to the fuselage mounted tanks, carried fuel in the leading edges of the wing. This gave the Spitfire a staggering total of 115 imperial gallons of fuel. The aircraft had a range of 1750 miles and was nicknamed the 'bowser' because it was considered to be a flying petrol tanker.

Getting his team together, and converting first the Blenheims then the Spitfires took time but by the last week in October Cotton's unit was operational. Officially it was known as the No. 1 Camouflage Unit. Unofficially it was known as Cotton's Club or Cotton's Crooks. With a wry sense of humour Sidney distributed little lapel badges to his team bearing the letters CC 11. The eleven stood for the eleventh commandment, Thou Shalt Not Be Found Out.

The Club grew rapidly. When it started in 1939 it employed twenty-seven people—eight officers and nineteen other ranks. By April 1940, 316 people worked at Heston; not just pilots but engineers, armourers, carpenters, instrument makers and various grades of fitter.

Cotton had traded his double-breasted business suit for a wing commander's uniform but it was hard to tell the difference. He ran the unit as if it were a private flying club. His chauffeur and manservant Cyril Kelson was in constant attendance.

Outside the hangar at Heston stood Cotton's crimson Hotchkiss sports car. Cotton was unconcerned if his officers failed to salute him nor if they wore strange hats or suede shoes or their hair too long. Fighter pilots wore their uniforms with the top button undone. Sidney would not notice.

'We were Sid Cotton's air force, members of an elite secret unit,' said Jack Eggleston, a photographer with the unit. Eggleston had seen the pale blue Lockheed coming and going and knew about its secret cameras. 'But to say anything was asking for trouble. We were on a need-to-know basis.' Eggleston was a lowly leading aircraftman from the north of England and found many regular officers supercilious and remote. The wrong school, the wrong accent and the wrong family background could all affect your chances of promotion. Sidney Cotton, however, was a different sort of officer who seemed to treat all his team like equals. 'To me Sidney Cotton was a god, but he didn't expect me to salute him, and I liked that.'

One afternoon one of the unit's Spitfires made a forced landing at Hornchurch, on the other side of London. There were vital pictures in its cameras and Eggleston was given the job of retrieving them. Sidney gave permission for the Hotchkiss to be used for the trip. It was evening and the fastest way to Hornchurch was straight across Central London. Eggleston climbed into the magnificent Hotchkiss with Cyril Kelson at the wheel. 'Off we went at a rate of knots along the Great West Road and straight through the centre of London.'

There had been a bombing raid and all the traffic lights had been switched off. Eggleston and Kelson hurtled through London at 60 miles an hour sometimes with a police escort. 'There was smoke and fire, firemen and rescue teams at work, and I remember seeing huge flames from broken gas mains,' Eggleston said. They arrived at Hornchurch, retrieved the films and sped back to Heston, Kelson as unflappable as ever. 'He never turned a hair. He seemed to know his way around London.'

Leslie Axon a leading aircraftman at Heston said: 'It was a very hush hush place. When I arrived I was introduced to the little nucleus of engineers who were to look after the Lockheed.' After a couple of days Sidney invited him into his office. 'He said:

"Anything you see here keep completely to yourself." He had a quiet authority about him. He didn't bawl or shout. He was the easiest man in the world to deal with so long as you knew the ropes.'

By the time Axon joined the unit the Spitfires were doing the photographic work and the Lockheed was being used to ferry men and equipment in and out of France. 'He knew all the aerodromes in France like the back of his hand.'

Once they were taking off from the L'Armée de L'Air airfield at Coulommiers when an air-raid warning came. Not wanting to get the Lockheed strafed by the Germans, Sidney taxied the aircraft out of the airfield and took off along the main road. On another occasion Sidney landed at a field in France and told Axon to stay behind to look after the aircraft. He was gone for five hours. 'When he came back he said, "You haven't had anything to eat, have you?" so he bought me some strawberries.' Axon got the impression that Sidney was not overly fond of the officers of the French air force. 'If we had to carry an officer, Sidney would make him sit in the back of the plane, and he would ask me to sit up the front.'

Between the beginning of June and the Fall of France on the 21st, Leslie Axon spent forty hours in the air, mostly in the Lockheed. 'Heston was like a London bus station at times. Sometimes there was so much coming and going I didn't where I was.' Before the establishment of the special flight, Sidney had never carried guns in the Lockheed. But now that the war was on he carried a revolver and the Lockheed carried four rifles. At Le Luc near Marseille the airfield was attacked by German fighters. 'Sidney said, "Get the rifles." We jumped into a slit trench around the airfield but most of us couldn't hit a bloody haystack.'

When Sidney returned to Heston he was whisked away in the red Hotchkiss by the ever diligent Cyril Kelson. 'Petrol was short so he used to fill up the Hotchkiss from the tractors.'

But this informality and lack of respect for service traditions did not suit everyone. An early casualty was Squadron Leader Alfred Earle, the unit's first photographic officer, who found that he was not at all in sympathy with the 'highly unorthodox and non-service methods adopted by Cotton' and he asked to be transferred from Heston. To replace him was Paul Lamboit, an old friend who had formerly worked as a technical representative for Cotton's company, Dufaycolor in New York. Commissioned as a pilot officer, Lamboit found himself swiftly promoted to squadron leader which Cotton considered more in keeping with his position. This lack of discipline suited many of the civilians that Cotton had hired but it only served to provoke the regular officers who had grown up to respect the traditions of the service. Cotton might be an Australian who called a spade a bloody shovel but as far as the Establishment was concerned he was a bloody colonial upstart.

During the period of the phoney war in the autumn and winter of 1939 the expected German invasion of the low countries and France did not come. Hitler had invaded Poland and stopped. France and the Low Countries held their breath with anticipation. Italy was not yet in the war, but it too was Fascist and had a border with France. The English Channel lay between Europe and England but only the River Rhine stood between Germany and France. To prove its worth, Sidney Cotton's Circus had to get closer to the action. To France.

The idea was that one of the Spitfires should be based in France to make trial flights over the German border. The airfield chosen was at Seclin outside Lille which was also home to two squadrons of RAF Hurricanes. The officers and men were billeted at a hotel in Lille. They were told they could socialise among themselves but not to discuss their work with others. In the bars and restaurants of Lille they kept their own company.

Jack Eggleston who had first been with Cotton at Heston, was stationed at Seclin. It was his job to remove the exposed films from the cameras in the aircraft. There was no proper dark room so they commandeered a large metal box in which the French kept their fire extinguishing equipment. It was big enough to take a man. 'We used to jump inside the box, pull the lid down and remove the film from the cameras. With the lid down it was quite dark enough.

Then we would put the film in a canister and send it to England to be processed and developed.' It was primitive, but it worked.

The Spitfire was kept in its own hangar under lock and key. Cotton told the pilots not to mix with any of the other RAF pilots or to discuss the nature of their mission. It was natural that the Hurricane pilots should be curious about a lone Spitfire painted a strange colour. They would see the pale green unarmed aeroplane taking off but could only speculate as to its purpose.

On 22 November the Spitfire made its first successful operational sortie. Flying at an altitude of 31 680 feet Flying Officer 'Shorty' Longbottom photographed the Eupen–Elsenborg region of Belgium. This was first time that photographs had been successfully exposed at high altitude under wartime conditions by cameras mounted in a Spitfire. History was being made! Two days later he made his first flights over German territory but the weather deteriorated and for nearly a month no flights could be made because of fog and snow.

At this time all the photographs taken were rushed back to Heston for processing, then the prints rushed to General Gort, the commander in chief of the British Expeditionary Force at Arras. Gort was convinced that the Germans would avoid the Maginot line and the Ardennes forest and advance through northern Belgium, so the pictures taken over Belgium were of vital importance.

But although Cotton had proved he could get the pictures, there was still the matter of interpreting them—identifying tiny details in pictures shot from high. The solution was provided by an aerial survey business at Wembley run by an old friend of Cotton's, Major Lemnos Hemming. If Cotton was a buccaneer, Hemming looked like a pirate. He had lost an eye in a plane crash in Newfoundland and wore a black eye patch. The nickname was a curious one, taken from a Greek island where all the women had murdered their husbands.

Hemming's company possessed one of the revolutionary Swiss *Wild* (pronounced Vilt) machines, whose stereoscopic glasses enabled the viewer to measure, in 3D, the tiniest detail of an aerial picture. The *Wild* looked like a brass bedstead with binoculars attached to it. It was a heavy expensive piece of equipment but it had the ability to make precise measurements from a set of aerial photographs. On 7 December 1939 Cotton gave Hemming a set of five inch square photographs and said, 'See how much information you can get out of them.'

Hemming made his money out of aerial mapping and survey work but, since the war began, his business had fallen off. He was keen that the Air Ministry would take his operation over but they were not interested. However Sidney had a backlog of undeveloped film so he began to make unofficial use of Hemming's facilities. Sidney swore Hemming and his team to secrecy and guaranteed that they would be paid out of RAF funds. 'There's a war on,' he said by way of justification. In the first three months of 1940, Hemming's company earned £1300. In fact this unauthorised spending on a civilian enterprise was to get Sidney into trouble later.

The man that Hemming entrusted to interpret the photographs was Michael Spender (brother of the poet Stephen Spender and the artist Hugh Spender). Through the viewing mechanism of the Wild machine, Spender could see everything in three dimensions and was able to make accurate measurements of the length and height of buildings even though the pictures were taken from six miles above. If the brilliant Mr Spender and his machine could measure the length of buildings, reasoned Cotton, they could also measure the length of ships. Especially German ships.

Cotton was already unpopular with the air force for telling them how to do their job. Now he was about to give the Royal Navy a little present. Cotton had been told by Cyril Newall at the outset that he was to have a free hand in setting up the unit, but that was easier said than done. He chafed at every bureaucratic delay and bombarded the Air Ministry with an avalanche of letters.

Before the war it was unusual for aircraft to fly any higher than 20 000 feet. As Cotton put it: 'What we are doing today the fighters will be doing tomorrow, the bombers the day after tomorrow and civilian aircraft after the war.' Sidney was now asking his pilots to fly up to 1000 miles inside German territory in an aeroplane without a gun. It required a special breed of pilot, and not necessarily a fighter pilot.

An Air Ministry report spelled this out:

> The fighter pilot is not ordinarily suitable. Long distance reconnaissance in a single seater requires a skilful air pilotage and a temperament or aptitude different from that primarily required of a fighter pilot. The knowledge which strategical reconnaissance bomber or army co-operation pilots possess is most valuable and suitable. As the Spitfire aircraft is unarmed it is most desirable that the pilot should have had experience of the war conditions which will confront him in the air, otherwise he runs the grave risk of being surprised. In view of the great height which has to be maintained for long periods by the Spitfire pilots, special physical endurance and resistance to effects of altitude are necessary.
>
> In plain terms this meant that the ability to fly a Spitfire was the least of the qualifications required. The pilots they were looking for had to be capable of finding their way to selected points and doing this alone and unarmed. All in all the work called for a rare combination of conscientiousness, daring, self reliance and initiative.

What was it like to be one of these brave lonely men who flew unarmed photographic aircraft high over enemy territory? Some idea of how uncomfortable it could be is found in a report written by the Canadian Bob Niven entitled 'High Altitude Flying: Care of the Body'. He recommended that pilots ate and drank very little before a flight, as this caused the stomach and bladder to distend, which could be very unpleasant. It was like a diver plunging to the depths of the ocean, a journey to a hostile environment 'decked out in barbarous equipment and encased in a framework of dials and instruments and gauges'. The change in pressure at rarified atmospheres produced headaches and a feeling of drowsiness which could be difficult to shake off all day. If a pilot was starved of oxygen the results could be fatal—so likely was this that a second oxygen bottle was installed in the Spitfires. At great heights the cockpits started frosting up, so warm air was diverted from the radiator into the cockpit to give the pilots some sort of comfort.

To photograph the targets successfully the pilot had to be as dexterous as a one-armed paper hanger. Sitting in the freezing cockpit, his right hand on the control column, his left would alternate between the throttle lever and the map on his left knee. There was no airborne radar set to tell him of hostile fighters or missile attack. Before taking off he would give the weather, height and speed to the ground team.

The photographers would then set the shutter speed and apertures of the cameras. In the cockpit the cameras were controlled from a small box above the instrument panel—the type 35 push button camera electrical control which could be set to take a picture from two to every fifty seconds, the average fourteen seconds. The camera mechanism continued automatically to expose frames at regular intervals until switched off. And all this in a machine travelling at speeds of up to four hundred miles an hour!

The high flying Spitfires were usually invulnerable to attack by German fighters but it soon became obvious that they could still be seen from the ground (a phenomenon all too common in these days of high flying commercial airliners) even if they could not be intercepted. At altitudes between 27 000 and 40 000 feet, depending upon humidity and temperature, the water vapour in the exhaust from an aero engine condenses to form a visible trail. These dense white plumes of condensation started at the engine exhausts and widened out into a trail many times the width of the aircraft. Painting the aircraft blue was effective but only if the aircraft was not leaving vapour trails. Types of aircraft which could cruise in the stratosphere without being detected were constantly being sought.

Group Captain Desmond Sheen was one of the first Australian pilots to join the unit. 'If you were leaving a contrail you either went up or down,' he recalled. 'We had a little control panel where the gunsight used to be and the cameras were mounted in the wings. You had to position yourself over the target which is not as easy as it seems.' Fighter pilots were told never to fly straight and level for more than thirty seconds to avoid being bounced, but reconnaissance pilots had no choice; they had to fly straight and level to get their mosaic of pictures. Fortunately in 1939 no anti-aircraft gun could fire a shell to a height of 30 000 feet. On two occasions however Messerschmitt Bf 109s lay in wait for the Spitfires at 30 000 feet but both times the Spitfires were able to outrun them, being about forty miles an hour faster.

It was inevitable, however, as the war progressed that the Germans would discover ways of shooting the aircraft down. By the end of 1942 it was estimated that a photographic reconnaissance pilot had only a thirty per cent chance of coming back alive.

It was irksome to Cotton that the pictures taken by his pilots had to be printed and developed in England. Sometimes it was five days before the prints reached the military. What was needed was a mobile unit which could be deployed in the field. By March 1940 he had managed to get two photographic trailers delivered to the squadron. Sergeant Jim Muncie recalls: 'Wing Commander Cotton in his own private Lockheed 12 flew some of us, including myself, over to France to join our photographic unit. We landed at Coulommiers in early March and drove down to the village of Tigeaux where our mobile photographic trailers had arrived at the Château de Bessi. The photographers were billeted in the chateau and our two trailers were hidden under covers in the stable yard. When the Spitfire returned from a photo mission, instead of printing and processing at Heston, we were now in the field only several kilometres from both the army and air force headquarters. They could receive their photo-recce pictures within a few hours, which helped to speed up information.'

The photographs were being produced not only for the army but for the RAF and Cotton struck up a good relationship with Air Marshall Sir Arthur Barratt who commanded the RAF in France.

Cotton was also on good terms with General Joseph Vuillemin the French Chief of the Air Staff. In return for certain photographic favours he gave him access to his airfields. He even had a special hangar built at Coulommiers. It was big enough to contain the Lockheed and two Spitfires and it had a thatched roof so that from the air it looked like a haystack. When the Luftwaffe attacked the airfield in May 1940 it was one of the few buildings to survive.

It was Vuillemin who provided Cotton's pilots with a carnet de passage. Stamped *'Très Secret'* it authorised the pilot to land at any RAF or French air force airfield and asked those on the ground to place a strict guard on his aircraft by day and night.

As news of the unit's achievements spread, the word got out that Cotton was looking for volunteers with navigational experience to fly something very fast in an exciting hush-hush unit. Most of the applicants were young officers from various RAF squadrons in France. One pilot who was approached was Alex Henshaw (later to become better known for the testing of the Spitfire), who had established a number of records for long distance flights to Africa. 'As a friend I used to run across Sidney Cotton in various parts of Europe but sometimes way off the beaten track. Neither of us would expand upon the purpose of our visits as we were conscious that, in the tense political climate of that pre-war period, discretion was always advisable.' Sidney had shown Alex some of the more innovative features of the Lockheed: 'I was aware that more than one camera equipped with specialised film was secreted on board, so that G-AFTL was more than a private aircraft.'

Cotton invited him to lunch at the RAF Club and showed him the pictures of the Rhine he had taken from the Lockheed during the Frankfurt flying meeting in July. 'He took from his briefcase a number of very clear photographs and with a flourish laid them in front of me. They really were superb, with bunkers and concrete tank traps extending as far as the eye could see.'

Sidney told Alex that the RAF had told him they had been trying to get pictures of the Siegfried Line since September without success. He then produced a sheaf of prints which he had shown to the Minister for Air, Sir Kingsley Wood. But Henshaw realised that these had been taken four months ago en route to the Frankfurt flying meeting! Henshaw remembered that the Germans had imposed flight restrictions not to allow foreign aircraft to cross their defence lines, and the long 'dogleg' was being enforced. Henshaw had been flying the same route on the same day and recalled how he had seen the massive white line of concrete defences snaking over the countryside below him.

'You old scoundrel,' he blurted out to Sidney. 'These were taken when we flew to Frankfurt in July.'

'Yes,' said Sidney 'But the Minister didn't know that, did he?'

'Sid Cotton was an adventurer and a very able one, but as Tommy Rose once said to me, "You never know with Sid, he's either a multimillionaire or flat broke",' Alex Henshaw recalls. 'Sid put an astonishing proposal to me and at that moment it seemed a heaven sent opportunity. The idea was to collect a small team of competent pilots and in consultation with political and service chiefs to send them into enemy territory to photograph highly strategic targets.'

Cotton asked Henshaw to take charge of flying operations, an offer that he seriously considered but passed up because he did not want to be in uniform. Instead he became the chief test pilot at the Castle Bromwich Spitfire factory near Birmingham and flew one in ten of all the Spitfires that were built.

Often photographic missions were abandoned because of cloud cover.

Photographing the industrial Ruhr Valley presented a major problem because the target was frequently covered by a pall of smoke. The Ruhr was where the important factories were, including Krupps steelworks, and the Amalia factory. Cotton decided that if the industrial Ruhr was to be photographed it was necessary to get as close to the subject as possible so he moved the Special Survey Flight to Nancy making it the most easterly RAF unit in France.

It was left to Bob Niven, the former bus driver from Calgary, to get the results. On 29 December in less than half an hour he covered the whole southern half of the Ruhr. During the clear winter days that followed, he photographed Cologne, Dusseldorf and the Siegfried Line.

In January 1940 the Special Survey Flight changed its name once again, to the Photographic Development Unit. It was now charged with two distinct tasks: to keep a watch on the German fleet at Wilhelmshaven and to provide reconnaissance pictures of the Siegfried Line. But Cotton still had only two Spitfires, one in England and one in France.

In early May 1940, the long awaited German push into France began, and tanks rolled into the Ardennes forest. The Spitfires flew mission after mission, covering their advance. In the stifling heat of the photographic trailers Jim Muncie and his team worked stripped to the waist developing and printing the pictures. The work went on day and night to get the photographs to the commanders in the field. Each Spitfire was by now carrying three cameras with 125 exposures in each magazine. Six contact prints had to be made of each negative and rushed to the army and air force headquarters.

If France fell, it was likely that Italy would enter the war. That reality was not lost on Sidney Cotton. He was now charged with carrying out spy flights from bases in the south of France over targets in Italy. He organised for two Hudsons and a Spitfire to be flown to Le Luc near Toulon, and an advance party with processing equipment and a mobile radio van to go down ahead. All this was achieved in one long day but, as Cotton wryly observed, there was some consolation in spending the evening in Cannes.

The Spitfires were no longer the only aircraft used for photographic missions. In February the Photographic Development Unit had acquired three Lockheed Hudsons to reconnoitre above the clouds, check the weather along the Spitfire's intended route, and report by radio. If the conditions were unsuitable for the Spitfires the Hudson would drop below the clouds and take pictures. This made them more vulnerable to fighters and anti-aircraft fire. The Lockheed Hudson shared the same lineage as Sidney's famous Lockheed 12 and looked externally similar.

With a range of a thousand miles and a cruising speed of nearly two hundred miles an hour the Hudson was a useful addition to the unit. One of them was to be used on another clandestine photographic mission, this time not to Germany but to photograph the Russian airfields at Baku. The aircraft was piloted by Flying Officer Frederick Burton and Squadron Leader Hugh MacPhail. Accompanied by two leading aircraftmen and a civilian radio operator, Mr Norrington, they set off from Heston to fly to Habbaniya. When the aircraft left England it had the bulls-eye roundels of the Royal Air Force and the military registration N 7364.

But by the time it left Habbaniya it had been transformed into a civilian aircraft G-AGAR and once again painted in the Camotint blue-green camouflage. The Hudson made an uninterrupted survey of the Baku oilfields and six days later photographed Batum on the Black Sea coast. Russia was still neutral at this stage of the war. If the Russians had known they were being secretly photographed they gave no sign.

In reality the French had thousands of troops stationed in the area and, in the event of Russia coming into the war on the German side, Baku was to be bombed.

Ironically, when France fell, copies of these pictures were seized by the Germans and they used them as a propaganda coup with Stalin. Then after the Germans invaded the Soviet Union in 1941, the Luftwaffe relied upon the same maps when they attacked the Russian oilfields!

With the Germans moving closer to the forward airfields like Seclin, it was decided to shift the operations to the A flight base at Meaux, north-east of Paris. B flight was brought back from Nancy and C flight from Seclin. Their job was twofold, to find targets for the bombers to attack and to plot the German advance.

The British expeditionary force was being driven back towards the Channel coast and German fighter aircraft were flying deeper into France looking for targets of opportunity. The Luftwaffe had mounted Operation Paula, putting three hundred bombers and Stukas in the air to destroy airfields and factories.

Sidney Cotton, meanwhile, was still coming and going from England, either flying in the Lockheed or being driven by his loyal chauffeur, Cyril Kelson, via the car ferries. Generally he used the big red Hotchkiss which bore the personalised numberplate RAF-X and a Union Jack which illuminated at night. The Hotchkiss was typically Sidney. It was an exotic car made only in small numbers, designed by an Englishman, and made by a French company best known for its manufacture of machine guns.

Occasionally the Lockheed was used for humanitarian flights. The airmen based in France found the French beer too weak so Sidney flew over some barrels of English bitter. Unfortunately he flew too high and the barrels burst. When the plane landed in France the cabin was awash with beer froth.

These days businesses use cars as mobile offices but in 1940 this was the exception rather than the norm. Sidney Cotton had three dictaphones, one in his car, one in his office at Heston and one in the Lockheed. While not flying or being driven he would produce copious letters to assorted authorities. On 29 May Cotton was standing on the edge of the grass airfield at Meaux in the middle of dictating a letter to Lord Beaverbrook on how the war could best be won. Nearby stood the ever diligent Cyril Kelson. Discreetly camouflaged, his mobile photographic vehicles were partly hidden under the trees. Suddenly, without any warning, yellow-nosed Messerschmitt fighters came hurtling over the hedges, bullets kicking up the turf.

Cotton told Kelson to drive the red Hotchkiss sports car under the trees near a ditch. 'If any aircraft heads our way you are to jump into the ditch immediately,' he told Kelson. Kelson, ever the gentleman's gentleman, started rummaging in the car and produced a travelling rug.

'Will you be jumping in the ditch too, sir?' asked Kelson.

'Yes, Kelson, I certainly will,' said Cotton.

How much Sidney Cotton was in haste can be judged by the fact that the Germans had entered the final phase of the Battle for France and were advancing on his French aerodromes. It was only a matter of time before they were overrun.

The Special Survey flight was stretched to the limits with more requests for photographic intelligence. They now had two more Spitfires but were flying up to five photographic sorties a day.

The missions were not always successful. On 7 June the unit lost its first Spitfire. Flying at 30 000 feet, Flight Lieutenant Tug Wilson accidentally pulled the oxygen mask away from his face. He passed out, and when he recovered, the aircraft was flying at only 8000 feet. Short of fuel he decided to make a forced landing on an airfield at Champagne near Rheims which had already been abandoned in the face of the advancing Germans. Vain attempts were made to destroy the aircraft but it was finally captured intact by the Germans.

At Arras General Gort's photographic intelligence officers were given the job of destroying their entire print library in a matter of hours rather than let them fall into German hands. Unfortunately, the stacks of shiny photographs stuck together and would not burn. Finally the smouldering heap was shovelled into the back of a waiting car and driven to another location. Three attempts were made to burn them before they were finally reduced to ash.

Jim Muncie describes the evacuation from Tigeaux: 'After Dunkirk we were forced to move. We packed up and headed south to Orleans at 5 a.m. With a hundred miles ahead of us, the road was packed with refugees and it took us all day. During the drive a Frenchman on a bicycle swerved in behind the photographic trailer and was run over by a power unit trailer. He was killed and we put him in the back of the lorry until we reached the next village.

After a lot of argument by Sergeant Walton at the point of a revolver the local police took him off our hands. We duly arrived at the Duke of Orleans estate and set up our trailers near the mill stream.'

Cotton continued the photographic operations until the very end. His team were nothing if not resourceful.

The caravans became unbearably hot in the June heat. The aircraft came and went, the exposed films were taken from the magazines. There was no tap water in the caravans so the films and prints from the sorties were washed in a trout stream. The still wet prints were rushed to Arthur Barratt's headquarters at Châteauneuf and the army headquarters near Orleans.

It was safer for the little unit to push south towards Poitiers and then retreat west to La Rochelle. By now it consisted of two or three RAF officers, a number of NCOs and other ranks. They had two Spitfires and a Lockheed Hudson and every day they ran a shuttle flight to Heston, the Hudson overloaded with troops.

By 16 June 1940 they were down to twenty men and had managed to reach the small strip at Fontenoy-le-Compte, inland from La Rochelle. There was now nothing but the Wehrmact in between them and the Channel coast. The French army had as much fizz as a wedding party after the bride and groom had departed. Many French officers had shamefully abandoned their men and fled to the brothels of Paris leaving their men wandering aimlessly around the countryside. The German army roamed at will encountering only token resistance and captured scores of bewildered French poilus.

Sidney, meanwhile, was telling his superiors that the fall of France could still be averted and the French motivated to fight.

A letter to Beaverbrook, marked 'Secret and Private and Confidential' was written on 29 May 1940, only days before the fall of France. 'I urge,' wrote Cotton 'that the present situation is most delicate and prompt action can avert a disaster.' What was wanted, said Sidney, was a rallying cry. 'The old spirit of 1914,' he wrote, 'was missing.' Look where you will, round the streets of Paris, in the country, in cafés and restaurants, everyone has long faces and no spirit is shown at all.'

'It was imperative,' wrote Sidney, 'that some effort was made immediately to revive the spirit of France. The arm of the service lending itself to spectacular and romantic exploits is the air force, and in order to combat the lack of spirit shown on French aerodromes I recommend that a few British fighters be put on each of the French aerodromes around Paris, thereby enabling a better spirit to be awakened among the pilots.'

Sidney suggested that the press be given free rein to build a little romance into the war. He believed that if Italy could have been kept out of the war for another two to three weeks the spirit of the French people could be revived. But if the Germans did come south, adequate steps should be taken to evacuate the RAF. 'The only practical point of evacuation is Bordeaux and I suggest that stores should be directed towards both Nantes and Bordeaux.'

British fighters could be left behind in the fields between Paris and Bordeaux to keep the German bombers at bay. Beaverbrook was already entreating the British housewife to give up her aluminium saucepans so that the metal could be used to build Spitfires.

'I strongly urge,' Sidney told the Minister for Aircraft Production, '. . . that every effort be devoted to producing more and more fighters in the greatest possible numbers, leaving bombers alone for the time being. I have another meeting in Paris shortly and if it is satisfactory propose returning to London late today, when I will get in touch with you.' Cotton was not overly fond of Beaverbrook. 'I never trust anyone whose writing slopes backwards,' he said.

The escape from France was not going to be that easy. The men scoured the airfield and found two Tiger Moths and a lumbering Fairey Battle day bomber which had been abandoned with a damaged wing. With great ingenuity they bent the branch of a tree to form a makeshift wingtip which made the aircraft just flyable.

There wasn't much else in the way of escape craft. The Tiger

Moths were two seaters and did not have enough range to get to England without stopping to refuel. The aircraft was normally flown from the backseat, with the pupil in front. Nothing daunted, a pilot was put in each aircraft and the front cockpit loaded with petrol cans. The Tigers sputtered to Brest and landed in a field. With a top speed of 90 miles per hour they pressed on across the Channel and somehow made it home. Normally the Battle carried three people but eight people were stuffed into the bomb bay. The aircraft, grossly overweight, just managed to struggle into the air and the terrified passengers flew back to England in great discomfort.

If the evacuees wanted to avoid being captured or shot down they could not expect to use the Hudson much longer.

Sid caught up with the remains of his unit in the early hours of 17 June when he landed the ambassadorial Lockheed at Fontenoy-le-Compte. He took off again almost at once saying he would fly to Bordeaux and requisition a larger plane to fly them out. He promised to return by mid-morning, but at 4 p.m. when he still had not shown up, the group decided that the only thing to do was to destroy the equipment. An NCO was dousing the trucks with gasoline when Sidney returned. The precious photographic trailers and the trucks which towed them were arranged in a circle around a petrol bowser which was then blown up. When Sidney saw the clouds of black smoke rising from the burning lorries he was furious. He took off for England with all his passengers. One of the officers, Douglas Kendall, stayed behind until a troop-carrying plane landed, hoping to reach Nantes with whatever fuel was left in the tanks. They scrounged enough fuel to reach Jersey and finally made it back to England.

But it was hopeless. The Germans had entered Paris on 14 June and it was time to go. Cotton asked Barratt for permission to fly his Spitfires back to Heston from where they could continue to operate in greater safety.

The other members of the unit escaped by ship from La Rochelle. Given that German fighter aircraft were marauding around the point of departure it was a miracle that Cotton's civilian

Lockheed was not attacked. It was just as much of a miracle that he was not shot down by the RAF. The Lockheed had no ability to transmit the IFF (Identify Friend or Foe) code, simply because, as Cotton said, 'No one had ever suggested it.' When he took off anywhere he would transmit over the radio 'White flight taking off' on a frequency that would be heard by Fighter Command.

Once again Sidney's stubborn refusal to obey orders had got him into trouble. He had been ordered to evacuate his squadron some weeks previously but in blind faith clung to the notion that France could be saved. Instead all the equipment was either lost or captured by the Germans and the members of 212 Squadron narrowly missed being captured or shot down. This episode contributed to Sidney's downfall.

After the Germans entered Paris they plundered the files of the Deuxième Bureau and found Sidney's pictures of the Siegfried Line fortifications supplied to the French. Just before leaving La Rochelle, Cotton again bumped into his old friend Ian Fleming who had been supervising the evacuation of refugees from Point Verdon at the mouth of the estuary.

Pat Martin hadn't seen her lover, Sidney, for three weeks and didn't know where he was. She was having her own problems getting out of France. After her intelligence-gathering mission to Italy she had stopped off in Paris to see a girlfriend.

'I was scared and I wanted to get home, but all the planes and trains were full and people were driving their cars to Calais.'

She was standing at the desk in the lobby of the hotel trying to arrange some sort of transport when there was a tap on her shoulder. She turned round to see a Scottish sergeant pilot wearing a kilt.

'What are you doing by yourself, woman?' he asked.

'He was like every Scotsman you have ever seen. He was enormous and he had legs about four feet wide.'

Pat explained that she was trying to get back home. He told her that he was heading out to Le Bourget airport to see if he could find an aircraft and fly it back to England. There was a seat for her if she wanted to take the risk.

'He said he thought I was cute, and I thought he was cute, so I agreed.'

At Le Bourget, there were rows of RAF aircraft on the airfield but very few of them had any fuel. The Scotsman commandeered a Blenheim bomber and went to find some fuel for it.

'There was a little Frenchman behind a desk. When we asked for petrol he kept on saying "Non, non, non, monsieur". He would not give us any fuel.'

The Scotsman produced a revolver and said: 'This says you will.'

The Frenchman picked up the phone and made a call to the other side of the airfield where there was another fuel dump. The Blenheim was pushed across the airfield and tanked up. Pat squeezed in behind the pilot who then announced he had never flown an aircraft with two engines before! Whether or not this was true he successfully piloted the Blenheim across the Channel and landed it safely at an airfield in Kent

'I rang Sidney,' said Pat, 'and told him I was back in England a day early. We went out to dinner. And then we went to bed.'

The fast bluey green Spitfires had proved their worth. Back in England they ranged across Europe from Norway to Spain. 'There was little that escaped the eyes of these Spitfires whether it was over Western Europe or over Belgium,' said Winterbotham. 'It was these same Spitfires which spotted the concentration of German tanks ready for the breakthrough in the Ardennes.'

But Cotton's behaviour in France was already making waves in England. No one doubted that Sidney could get the results but he only devoted half of his time to the aerial espionage operation. He was still running his civilian business, the Aeronautical Research and Sales Corporation. This company's operations were not exclusively concerned with aviation—Sidney had interests in oil exploration, civil engineering, building and construction and air conditioning equipment. And of course gun running.

Winterbotham was severe: 'His conduct was absolutely disgraceful everywhere but he got the photographs.'

Some of the charges were trivial such as that he played the fool in the company of women by dancing around in silly hats in the French air force mess. So what? one might have asked. There was a war on and fighter pilots tended to let their hair down. Some of the other charges were more serious.

'There were always women mixed up with the whole thing,' said Winterbotham. 'He really played the fool and you know the French are very particular about that sort of thing. He was a liar, he was an extrovert and the French simply hated him. I had an awful time with the French over it. They wanted to put him in prison there and then in Paris and I said no, for God's sake let him come home.'

The high flying operations over Germany were proving exhausting for Cotton's pilots so he asked if SIS could rent a flat in Paris so that they could relax. Winterbotham, who knew the exacting nature of aerial photography, quite reasonably agreed.

'So I thought, well this is a good idea in a way—those poor chaps—I know what it is. But I was to find out that he'd at once established a brothel there, not only for himself and his pilots but also for the Chief of the French Air Force (General Joseph Vuillemin). So I'm afraid we had to close that one down.' Whether or not Sidney frequented brothels he certainly had a reputation as a ladies' man. One female associate who knew him at the time said that Cotton was 'a tremendous skirt chaser. He ran a whole string of mistresses and when he was finished with them he would invariably marry them off to some unsuspecting fool or other.'

## Chapter 9

# Plying for Hire

General Joseph Vuillemin's name crops up frequently in Cotton's memoirs. Cotton, a six footer, towered over the tiny Frenchman, but they had a lot in common. While operating in France, Cotton preferred to use French airfields rather than RAF ones because of the open hostility of some of the RAF station commanders.

Vuillemin was later to give Cotton a carnet de passage giving him and his pilots access to the airfields of L'Armée de l'Air. It was Vuillemin who had disguised as a haystack the aeroplane hangar where Cotton could store the Lockheed and other aircraft from the flight.

This letter, marked 'Très Secret', read:

> Le Pilote anglais porteur de cette lettre est autorise a atterrir sur tous aerodromes en FRANCE y compris les Bases d'Opérations de l'Armée de l'Air et de la Royal Air Force. Les autorités sont invitées:
>
> 1. a lui preter aide et assistance

> 2. a faire assurer une garde très stricte de l'appareil de jour et de nuit, en vue d'en interdire l'approche a tout personne autre que le pilote lui même et les mecaniciens employe a son entretien et a son ravitaillement.

('The English pilot carrying this letter is authorised to land on all aerodromes in France which comprise the operational bases of the French Air Force and the Royal Air Force. The authorities are invited to give him aid and assistance, to place a strict guard on his machine by day and night and to apprehend anyone who approaches other than the pilot himself and the mechanics working on his behalf and his provisioning'.)

Certainly the classified material, which Winterbotham was anxious to retrieve from Paris before the German occupation, took a back seat to Cotton's business interests.

Desmond Sheen, the Australian who briefly flew with the Special Survey Flight, accompanied Cotton in the Lockheed on a flight to Le Luc in the south of France. When they arrived Cotton gave him 'a sheaf of French banknotes' and told him to enjoy himself. The Côte d'Azur, unlike the rest of France, did not seem to be on a war footing. 'I was invited out on a yacht full of popsies,' Sheen said. 'They mostly seemed to be nicely elegant English people avoiding the war.'

Like many others, Sheen could not keep up with Sid's coming and goings. 'He had other business in France. It involved American carbines but I am not sure of the details.' In reality Cotton was selling weapons to the French.

Fred Winterbotham had his own view of the situation: 'Alas the success of the unit went to Cotton's head once more and just before the fall of France he could not resist poking his nose into politics.'

Cotton had been told to fly the Lockheed to Paris to pick up 'essential equipment and personnel'. The key figure among the essential personnel was a Polish Jew who went under the name of Richard Lewinski. Lewinski had earlier provided MI6 with details of the German Enigma encoding machine. The Enigma, which looked like a cross between a cash register and a typewriter, was able to translate secret messages into a code. It was described as the ultimate writing machine and could produce an infinite number of different cipher alphabets simply by changing the keying procedure. Its acquisition by British intelligence would mean that the Allies would know every move the Germans made.

Lewinski had worked as a mathematician and engineer at the factory in Berlin where Enigma was produced, but he had been expelled by the Nazis because of his religion. Lewinski said he would sell MI6 the secrets of the Enigma machine for £10 000, a British passport and a resident's permit for France for himself and his wife. Lewinski said he knew enough about the machine to build a replica. MI-6 smuggled Lewinksi out of Poland to Paris, travelling through Gdynia and Stockholm to avoid Germany. They set him and his wife up in a flat on the Left Bank in Paris where he beavered away building the replica Enigma.

Lewinski was a dark man in his early forties. One of the British cipher experts who flew to Warsaw to interrogate him had said he was like a raven plucking at an abacus. Lewinski and his wife waited at Orly airport accompanied by a minder, Commander Wilfred 'Biffy' Dunderdale. The airport was full of French businessmen, their briefcases stuffed with thousand franc notes, clamouring to escape the Germans and ready to pay good money to fly to England.

Cotton, meanwhile, had been asked by Fred Winterbotham to fly the Lockheed to Paris, escorted by two fully armed Spitfires, to collect Lewinski and his wife and fly them to safety in England. MI6 already knew about the Enigma machine and how to decipher its codes—the technique known as Ultra. Clearly if the Germans detained Lewinski he might crack under interrogation and give the secrets of Ultra to the Germans.

Dunderdale, who was well known socially in Paris, was spotted by a wealthy Jew, the textile merchant Marcel Boussac, who offered him a small fortune to fly him to London. Dunderdale refused.

By the time Cotton arrived in the Lockheed the crowd was verging on hysteria. There were industrialists in dark suits, a Jewish diamond merchant in a Homburg hat, women in fur coats tightly clutching the hands of their children. As Cotton taxied the Lockheed up to the terminal, the waiting crowd surged onto the tarmac. The tall figure of Cotton stepped from the rear door of the plane, and Marcel Boussac moved towards him with an outstretched hand.

'Bonjour, Marcel,' murmured Sidney. 'Comment allez-vous?'

Cotton and Boussac had been friends for a long time. Boussac had made a fortune out of the linen fabric which covered the fuselages and wings of early aeroplanes and turning it into women's dresses. He had a chain of shops called *Toile d'Avion*. A multimillionaire, he was later to found the Dior fashion house.

'Sidney, I am prepared to pay very handsomely for two seats on your aeroplane,' said Boussac.

The Lockheed had two spare seats. 'Well,' said Sidney, 'perhaps we can talk business.'

Wilfred Dunderdale was beside himself. Cotton's mission was a matter of national security and here he was plying for hire in an aircraft of His Majesty's Government. The aircraft was not even his! Dunderdale insisted that Cotton get Lewinski away without further delay. When Cotton refused he made an urgent phone call to London.

Winterbotham was incensed. 'Put Cotton on the line,' he shouted down the receiver. He threatened to have Cotton court martialled and thrown into the Tower of London. 'No doubt the Frenchmen had been willing to pay well for the flight to the UK,' wrote Winterbotham acidly.

The crowd was getting hysterical and Dunderdale and the gendarmes were having a difficult time controlling them as they tried to force their way onto the aircraft. Finally Lewinski and his wife were seated on the plane, the doors closed and the propellers started turning. As Sidney taxied away, he waved from the cockpit to the sad figure of Boussac. The little Frenchman, small and dapper with a pointed moustache, was left behind on the rain swept tarmac. He turned on his heel and walked dejectedly back to the terminal. Boussac owned some of the best racehorses in France. It would be six years before he and Sidney were to go to the races again.

The Lockheed flew north with its cargo of VIPs. As well as the Lewinskis, Sidney had collected a frightened English secretary and her collie dog, which had lain down in the back of the plane and gone to sleep. No doubt, Sidney reflected, there would be hell to pay when he got back to England. The dying rays of the sun made yellow squares inside the passenger cabin. Lewinski sat quietly holding his wife's hand. She was not a good flier.

Sidney had already throttled the engines back and started to descend when fog started swirling around them. There was no alternative but to seek somehere else to land. He flew back to the Channel Islands and landed in Jersey. The little party spent the night at a small hotel in St Helier and as Sidney's head touched the pillow he suddenly remembered that it was 17 June, his birthday. And what a great birthday party it had been! He awoke at daybreak to the sound of high-revving aero engines. German fighters were shooting up the town and if Sidney and his passengers were not to be caught on the ground they should leave as soon as possible.

The control tower confirmed that the English Channel was swarming with German fighters. Sidney filled the tanks of the Lockheed up to the brim and headed out into the Atlantic flying at low level, then turned north and then west, finally striking the coastline of south Wales.

At Heston, Cotton delivered his important passengers to two men in a black car who drove swiftly away. Lewinski was provided with accommodation and a police guard when he arrived in London. Then he disappeared without trace. One story was that he ended up in Australia where he had been rewarded with a farm.

Winterbotham was not there to welcome Sidney but there was a letter from Sir Arthur Street, the Permanent Under Secretary of State for Air. Effectively, Cotton had been given the sack. Street's letter read:

> I am commanded by the Air Council to inform you that they have recently had under review the question of the future status and organisation of the Photographic Development Unit and that after careful consideration they have reached the conclusion that the Unit which you have done so much to foster should now be regarded as having passed beyond the stage of experiment and should take its place as part of the ordinary organisation of the air force.

Control of the unit, the letter went on, would be handed over to Sidney's number two, Geoffrey Tuttle.

> I am to add that the the Air Council wish to record how much they are indebted to you for the inventive work you have done and for the great gifts of imagination and inventive thought which you have brought to bear on the development of the technique of photography in the Royal Air Force.

Sidney took it badly. 'However the pill was coated nothing could conceal the fact that this was a letter of dismissal and coming at the end of a period of great tension in which I had worked and flown myself to a standstill. It was a blow that for the moment I could hardly absorb,' he wrote. 'I had never felt so sickened as now.'

For some time, the Air Ministry had been irritated by the way Sidney had used the Lockheed to conduct his own business. That had been part of the original cover story when he had been flying over Germany in peace-time but now there was a war on. No one could keep track of his comings and goings to France, and many of the trips were in connection with his private business dealings. It was not that he was unpatriotic, but the pay of an acting wing commander was not keeping him in the manner to which he was accustomed.

Cotton was still quietly acting as the British agent for the American Armaments Corporation run by Albert and Ignacio Miranda. The French needed weapons and the Mirandas could supply all the latest American *matérial*. It seemed that he was never available when executive decisions had to be made, and there were many people in England who conspired against him.

Even Geoffrey Tuttle, his loyal deputy, was concerned by his frequent disappearances in the Lockheed. On 13 June 1940 Tuttle wrote Sidney the following letter: 'Lionel and Mike as well as myself are very worried because you are still away. I can't say anything about it myself as my lips are unfortunately sealed and one must keep one's word. It is however essential that you return as quickly as possible. Can I take over the Southern end for you for a bit? Geoffrey.'

The 'Southern end' referred to the aerial operations which were conducted from the south of France ranging over Italy, the Mediterranean and as far as North Africa. Sidney was supposed to be running a photographic intelligence operation, not an airline. Boussac was not the only high profile Frenchman to whom he had offered rides. There were also a number of French politicians.

Winterbotham and Cotton had been good friends in the beginning. Now there was a rift in their relationship which would never heal. Why had the relationship soured? The two had shared a passion for their work and had lived very much in each other's pockets. They had wined and dined together and had enjoyed the company of pretty girls. Before the war they had even owned an aeroplane together. But Winterbotham himself had wanted the job as commanding officer of the Photographic Development Unit and was miffed by Sidney's appointment.

Long after the war, Winterbotham was still clinically dissecting Sidney's reputation in his books and in a famous radio interview on the BBC. Much of what he said about Sidney, however, was after Cotton's death. 'There were three things in his life,' said Winterbotham, 'Flying, money and of course women.' It could also be said that there were women in Winterbotham's life.

Some may have objected to Cotton's abrasive style but not the charming and diplomatic Geoffrey Tuttle. Unlike Cotton, he was a regular serving officer in the RAF. He was clearly embarrassed by the fact that he had been asked to step into Cotton's shoes. Even years later when Tuttle had risen to the rank of air marshal and been knighted, he was still to address Sidney as 'Sir'. In fact, Tuttle publicly stated that Cotton was the greatest leader he had ever met. Tuttle, a lifelong bachelor, shared Cotton's passion for fast cars. A capable pilot, he had flown dangerous missions on the North West frontier in India during the 1930s.

Tuttle was in contact with Cotton several times a day using coded radio signals. But the communications were not always of a military nature.

On 11 June 1940 Sidney sent a letter to Tuttle which ended: 'You might ask Mike to order me two sets of tropical shorts, shirts, etc from Gieves and he could pay them say £20 on account out of the £80 he holds for me. The balance he can send to Mary (his secretary) or Mrs Pratt and ask them to pay my kiddies school fees if that hasn't already been done.' Sidney's children's school fees were always in arrears.

There were a number of things for which the Air Ministry never forgave Cotton and they had resolved to get rid of him as soon as they could. There had been the disastrous meeting in the Admiralty War Room at which he had seriously antagonised the Air Staff. The Air Staff had always resented the references to the Photographic Unit as Cotton's Club, which latterly had become known as Cotton's Crooks.

Sidney was aware he annoyed those who preferred regulations.

'There was the way I had got my first Spitfires, the use of Lemnos Hemming's company at Wembley before it had been requisitioned, the continual war I had waged on apathy and delay and so on. All these things marked me down from the Air Staff's point of view as a nuisance.' He also said: 'The Air Ministry is not geared to deliver goods over the counter.' Although this might have been true, the Air Ministry replied that a considerable amount of delay in supplying the requirements of the Photographic Development Unit were mainly due to Cotton's personality, which aroused hostility.

Cotton had little patience with going through official channels.

The last straw was when Cotton, rather than wait for Air Ministry approval, had entered into a personal commitment for photographic equipment worth £10 000.

Clearly he had already done what was expected of him. The Photographic Unit was established and successful. Because he was only an acting wing commander it was a simple matter to have Cotton pushed to one side and replaced by a regular serving officer. That way the RAF could save face, Cotton's real and alleged indiscretions could be swept under the carpet and the whole unit incorporated into RAF Coastal Command.

Effectively Cotton's war was over even before the Battle of Britain. But if he was unpopular with the RAF there was still the Royal Navy.

Joan Henry was having quite a good war. She had got used to not seeing much of Sidney but now her new man, Peter, had gone off to the naval college in Dartmouth. The farm at Checkendon, however, was the next best thing to going back to live in Newfoundland. It was safer than London with the constant air raids and she had her farm animals for company. Sidney never paid her a regular allowance but occasionally he would turn up with extravagant gifts.

'Once he fished in his pocket and produced a diamond bracelet. He said that diamonds were a girl's best friend and that it would never go down in value.' Some time later he bought her an emerald ring. 'Then he saw the mounting was loose so he took it away and said he'd get it fixed. I never saw it again. Perhaps he pawned it.'

'You'd never get any money out of Sidney. Sometimes he would come in and say "any of you kids got any money?". When he'd got the money he didn't care where he spent it. And he was not above using privileged information to get money.'

The First Sea Lord, Admiral Sir Dudley Pound, was an ally of Cotton's, as was Rear Admiral John Godfrey, the Director of Naval Intelligence. In August 1939 Ian Fleming had approached Cotton on behalf of his boss Admiral Godfrey asking him if he wanted to join the navy with the rank of captain. Now it was Sir Dudley Pound who arranged for him to be reinstated as a naval oficer. The admiral did not want to rely upon the RAF for his pictures. He wanted control of his own Photographic Reconnaisance Unit aircraft and always dealt with Cotton direct when he wanted pictures in a hurry. Pound had a reputation as a stern taskmaster, long on asperity and short on humour. But Cotton had taken the pictures of the German fleet when the luckless 'professionals' flying Royal Air Force Blenheims had all been shot down.

On Pound's instructions Sid ordered a brand new naval uniform the first he would wear since he resigned his commission in World War I. Pat Martin was with him when he went shopping for his new uniform. 'We looked at all sorts of materials, heavy and lightweight wool. Sidney was quite enthusiastic about going back into the navy.'

But his reappearance in the senior service was to be stillborn. He had worn naval uniform in World War I but it was not to happen again.

Before the commission was confirmed a letter arrived from the Air Staff. It said that the RAF had had a great deal of trouble with Sidney and if the navy now took him on they would consider it an unfriendly act. The navy had abandoned its right to operate land based aircraft before the war, and was now only operating modified land based aircraft from aircraft carriers. Consequently it had to beg the Air Staff for spares and equipment. If the navy ignored the letter effectively blackballing Cotton it could go against them.

Cotton then offered his services to the navy as an unpaid civilian adviser. 'It was clear to me now,' he wrote, 'that the Air Staff were determined to obstruct me in anything I might attempt and about this time I learned that they were actually contemplating positive action against me.'

But what sort of action?

All Cotton's efforts to get back into the Photographic Development Unit proved abortive. He had lived his life at a frenetic pace as commanding officer of the PDU; the long hours in the air, the comings and going from France; the battles with bureaucracy; not to mention his business dealings on the side. Suddenly everything had ground to a halt. Sidney's three telephones did not ring quite so frequently as they had before. He was posted to the pool depot at RAF Uxbridge and moped around looking for something to do. The war was continuing with no end in view. Peck, who remained an ally, told him that the RAF still had other plans for Cotton's considerable abilities.

Sidney was as quick as ever to recognise a good idea. He was now to get involved in a plan that would light up the sky. After his sacking from the Photographic Development Unit, Cotton had bumped into an old friend, Bill Helmore. Helmore, a brilliant scientist, was one of the boffins working for Sir Henry Tizard who was in charge of the Committee for Scientific Survey of Air Defence. The Battle of Britain had been fought and won by a narrow margin, and the Luftwaffe had learned the folly of bombing by day. By October 1940 the Luftwaffe had switched to night raids on Britain, which were much more successful.

While the RAF had the edge over the Luftwaffe with its day fighters like the Spitfire and Hurricane, it lacked a successful night fighter and had no means of directing attacks on the German bomber streams.

The anti-aircraft batteries, although providing a boost to civilian morale, rarely hit anything. The bombers could be illuminated from the ground and flak directed against them but it was difficult to hold the target in the light long enough for the night fighters to find them. All the anti-aircraft guns succeeded in doing was forcing the the bombers to fly higher. How much more efficient, reasoned Helmore, to have a powerful light in the nose of an aeroplane which could light up the bombers in the air and illuminate them long enough for the fighters to do their work. The official name for the idea was to be Aerial Target Illumination or ATI and the device was to be known as the Turbinlite.

Cotton and Helmore, who was now a wing commander, decided to develop the idea 50:50. The idea was that the aircraft with the light would stealthily advance to within 600 yards of the target and then switch the light on. The fighters would then close in for the kill. Neither Cotton or Helmore believed that any existing light was powerful enough for their purpose so the General Electric company was given a contract to build one.

The aircraft chosen to carry the light was the American Douglas DB-7 Boston (or Havoc) which were in plentiful supply. The Boston was a twin motor medium bomber with a respectable turn of speed. Initially the Turbinlite gained the support of Air Marshal Hugh Dowding, the boss of the Fighter Command. On 19 October 1940 he wrote to Lord Beaverbrook:

> Dear Lord Beaverbrook,
>
> Helmore has been to see me about a scheme for searchlight interception which Cotton has devised. The proposal has been made before and always turned down. At the same time I am a believer in trying anything which may be useful and I cannot think of any two people better than Cotton and Helmore to put such a project through. If you agree to let them go ahead with their plan, I will provide a fighter or fighters to give it a practical test when it is ready for trial.
>
> PS Helmore is a friend of mine and I have great admiration for him which I would like you to share. He wants nothing for himself—neither pay nor position.

As a result of Dowding's letter, Cotton had a Boston delivered to Heston in October 1940 and once again Airwork were engaged to make the modifications to the plane. A retired marshal of the RAF, Sir John Salmond, was chairman of the Night Defence Committee and at first seemed favourably disposed towards Cotton. Unfortunately for Cotton the Air Staff got to hear of Cotton's latest venture. Thinking that once again that he had gone over their heads or behind their backs, they told Salmond to have nothing further to do with Sidney.

'My relations with Salmond up to this point had been good. Now they deteriorated rapidly,' wrote Sidney.

The exchange of letters between December 1940 and January 1941 became increasingly acrimonious. Sidney put in a bill to the Ministry of Aircraft Production for £200 a month for expenses incurred in developing the Turbinlite.

On 27 December, Salmond replied:

> This appears to me to be a very large sum if it is your computation of money for value given hitherto—apart from what may be the incidence in the future. The fact is that in so far as a particular experiment is concerned you have got a DB-7 (Boston) which requires maintenance and nothing more up to the moment.
>
> I cannot see why this necessitates your keeping three cars and an office staff.
>
> Will you please forward a statement of expenses up to the 31st December and subsequently a weekly statement.

In a letter marked PERSONAL AND CONFIDENTIAL dated 25 January 1941 Salmond put in writing what Cotton had suspected—that the Air Staff had blackballed him: 'I had been informed in confidence by members of the Air Staff that they had found you difficult and unsatisfactory to deal with and for those reasons they felt I should be well advised not to have dealings with you. The members of the Air Staff in question made no attack on your honesty or personal integrity nor have I ever done so.'

Cotton had also upset Air Marshal Sir W. Sholto Douglas of Fighter Command. On 22 January 1941 Sholto Douglas reluctantly agreed to let one of his 23 Squadron DB-7s be fitted with twin searchlights. 'But I am not prepared to hand over a DB-7 lock stock and barrel to you. What I want you to do is to fit one of the squadron aircraft and do both the fitting up of the aircraft and the actual trials at Ford.'

To pursue the airborne searchlight idea, it was necessary for Cotton to become a civilian again. The Air Ministry were not all that sorry to see him go.

On 3 March 1941 they wrote to him:

> I am commanded by the Air Council to inform you that as it is no longer necessary for you to retain the acting unpaid rank of Wing Commander or to wear RAF uniform, the authority granted in this department's letter on 3rd October 1940, numbered as above, is hereby withdrawn with effect from the date of this letter.
>
> You will therefore remain on the Unemployed List of officers of the Royal Air Force Volunteer Reserve in your substantive rank as Squadron Leader, but as it seems unlikely that your services will again be required on the active list of the Royal Air Force, the Council would be prepared to give favourable consideration to an application by you to resign your commission, in order that you may feel entirely free to follow civilian employment.
>
> I am, Sir,
> Your Obedient Servant
> Arthur Street

On 3 October 1940 Cotton obtained his release from the air force, retaining the acting unpaid rank of wing commander and wearing RAF uniform when military duties made it necessary.

Flight Lt Jim Wayne was attached to 1451 Flight at RAF Hunsdon near Bishops Stortford flying Bostons fitted with the new light. 'It was a brilliant light, four feet in diameter,' he recalled. 'It was just that the batteries that powered it weighed two tons.' The aircraft carried a crew of two and the fuselage was packed with two tons of accumulators which could illuminate the light for a maximum of thirty seconds. The added weight of the accumulators meant that the aircraft was extremely dangerous to fly on one engine.

The Bostons were accompanied by two cannon-armed Hurricane fighters. The Turbinlite aircraft would be guided by ground controllers to within five miles of the enemy aircraft when the radar operator in the back of the Boston would take over. When they were 200 yards from the aircraft they could surge ahead and switch on the light—the Hurricanes were then supposed to attack the illuminated aircraft.

In practice the experiment was a disaster. The brightly lit Boston was a prime target for the rear gunner of a Junkers 88 who would immediately shoot out the light. The Turbinlite operation was abandoned after fighters inadvertently shot down an RAF Stirling bomber returning from a raid over Germany.

Whether the Turbinlite would have been a success or not, its very development was to get Cotton investigated by MI5. The charge: passing information on this highly secret device to a foreign power. The foreign power was the United States of America. In August 1941 the United States was not yet in the war, and the Japanese attack at Pearl Harbor was four months away. However, Churchill had cemented the special relationship with Roosevelt. American pilots were flying in the RAF and shiploads of lend lease aircraft were arriving at Liverpool and Southampton docks. It might have been a foreign power but it was scarcely a hostile one.

On the afternoon of 22 August a despatch rider drew up outside Sidney's flat in Curzon Place with a letter from Sholto Douglas. It read: 'I regret that I have to tell you that acting on Air Ministry instructions I shall have to withdraw the permission I gave you to visit Hunsdon. This ban also applies to other stations in Fighter Command and is to take effect immediately.'

Cotton was told he had been discharged from the Airborne Turbinlite Project and was asked to leave Heston. When he went down to the airfield a few days later to collect his private effects he was arrested.

'I was escorted to see a new wing commander who had been appointed as No. 2 to Geoffrey Tuttle. He told me how upset they had all been about the new order but it had come from the Air Ministry and there was nothing they could do about it.'

Sidney had suspected for a while that he was being followed. Now he would be interviewed by MI5. He was summoned to the office of the Director of Intelligence Security, Air Commodore D. L. Blackford. A shorthand writer sat in the corner sharpening her pencil and two other men, to whom Sidney was not introduced, looked at him with curiosity. Blackford said that he understood

Cotton had been a consultant during the early stages of the Turbinlight project, but had been told that his part in its development was now finished. Despite the fact that a ban had been placed on him, had he not visited the RAF station at Hunsdon and had he not also passed the details of the invention to the American authorities in London?

Cotton said that he had not been called in as an adviser on the project. He had invented it. He denied passing any of this information to the Americans. He knew they had expressed an interest in the idea and he had referred them to the Ministry of Aircraft production.

For the rest of the morning, Sidney was subjected to a thorough grilling by Blackford. Where was he on certain dates? Where did he go between this date and that? Who had visited him?

Sidney slunk back to his apartment, drained of emotion. 'It was obviously a frame up,' he wrote. 'The Air Ministry were trying to get me put away under section 18b of the Official Secrets Act.'

That night Sidney dined with an American, one of Roosevelt's special envoys to Britain, who told him he had received a letter from the Air Ministry saying they should have nothing whatever to do with him.

The next day at 11 o'clock Cotton again presented himself at Blackford's office. The interrogation began again but Sidney quickly interjected: 'This whole thing, as you know well enough, is a frame up.' He then produced a letter from the Ministry of Aircraft Production which proved without doubt Sidney's bona fide association with the searchlight project.

'As for the Americans, you invited them out to Heston, or the Air Ministry did.'

Blackford seemed convinced and Sidney heard no more about the affair. But although the case against him seemed to have collapsed, Sidney still found himself out in the cold. No one in the military seemed inclined to engage his services and what he did for the rest of the war seems to be a mystery. Later he was to receive a paper from Winston Churchill to be placed in his files to the effect that he was to be cleared of any suggestions of malpractice. But some of the mud stuck.

There was no doubt that Sidney was a marked man. He did however take the precaution of placing all his personal papers in the safekeeping of a fellow Australian, Stanley Bruce, the then Australian High Commissioner in London, in case a fresh action was mounted against him.

Like Cotton, Bruce had spent most of his time in England and had been educated at Trinity College Cambridge. He had served with the British Army in World War I winning a Military Cross at Gallipoli and had become Prime Minister at the age of only thirty-one. Bruce had lost his seat in 1929 and had spent most of the rest of his life in England, being Australian High Commissioner from 1932 to 1945. Debonair, in a pin-stripe morning suit and spats, Bruce was more British than the British. He spoke in the carefully modulated tones of the Melbourne Establishment, and was a member of all the right clubs.

It was to Bruce that Sidney appealed when he was being grilled by MI5 over a possible security leak.

In his papers held by the National Archives of Australia, Bruce told his own version of Cotton's relationship with Churchill.

> After the war broke out and Winston went to the Admiralty about October or November 1939 and demanded information as to where the German fleet was, and raised the question as to why the Air Ministry could not get photographs.
>
> He took the matter up with the Air Ministry but their reply was that they could not get the photographs. At this stage the Admiral (Rear Admiral J. H. Godfrey, director of Naval Intelligence) came into it and told Winston he thought he had got the man who could get the photographs, and proceeded to send for Cotton. The result was that Cotton got all the photographic particulars of the location of the German fleet in Kiel and Wilhelmshaven etc.
>
> With his usual impishness Winston rang up Sir Kingsley Wood (the Secretary of State for Air) and twitted him on the incapacity

of the Air Force to get information. At the Conference Winston put Cotton on his right and the air representatives on his left produced all the photographs—and was eulogistic towards Cotton and twitted the Air Force on their failure.

This laid the foundations of an undying vendetta against Cotton.

They were however forced to take him into the Air Force and he was sent out to France where he had something of a roving commission.

He apparently got on quite well with the heads of the Air Force in France and there does not seem to have been any trouble while he was there.

In the last stages [of peace] in France Cotton had nothing particular to do and spent most of his time flying important people back to England as part of the evacuation.

When in England, on one of these trips, Beaverbrook who had then become a Minister asked him to bring an American out of France—which he did. This American turned out to be a man who was on the Security people's black list. Not for anything very vicious, but because he was always prepared to pass onto the Germans anything he knew. Cotton was immediately pulled up for having done this unauthorised action.

He told the story that Beaverbrook had asked to bring him out but Beaverbrook said he had never done any such thing.

Clearly Winston Churchill admired Cotton's bravura and preferred the directness of the plain speaking Australian to the bluster and pomposity of the air force top brass. Churchill's aide, Desmond Morton, became Cotton's champion. Bruce reported:

Morton proceeded to tell me that he had seen all the files in the Air Ministry about Cotton and that in his view they constituted the worst example of persecution and relentless persecution of a vendetta that he had ever seen in his 30 years experience of the United Kingdom Civil Service. He said that every possible

> opportunity of prejudicing the records against Cotton, without actually falsifying them, had been taken.
>
> Morton has said that this had been done with great skill and that the real villain in the piece was a man who was still in the Air Force, and is in fact an Air Marshal. He asked me not to press him as to who this individual was.

Could the Air Marshal in question have been Air Marshal Sir Richard Peirse? Cotton had taken his seat at the table.

Bruce continued:

> Morton finished his story at the point where Pound's personal assistant committed the indiscretion of putting on paper that there was a gentleman's agreement between the Admiralty and the Air Ministry that Cotton was not to be employed. The present position I gather is that owing to Morton's intervention the Admiralty has now written Cotton a letter which completely clears his character, and would enable him to meet any charge that might in the future be brought against him.

On 2 February 1944, Stanley Bruce met Cotton at Australia House in the Strand: 'I continued to see him as I had a feeling that what he was telling me true, whereas his story was so fantastic that what I should have done was to have thrown him out and refuse to see him any more.'

Cotton was looking for a new job. Doors had slammed shut in Britain. But now that Australia was in danger from Japan was there a role for him in the Pacific theatre?

'I explained to him the position which existed at present with regard to the Australian forces in the South-West Pacific area and told him I did not think it would be the slightest use for him to be attached to the Australian Air Force even if they were prepared to give him a commission.

'I suggested the only possible way of his getting a job of work to do would be put himself over on General Douglas McArthur.'

Bruce offered to put Cotton's case to John Curtin, the Australian

Prime Minister, during his forthcoming visit to England. 'I would then be quite prepared to arrange for him to see the Prime Minister, having given the Prime Minister . . . the story of what had happened to him here.'

Years after he had first been investigated by British Security Cotton was still a marked man. Another enemy was Air Chief Marshal Sir Philip Joubert de la Ferté the chief of RAF Coastal Command in World War II. The two men had originally been friends—in fact after Cotton had been replaced as head of the PDU Joubert had invited him to join his night interception unit. But after being discharged from the Aerial Target Illumination project he received a letter from Joubert. It read:

'Sir Philip regrets that owing to the action taken by the Ministry of Aircraft Production it will be no use you seeing him again.'

After the war Joubert published his memoirs in the book *Rocket*. Sidney took exception to it and launched a libel action in the High Court. Joubert's version of the creation of the PDU is different to Sidney's but it is difficult to see what would have angered the Australian. Joubert describes how photographic intelligence had a low priority in between the wars.

'Into this pleasantly conventional peace time picture had intruded a rather unusual individual, Mr Sidney Cotton, and with him other associates.' He says that Cotton was much encouraged by the support of Air Vice-Marshal Richard Peck . . . 'a man of rare intelligence, who as an amateur photographer of some skill had fully appreciated what the latter was trying to achieve.'

Joubert's version of the evacuation from France also differs from Cotton's:

'No. 212 Squadron worked in France until evacuated in June 1940, almost too late to get away owing to Cotton's insistence that the French would not collapse. As a result of this piece of wishful thinking, Cotton was relieved of all further control of operations and PRU became a normal air force unit.'

The air raid sirens had already sounded and the searchlights were probing the blackness when the bell rang at Joan Henry's mews flat in Kensington. She had already taken the precaution of placing her tin helmet and gas mask on the hat stand in the hall. Joan Henry was not expecting visitors.

Outside, his spectacles glinting in the dim light was her estranged husband Sidney Cotton. From somewhere up in the sky above came the erratic beat of aircraft engines. 'Come on, Joey, let's go and watch the fireworks,' he said. 'Let's go to the Dorchester.'

The Dorchester Hotel was several blacked out streets away. Sidney, she noticed, wore no tin hat. They decided to stick to the main roads, along the Brompton Road to South Kensington tube station then past the Victoria and Albert Museum to Hyde Park Corner. Sidney strode purposefully. The sky was lit by the flash of exploding anti-aircraft shells. Bombs were falling all over London.

'We walked along Rotten Row and I looked up through the trees and the bits and pieces of shrapnel was falling everywhere,' she said. 'I said to Sidney "Where's your tin hat?" "What's the good of that?" he said. Sidney had no fear at all. No matter how dangerous it was he wasn't frightened. He was born with no fear.'

Not a light shone at the Dorchester and the windows of the great hotel were covered with blackout curtains. The ballroom however was ablaze with light. The Dorchester which had only opened in 1931 was one of the first steel framed skyscrapers in London and said to be bomb proof, earthquake proof and fireproof.

The front entrance of the hotel had been heavily sandbagged within days of the first air raid. Its staff doubled up as both air raid wardens and fire watchers. With the outbreak of war many things had changed. The restaurant had moved to the Gold Room where diners had the reassuring protection of eight floors of reinforced concrete instead of the glass domed roof. The grill room had transferred to the Ballroom lounge which avoided the danger of flying glass. Guests slept in the air raid shelter, cubicles in the gymnasium, the Turkish baths in the basement, the kitchens, and some even slept in the corridors. Those more fatalistic stayed in their beds and hoped for the best. Layers of shingle on the roof offered some protection from incendiary bombs.

But although it was often ringed by falling bombs, the Dorchester's claim to be bomb proof was never put to the test. Confidence in the building however was enough to persuade many government ministers to become residents. Occupants included the Foreign Secretary Sir Anthony Eden, Sir Charles Portal, Chief of the Air Staff, and General Eisenhower.

Small wonder then that the well heeled residents of the West End chose this as a place of sanctuary rather than a damp air raid shelter. Cecil Beaton the society photographer compared the scene in the hotel lobby to 'a luxury liner with all the horrors of enforced jocularity and expensive squalor'. Ian Fleming's wife Ann said the whole place 'had a strange feeling of synthetic safety with a mass of cabinet ministers, crooks and Mayfair remnants milling around'.

The lobby that night had quite a few Mayfair remnants; politicians, diplomats, musicians and members of the aristocracy. People in evening dress stood around the walls as if they offered protection. The room was rocked by explosions and a thin drizzle of plaster fell from the ceiling. Some people were clearly drunk. Women were weeping uncontrollably. As Sidney and Joan walked into the room, the Duchess of Newcastle was having hysterics. 'The Duke was trying to calm her down and she turned round and gave him a fourpenny one,' Joan said.

Dame Myra Hess the celebrated concert pianist had also sought refuge in the ballroom, but she was in no state to play the piano.

'She was in hysterics. So Sidney said "For God's sake see if you can calm her down a bit."'

Joan led her over to the grand piano, put her arm comfortingly around her shoulders and placed her hands on the keys. 'I said: "Play something to calm all the others down." Once I got her hands on the piano she couldn't stop. It did a lot of good. She was sobbing at the same time but she was still playing. It was a very exciting evening.'

## Chapter 10

# War Surplus

Sidney was not idle during his time in the wilderness and was constantly thinking of ways of improving the high flying photographic aircraft . . .

In 1940, he produced drawings of his own aircraft the PDU-1. It looked like a cross between a Spitfire and a North American Mustang. The aircraft was a single seater with a maximum speed in level flight of 470 miles an hour at 25 000 feet, 330 miles and hour at 32 000 feet with a range of 1050 miles.

'The PDU-1,' wrote Cotton, 'has a performance that will be hard to equal by any fighting aircraft for at least three years. The photographic reconnaissance work carried out by the Photographic Development Unit has proved the justification for the design and production of a purely photographic aeroplane but at the same time the potential usefulness of such a machine in other spheres has been borne in mind.'

The aircraft was to be powered by a supercharged version of the new Rolls Royce Griffon engine which in 1940 was not yet in production. Like the Mustang its air intake was set well back on the belly of the aircraft, almost behind the wing. The cockpit was pressurised (unlike the early PR Spitfires) and the floor of the cabin had Perspex panels so that the pilot could see the photographic target. Two Eagle IX cameras were to be fitted in the fuselage behind the pilot each angled at 80 degrees, with provision for another two F 24 cameras.

Early Spitfires had exposed rivets, unlike the German Messerschmitt 109 which incorporated rivets flush with the skin. Any obtrusion on the skin of an aircraft leads to drag, so to make them more streamlined, the PRU Spitfires had been coated with plaster of Paris which was then sanded back and painted.

The airframe of the PDU-1, however, was to be of flush riveted alclad sheet with no exposed rivets. The undercarriage was to have rigid wheel fairings which fitted flush with the skin when the wheels were retracted. 'A flush and airtight sealing of the wheel housing is thus achieved by the simplest means and no use is made of questionable flaps or dangerous mechanisms,' wrote Cotton. 'All present day single seaters are seriously handicapped by undercarriage problems which detracts from the efficiency of the aeroplane as a whole. Although the design is conventional in order to make certain that a practical aeroplane with good flying qualities and moderate landing speed will be produced, the PDU-1 has an aerodynamic form not previously attained. No structural difficulty interferes with the shape,' wrote Sid, who had certainly done his homework on streamlining .

The PDU-1 was purposeful rather than beautiful. There is however no record of it being built. In 1940 Britain had a dozen aircraft manufacturers and the competition was fierce for contracts. It is unlikely that Sid's aeroplane would have had a sympathetic reception, especially now that he was out in the cold.

Sidney Cotton's work at establishing the Photographic Development Unit had been an unqualified success. The Lockheed might have attracted some suspicion among the Germans but the regular overflights by the Spitfires must have confirmed the existence of a photographic reconnaissance. So how did the Germans respond?

Sidney's opposite number in the Luftwaffe was an Oberstleutnant Rowehl. Throughout 1939 he had experimented with both pressurised and unarmed versions of the Junkers 86 medium bomber. By the summer of 1940 he had managed to coax one of these obsolete machines up to 41 000 feet—far higher than Cotton's Spitfires. He also experimented with the long range Dornier 217As which had their fuselages extended to carry two vertical cameras. These obtained excellent high altitude photographs of every important airfield and British city, as well as industrial targets like aircraft factories.

In his early discussions with Sir Cyril Newall, Cotton had insisted on operating from Heston rather than a military airfield. The cover was perfect. But ironically, Germany's national carrier, Lufthansa, was operating civilian flights from Heston at the same time as Sidney had begun operating spy flights.

The German airline flew its distinctive Junkers JU-52 trimotors on regular scheduled services to Hamburg, Cologne and Berlin in conjunction with British Airways. It has also now been established that the Germans were playing the same observation game. Some of the civilian registered *Tante-Us* combined their passenger carrying duties with spy flights over Britain, taking pictures of airfields, factories and other potential targets. It was inevitable that the Germans would sooner or later put two and two together. The huge concave Airwork hangar at Heston where the Lockheed had originally been modified to carry cameras and long range tanks dominated the airfield and could be seen for miles.

In the autumn of 1940 when the Luftwaffe switched from daylight to night raids, Heston was one of the first targets. On 19 September, the Germans raided the airfield and a magnetic mine exploded outside the Airwork hangar which was demolished. One visiting Miles Magister, a low wing light aircraft was destroyed, and fifteen other aircraft including Sidney's famous Lockheed were damaged.

Leslie Axon was a leading aircraftman with Sidney's unit when the Germans attacked Heston. Today he lives in retirement in Minehead in Devon. 'In the first raid the Germans tried to set fire to the aerodrome with incendiaries and we were all called out with blankets to beat the flames out. Then there was a terrific air raid. So big we weren't allowed out of the air raid shelter. We heard a big thump but fortunately they didn't hit the petrol dump.'

The explosion however blew down the doors of the hangar containing the Lockheed. Leslie remembers that by this time the aircraft had been painted a sand colour on top and pale blue underneath. The Lockheed was shipped back to the Lockheed plant at Burbank in California for an extensive rebuild.

The day after the raid, Geoffrey Tuttle was told that His Majesty the King was at the gates to the airfield. He thought someone was pulling his leg but when he went to the gate he saw the royal car. Tuttle threw up his best salute. The King said: 'I was driving from Windsor to London when I looked out and saw that the big hangar wasn't there any more. So I called to see how you were all getting on.'

After Sidney was kicked out of the PDU, the old team went their separate ways. Pat Martin had found herself a new boyfriend, pilot called Guy Conran who she later married. Pat did not have much luck with pilots. Conran was shot down over Holland and spent the rest of the war in a German POW camp. After leaving Heston, Bob Niven, the tall Canadian, toured Britain for Sir Alan Cobham looking for satellite landing fields. Britain was gearing up for the huge bomber offensive against Germany and large areas of farmland were turned into makeshift airfields.

Later Niven was given the job of ferrying new aircraft across the Atlantic from Canada. These were Lockheed Hudsons, a larger version of Sidney's Lockheed 12.

Then in 1941 he became the commanding officer of 59 Squadron based at North Cotes in Lincolnshire. The pre-war flying had been dangerous enough. Now Bob would be taking part on low level raids over Germany. In May 1942 he left home to go to the base and said to his wife, Andrea: 'I might be a bit late this evening. I'm seeing the chaps off on a mission.' Bob Niven did not see his pilots off on the mission. He joined it.

That night the Hudsons attacked German convoys off the coast of Holland and Bob's aircraft was shot down. Two of the three bodies were recovered. The third was never found. Andrea Niven had had trouble sleeping that night. There was an air raid and a bomb had dropped nearby. 'I had a bad feeling about that day. I had this feeling that this might be the last time. Then the phone rang at about 6 a.m. and the voice on the end seemed a bit strange. Later on a fellow officer of Bob's came in and said "I have to tell you that Bob was shot down tonight". It was the worst day of my life.' The tragedy was compounded by the fact that Andrea was pregnant. Three months later she gave birth to Robert junior.

It would be nearly a year after his dismissal before Sidney's work with the PDU was officially recognised. The men in his unit put forward a recommendation that he receive the Distinguished Service Order, but it was not forthcoming. In the New Year's honours list in 1941, he was awarded the Order of the British Empire. 'OBE stood for Old Buggers Encouragement,' sniffed Joan Henry who thought he should have had at least a knighthood.

After Sidney had been sidelined, the Photographic Development Unit went from strength to strength. In July 1940 it was renamed the Photographic Reconnaissance Unit (PRU). It was obvious that after the big air raid on Heston the unit could remain there no longer so in December 1940 it moved to Benson in Oxfordshire.

Bombers were now taking flash pictures over their targets at night so a second PR unit No. 3 PRU was formed, followed by No. 2 and No. 4, both based in North Africa. Many new squadrons of photographic aircraft were formed, not just Spitfires but Mosquitos, and American Lightnings.

Aerofilms, Major Hemming's photographic interpretation unit at Wembley, was also damaged in an air raid so it was decided to seek a safer place outside London. In April 1941 the unit—now renamed the Central Interpretation Unit—moved to Danesfield House at Medmenham on the River Thames.

Cotton's Crooks had earned a reputation as a hush-hush glamour unit—now the unit was to engage the services of some glamorous women in uniform. Both Cotton and Geoffrey Tuttle believed that women would make good photographic interpreters.

'Looking through a magnifying glass at minute objects in a photograph required the patience of Job and the skill of a good darner of socks,' said Sidney.

Women in uniform had been with the unit ever since the Heston days. At Medmenham WAAFs were to soon outnumber the men. Among them was Churchill's daughter Sarah Oliver who brightened the scene with her elegance, glamour and wit. But the brightest star was Constance Babington-Smith, the daughter of the Director of the Bank of England. Constance, an attractive vital woman, liked Sidney enormously and was impressed by his single mindedness and drive. It was she who first described him as a 'buccaneer'. The operation started as a 'one woman band' and grew steadily until by 1943 she had eleven specialist interpreters working underneath her.

'Babs', as she was known, was one of the first WAAFs trained to interpret aerial photographs—how to identify airfields and railway stations and how to differentiate between roads, which usually follow the lie of the land, and railways with their gentle curves. She learned how to use the stereoscopic viewer in which two overlapping pictures were placed side by side underneath something which looked like a pair of spectacles mounted on four legs. By juggling the pictures the two images fused together to achieve a three dimensional effect which leapt out of the picture. Later, Constance Babington-Smith was to make one of the most important discoveries of the war—a small egg shaped machine with wings—the rocket powered Messerschmitt 163 fighter.

By the end of the war nearly seventeen hundred people worked at Medmenham, which Churchill christened The Chalk House With Tudor Chimneys. The CIU and PRU were involved in every major operation of World War II. The photographic aircraft would fly over before and after a bombing raid. If the pictures showed that the bombs had missed, the target would be raided again. The eyes of the PRU were able to show that the vast majority of British bombs were failing to hit their targets, which was a constant source of irritation to the chiefs of Bomber Command.

The aircraft returned with pictures of invasion barges in the Channel ports which confirmed Hitler's preparations for the invasion of England. They photographed radar installations, tank movements and trainloads of weapons. They found the Moehne, Eder and Sorpe dams, later destroyed by the Lancaster bombers of 617 squadron. In northern France the photographic interpreters found the ski sites for the pilotless V-1 flying bombs which were launched against London.

Operation 'Crossbow' was launched to destroy the sites. An even more devastating raid, was later launched against the Peenemunde facility on the Baltic coast, which was producing V-2 rockets.

The importance of photographic intelligence was not lost on the Germans. Even in 1938 Generaloberst Werner Freiherr von Fritsch had warned his superiors that: 'Military organisation which has the most efficient reconnaissance unit will win the next war.' The prophecy had come true. That victory was in part certainly due to Sidney Cotton.

Sidney Cotton was not there to witness the continuing success of the Photographic Reconnaissance Unit. He had already hung his wing commander's uniform in the closet and moved on.

The British war machine was winding down and people didn't want aeroplanes and pilots to fly them any more. Sidney was not however going to sit around licking his wounds. There were deals to be made and huge amounts of war surplus equipment were lying around in Europe. It was business as usual.

It was time to pick up the threads of his family life, too. Sidney had seen little of his daughter, Jill, during the war. Then in 1944 she had returned to England from America.

By this time Sidney was living in London and Joan was living on the farm at Checkendon. 'When Sidney did come to stay for a few days he was very affectionate with me and it was fun to see him,' said Jill. 'But I really did not get to know him until I came back from the States. I was at boarding school in Dorset then and used to spend quite a lot of time in London in the school holidays. He could be extremely amusing and we got on well together. I think he wanted to be a good father but business definitely came first.'

The last time that Sidney had seen Marcel Boussac was in Paris in 1940 when he had offered him a great deal of money to escape to England in the Lockheed. Boussac had stayed behind during the German occupation and had managed to retain at least some of his fabulous collection of race horses. However his most famous horse, Pharis, had been stolen by the Germans and was being held at a stud farm outside Erfurt in Germany.

De Gaulle had entered Paris at the end of August but it was still out of bounds to civilians travelling from England. Sidney, however, still had an entrée to 'a gentleman who smoked a cigar'. Desmond Morton, Churchill's aide, arranged a passage for Sidney on a British destroyer from Newhaven to Dieppe.

In Paris, the little Frenchman poured out his heart to Sidney. Could he organise a rescue mission to bring Pharis back to France? The Americans were already advancing into Germany. It was quite likely they would seize the famous stallion for themselves. Sidney agreed to mount a rescue operation to follow the Americans into Germany, grab the horse and bring it back to France. In his account, he is suitably vague as to how this was actually accomplished.

'I was able to enlist a formidable array of officers of various nationalities and services to carry out the rescue. Our mixed party would give us the necessary liason with whatever forces we encountered on the way.' The famous horse was rescued and restored to its owner. All this had been accomplished, said Sidney, by a bribe of a horsebox full of champagne!

Sidney had reluctantly had to part with his famous Lockheed when he was sacked from the PDU. He still considered it the best executive aeroplane around so now he tried to buy another one. In 1945 this was easier said than done.

The Royal Air Force had quite a few of them but they could only be bought with US dollars. An American friend loaned him the money and he bought two aircraft, keeping one of them, a former US navy aircraft which he named *Caprice*. As soon as he had the aeroplane he wanted to travel to Italy where he knew that a huge amount of military equipment was up for sale. When he applied for a visa, however, he was told that he must get permission from the Board of Trade and that unless his visit was in the national interest he would not be allowed to go. There were three foolscap pages of questions which Sidney refused to answer. He announced instead that he was going to France and that he would get a visa for Italy while he was in Paris.

The Italian deal was in second-hand aircraft. Sidney bought seventy-five Douglas DC-3s for the bargain price of £250 000, with a huge amount of spare parts thrown in. There was a good market for DC-3s because they were rugged, dependable and suitable for passengers or freight. A man called Valetta, the boss of Fiat, had already agreed to buy twelve of them.

It was a shrewd business deal. In fact many airlines started their postwar operations using second-hand DC-3s. 'The pen was in his hand, ready to sign then the telephone went and he was called away to talk to a General Wilson the agent for Trans World Airlines in Italy. He had phoned to say, "Don't sign that agreement. TWA will make you a present of 12 Dakotas". So that blew up in my face,' Sidney later recalled.

Sidney flew on to India. This time he bought £10 million worth of war surplus road-making equipment which had been lying unused in Calcutta. He paid £250 000 and onsold it to an American oil company for £2 million. Sidney had nearly concluded the deal when the Indian Prime Minister Jawaharlal Nehru stepped in and placed a ban on the equipment being shipped out of India. Sidney then arranged with one of the Indian princes, the Maharajah of Baroda, to take over the operation and ship the equipment from the state of Baroda instead. Once again political events overtook him. India declared independence and Baroda was no longer a separate state. Sidney couldn't complete the deal.

Another of Sidney's postwar ventures was buying up war surplus bicycles. A visitor who had been seeking the toilet during a visit to Sidney's flat in London had opened the wrong door and found a room jammed from the floor to ceiling with bikes. He obviously had trouble getting rid of those, too.

It seemed that Sidney could not win a trick. Before the war he had the Midas touch. But in austere postwar Britain it was a different story. He spent long hours talking up business but most of his deals came to nothing.

'Most of my old friends have either died or dropped from sight,' he wrote. In the fifties he complained: 'I do not know so many people in this country as I did previous to the war.'

Sidney was unfailingly generous to his friends and business contacts and still believed that to make money one must be prepared to spend it. This attitude was to add to his ultimate downfall: 'I have never believed in the "penny wise and pound foolish" policy for one must spend money to make money and spend it on what might appear to be at time unnecessary expenditure. It all comes back in the long run provided the run is long enough. Money is a servant and I have always treated it as such. Many people, to their disadvantage I believe allow money to be their controlling passion and that does not make for constructive thinking or happiness.'

Before the war Sidney had relied upon his old boy contacts but: 'In postwar Britain his way of doing business was that of a dinosaur,' said Brian Brooke-Smith, later to become his brother-in -law. 'Sid used to say there were two sorts of fish. There were those just swimming about in the current snapping at everything that went by, and there was the one that sat in a hole in the bank waiting for the big one.'

The big one was not long in coming. It was called Hyderabad.

## Chapter 11

# The Buccaneer

Frederick Rowan, a thickset man in his early fifties, had one of the loneliest jobs in the world—operating a radio beacon on a disused airfield in the middle of India. At night he would listen with his ears straining to hear the sound of aircraft engines—converted Lancaster bombers that he would guide onto the airfield. The airfield at Bidar was set in a wilderness. It was as hot as hell during the summer and wet and miserable during the monsoons.

As soon as he had established radio contact with the Lancastrians Rowan would rush out to the strip and light the flarepath—gooseneck lamps fuelled by kerosene. This airport was no longer marked on maps. The airfield that he lived on had long since officially ceased to operate. It was close to Karachi but well away from the main civilian aerodrome.

Frederick Rowan missed his invalid wife seven thousand miles away in Gloucestershire. But jobs in aviation were scarce and the money was at least some compensation for being stuck in some hell hole where it never stopped raining for weeks on end. But had he known what was in store for him he would have packed his bags and got the next plane home.

Half a world away in London a great many pilots had just been demobbed from the RAF and were looking for work. It wasn't that difficult to fly an aeroplane and a life in civvy street looked dull by comparison—flying was certainly more interesting than a career in accountancy. There was just the problem that pilots were ten a penny. Air travel for the masses was still twenty years away. Flying was then too expensive, too uncomfortable and potentially dangerous. It was something that only rich people did. The major airlines re-established their pre-war routes with lashed up converted bombers that would not necessarily deliver you to your destination in one piece, or at all. The British were playing around with jets, but they weren't that good.

Sidney Cotton was about to offer a small number of pilots some very well paid work. Footing the bill was the richest man in the world. The big fish was the Nizam of the Indian state of Hyderabad.

The Nizam was the only prince in India to carry the title *Exalted Highness*. His fabulous wealth included £100 million in gold bullion and £300 million in jewels. Among the gems was the 185 carat Victoria or Jacob diamond (sometimes also known as the Imperial or Great White diamond) which he had bought from an Armenian Jew called Alexander Jacob. On his desk was the Nizam diamond which had been found in Hyderabad's own alluvial diamond fields. It weighed 277 carats but had been only partly cut. He used it as a paperweight but often kept it in his desk rolled up in an old newspaper. He had more than ten million dollars in cash wrapped in old newspapers stored in the basement. Although he had enough gold plates to serve a hundred, he ate his own meal off a tin plate on a carpet on his bedroom floor.

Despite his enormous wealth the Mir Osman Ali Khan, seventh Nizam, was known to be a misanthropic old skinflint who wore a cheap second-hand suit and a fez encrusted with dandruff and who smoked cigarette ends left behind by his guests. *The Times* of

London depicted him shuffling around his crumbling palace in carpet slippers fretting about the cost of maintaining his four wives, forty-two concubines and thirty-three surviving children. Others saw him as a great philanthropist who had created a model state in which Moslems and Hindus lived in harmony. The Nizam reigned over a a country the size of Italy. More than eighty six per cent of the population were Hindus but the administration was largely run by devout Muslims.

When the British Government announced its plan for the partition of India on 3 June 1947, the five hundred princes, maharajahs, rajahs and the Nizam were given the option of becoming part of India, which was predominantly Hindu, or joining the Moslem state of Pakistan. The Nizam issued a proclamation that he would resume the status of independent sovereign after Independence Day on 15 August, and would not be joining either India or Pakistan. He protested against the provision in clause 7 of the Indian Independence Bill that Dominion status could not be granted to any Indian state. He maintained that this amounted to the British Government abandoning its old ally and forcing him to sever his ties with the King of England who was also Emperor of India.

The Nizam decided he was prepared to fight to maintain his independence. In the months leading up to Independence Day the cauldron that was Indian politics bubbled over with intrigue. One rumour current in Delhi was that the Nizam was attempting to buy huge quantities of arms from Western countries. A large order of four crores (forty million rupees) was placed with Czechoslovakia, and the commander of the Hyderabad army Major General Sayyid Ahmed El Edroos left for Europe to arrange for its despatch.

The Nizam had given Britain financial aid during both world wars. In World War I he had given forty million rupees as an outright gift. Two Imperial Service regiments, the Deccan Horse and the Hyderabad Lancers, served in the war under the command of General Arthur Watson. The Nizam repeated this generosity in

World War II with men, materials and money. He made an outright gift of £6 million in cash, financed two Royal Air Force squadrons (both bearing the name of Hyderabad), and provided rest camps, coal, food, ambulances and grain. Hyderabad troops served in Malaya and the Middle East and air staff were raised and trained in Hyderabad.

At formal ceremonies he was the only one of the Indian Maharajahs to merit a 21 gun salute. In nearly forty years British advisers had counselled him on everything from finance to education. His personal adviser was Sir Walter Monckton who had brokered the abdication of Edward VIII and he was on good terms with Winston Churchill (then in Opposition).

Hyderabad was the subject of a furious debate in the House of Commons but it was cold comfort to its desiccated ruler. Its champion was a man who had once heaped praise on Sidney Cotton's clandestine photographic unit—Winston Churchill. Churchill compared the threatened invasion of Hyderabad to the Nazi invasion of Czechoslovakia. The blockade of Hyderabad, he said, was similar to that which was now being thrown around Berlin by the Soviet Union, except that the numbers of helpless people were far greater—seventeen million compared to two and a half million. No drugs and hospital equipment were getting into the country. It was three months, for example, since any chlorine had got through and chlorine was essential in India for the prevention of serious pestilences.

Churchill disliked the Cambridge educated Nehru, a protégé of the left wing intellectual Bertrand Russell. Nehru, he said, had circulated false rumours that the state of Hyderabad was run by gangsters. 'It seems to me,' rumbled Winston in that famous voice, 'that that is the sort of language which might have been used by Hitler before the devouring of Austria.'

As a student Clement Attlee had visited India in the 1920s and was convinced that independence was the inevitable course for this teeming nation. The Prime Minister said that it was perfectly obvious that after the end of British rule in India any obligations that Britain had towards the Indian states must go.

But, reasoned Winston, the Nizams had been loyal to Britain in more difficult times—like the Indian Mutiny of 1857. And as he pointed out, the assets of the Nizam had been frozen by the Bank of India. Hastings Ismay, one of Churchill's most loyal lieutenants wrote to Attlee:

'I have always been unhappy in my mind about the way in which the Government of India have handled the affairs of the Indian states ever since the transfer of power . . . the bloodless character of their so-called triumph only shows how ridiculous were their claims that Hyderabad was a threat to India.'

Sidney Cotton was used to mixing with the rich and powerful. But nothing had quite prepared him for his first meeting with Osman Ali Khan. The Nizam received the tall Australian in the magnificent Chow Mahallah palace, which by 1948 had lost some of its former splendour. Sidney had heard of the Nizam's wealth and had seen pictures of him wearing his fantastic sherwani decorated with diamonds and rubies.

The shrivelled figure who greeted him looked as nondescript as a ticket collector on the Hyderabad railways. The Nizam was a small man in a crumpled black coat and red fez. For years he had taken a daily dose of opium. As with most drug addicts this had made him careless about his personal appearance and reluctant to spend money on himself. His teeth were in a terrible state. He suffered from pyorrhoea but refused to go to a dentist.

Sidney, immaculate as ever in his white tropical suit and Sea Island cotton shirt, towered over His Exalted Highness. The Nizam, not known for his small talk, came straight to the point.

'I wish to buy weapons to protect my country. I want everything. Machine guns, grenades, mortars, anti-aircraft guns. I want them delivered very soon.'

Cotton cleared his throat: 'That is entirely possible Your Exalted Highness,' he said.

'I require five hundred tons of weapons and you have five weeks in which to transport them to my country. You will discuss the terms with General Edroos and my son Prince Berar.'

Cotton looked into the eyes of the Nizam. 'It will cost you twenty million pounds, Your Exalted Highness.' Before the Nizam had time to blink, Cotton added: 'In cash.'

But for a man who carelessly left gold bars lying around in his harem, twenty million pounds was not a lot of money.

To the Nizam, Cotton was a knight errant who was prepared to help a country unjustly blockaded by the Nehru-despised socialist. To the Indians he was a crook who was trying to make a fast buck by smuggling arms into a hostile state. Sidney however, was manipulating the media. In a newsreel shown in English cinemas Sidney is seen on a ladder unloading small cardboard boxes from the front baggage locker of an Avro Lancastrian aircraft.

The boxes contained medical supplies and carried the names of well known manufacturers of medical equipment, such as Merck, Sharp and Dohme. During the Indian union's blockade of Hyderabad there was a shortage of certain medical supplies but in reality Sidney was carrying a far more sinister cargo. Cotton had arranged to have British Movietone film the event to make his flights more plausible—in fact the main cargo hold of the aircraft was not full of syringes and cotton wool but weapons.

The Lancastrian aircraft, a civilian conversion of the Lancaster bomber was designed to carry the biggest load of any bombing aeroplane of World War II—ten tons of bombs. Without the heavy weight of its guns it could fly 4000 miles. But in some ways it was better equipped to carry cargo than passengers. The most it could carry was thirteen and the fuselage was so narrow that they had to sit with their backs up against one side of the cabin wall. With its cramped unpressurised rear fuselage the Lancastrian was not a comfortable .

If the newsreel photographers had been allowed to take their cameras inside the fuselage they would have found five tonnes of weapons lying on the floor. Cotton's fleet of aircraft transported 1000 anti-tank mines, 25 000 mortars, 1200 Biretta, submachine guns, bazookas, 3000 submachine carbines, 10 000 rifles, a lone ack-ack gun and six low calibre anti-tank guns besides a considerable amount of ammunition. The weapons were desperately needed. Many Hyderabadi soldiers were still using ancient muzzle loading rifles from the time of the Indian Mutiny and much of their best material had been supplied to the British army during World War II.

The clandestine flights were mostly made at night. 'It was next to impossible for our aircraft to intercept these Lancasters during their night flight,' wrote Jawaharlal Nehru, later to become India's first Prime Minister. 'We had no facilities or aircraft suitable for the purpose. Only by the rarest chance would we come across them and even then it would be difficult to take any action as the Lancasters flew very fast, about 250 miles an hour.'

The operations were a calculated risk. A great many British officers served in the Indian air force. Indeed Nehru's adviser on aviation matters was an Air Marshal Sir Thomas Walker Elmhirst. Whether the Lancastrians were carrying weapons or not, it is unlikely that British officers would have given orders to shoot down their fellow countrymen. These were unarmed civilian cargo planes. If attacked they could not retaliate. If any of them had been shot down the international outcry would have only benefited the Nizam. Besides were they not also carrying medical supplies?

Nehru consulted Air Marshal Elmhirst as to whether the Lancastrians could be converted back into bombers. 'This would require a heavy undercarriage being attached which could not be done here. But it was easy enough to use the Lancasters for makeshift bombing by dropping the bombs through the hold or through the floor. Bennett is a very capable man and could easily fix this up.' The Bennett referred to was Air Vice-Marshal Don Bennett, a Queenslander with a distinguished wartime record, the father of the RAF's Pathfinder force. He was also of the opinion that Hyderabad should be saved.

Reg Chasney, who today lives in Sydney, Australia, had trained on Beaufighters and Mosquitoes during the war but had no experience on Lancasters. He was one of the demobbed RAF pilots looking for work. In 1947 he was ferrying Spitfires from England to Turkey and being paid forty pounds plus expenses for the round trip. Cotton was to offer him much more than that.

Sidney shopped around in London and found that Aer Lintas, the intercontinental division of Aer Lingus had abandoned its plan to run an Atlantic service, and as a result a dozen flight crews were looking for jobs. Cotton hired eight three-man crews consisting of captain, first officer and wireless operator and paid £5000 a piece for five second-hand Avro Lancastrians.

Interested parties were asked to attend a briefing at Cotton's flat in Park Lane for a briefing. Reg Chasney was there. 'I recall Don Bennett was at the briefing. A very impressive man who did not suffer fools gladly.'

Cotton stressed that this was a potentially dangerous mission and offered to pay double the usual pilot's salary, plus danger money, to fly Lancastrians from Karachi to Hyderabad and land them at disused military airfields at night. The aircraft would be homed on a radio transmitter and Cotton arranged to have the flarepaths lit with a single line of kerosene lamps. The newly constituted Muslim state of Pakistan was favourably disposed towards Cotton and his team, so the aircraft would transit Karachi before flying on to Hyderabad.

Reg recalls: 'We got a thousand pounds each trip split between the crew and we gave a hundred pounds to the bloke who looked after the flarepath in Hyderabad. This was hazardous flying involving flying 1700 miles into Indian territory but it was the monsoon period, and there was plenty of cloud cover.'

On 11 May 1948, Sidney arrived at Heathrow airport to fly the first of the Lancastrians out to Karachi, picking up the weapons en route at Basle in Switzerland. The airport was seething with rumours and people were already taking sides in the dispute. Sidney did not expect an easy ride.The aircraft was empty of weapons but even so he was called aside when he tried to pass through customs. This is it, thought Sidney. The chief customs officer was known to

Sidney, and handed him a glass of whisky. 'We know what you are doing, Mr Cotton,' he said, 'and we want to wish you luck.' It was a nice gesture. Sidney touched the glass to his lips but as ever did not drink it.

At Basle they had to pick up Oerlikon cannon which had been ordered from the factory. When they arrived they found that the guns had been packed in boxes which were too big to go through the door of the aircraft. On the airfield, in full view of anyone who happened to be watching, they had to break the boxes open and stack the weapons inside the fuselage. Now everybody could see they were not carrying medical supplies.

Cotton knew that the heavily laden aircraft could not take off from the short runway at Basle with a full load of fuel. He had hoped to refuel at El Adem in North Africa but when they radioed the airfield they found it was suffering a sandstorm. Cotton wanted to avoid landing at British airfields in case they were stopped, so now they turned round and headed for Rome.

Rome was fogbound so the only alternative destination was Luqa in Malta, where Sidney had flown many times. In 1948 Malta was still a British colony, and the cargo of weapons could easily have been impounded there.

'What are you carrying, Mr Cotton?' asked the customs men. 'We are loaded to the roof with guns and ammunition,' said Sidney. The customs men smiled politely and stamped their papers without comment. An hour and half later they were on their way to Karachi.

Like everything else in Cotton's life, the mission was a gamble.

From the very first flight Sidney had been concerned about the heavy cargo moving during flight. His fears were justified. On 31 July one of the Canadian registered Lancastrians crashed on its approach to Mauripor airfield.

A field gun had broken loose during the approach, making the plane tail heavy, and it crashed on the field scattering guns over a wide area. This was seized upon by the Indian press as clear proof that Cotton was running guns, not vaccines. Four men were killed. Among them was Jerome Frewin, the pilot who had accompanied

Sidney on the first trip to Basle. Sidney was stunned. The operation was potentially dangerous, they had all known that.

'We all considered Frewin to be an outstanding pilot and one of our best,' he wrote. 'He was a mixture of natural flier and slide rule specialist and it was hard to understand how an accident could have happened to him.'

Cotton's planes flew to and fro night after night carrying thousands of tonnes of weapons and by now this was common knowledge in England. The gun running episode was to prove an intense political embarrassment to the British Labour government. Having granted India independence, an Australian resident in the United Kingdom and carrying a British passport was now supplying arms to an enemy of India!

Philip John Noel-Baker, a Labour MP wrote to Ernest Bevin, Attlee's foreign secretary: 'As you know the alleged gun running by United Kingdom persons and aircraft between Karachi and Hyderabad is most troublesome. It is public knowledge that Cotton has lately returned to this country in an aircraft in which he made his flight to Hyderabad last week.

'I think you will agree that if at the present stage he and his aircraft are permitted freely to leave this country we shall be faced with great political embarrassment vis-a-vis the Government of India.'

Noel Baker thought the way to stop Cotton was to get the immigration authorities to confiscate his passport: 'I understand that such instructions can readily be issued if a summons or warrant for his arrest has been issued . . . it would be possible for the immigration authorities to be told to stop him even in advance of the issue of a summons. I recognise of course that this would be a drastic step and one which would have to be defended in parliament, particularly as Cotton is a man with many influential friends.'

Another secret report to Attlee from the Foreign Office:

> Mr F. S. Cotton managing director of United Kingdom-registered company known as the British Industrial and Aeronautical

Cotton stands next to the De Havilland 14A which he later crashed on a beach in Italy while attempting a long distance flight to South Africa.

A rare picture of the Lockheed landing at Heston. The aircraft usually took off at first light and did not return till dusk—it was kept in a locked hangar when not being flown, to preserve it from prying eyes.

A high-flying PRU Spitfire. These stripped-down unarmed aircraft were so fast that German fighters had difficulty in catching them.

The Delage convertible, which Joan Cotton (nee Henry) entered in the RAC round Britain rally.

Sidney on board the *Amazone*.

Sidney unloads what appears to be a case of beer from his aircraft at Karachi. In fact, the plane was loaded with weapons.

The underside of the Lockheed 12 showing hatches removed from the hiding place of the secret cameras. The original sliding aluminium panels fitted flush with the skin and were difficult to detect.

Cotton and his dog Jerry in the house at Ford Manor.
This picture was taken only a few weeks before he died in 1969.

> Research Corporation appears to be primarily responsible for traffic between Hyderabad and Pakistan. Mr Cotton may also be responsible for, or associated with, the importation of arms from Europe. Our information concerning Mr Cotton is convincing but circumstantial. It is derived from secret sources or from Sir L. Grafftey-Smith's reports of gossip current in Karachi or statements made in conversation by officers of the Pakistan government.
>
> None of this could easily be proved in court. According to Sir L. Grafftey-Smith Mr Cotton makes no secret in Karachi of the fact that he is engaged in this traffic. He controls five Lancastrian aircraft based in Karachi which are stated to be loaded with arms at Malir, outside Karachi, and to do a shuttle service between there and Karachi. Of the five Lancastrians three are registered in the United Kingdom and two in Canada. Mr Cotton is an adventurer of very doubtful record, who was associated with Mr Kendall in Grantham Productions Ltd.

The effective action that could be taken by His Majesty's Goverment was, however, very small. 'We are not in a position to prove beyond question that Mr Cotton is in fact engaged in this traffic, and it may be taken for granted that the Pakistan government if they are conniving at it, as seems almost certain, would put every obstacle in the way of our obtaining the necessary evidence.'

Two of the aircraft that Sidney had acquired carried Canadian markings and the Canadians were just as concerned as the British about using them to carry arms.

V. K. Krishna Menon, the first Indian High Commissioner to Great Britain, wrote to Attlee: 'Canadian government have informed us through their High Commissioner that planes marked CF-CMW and CF-CMX were sold some time ago by Trans Canadian Airlines to a United Kingdom firm and taken off the Canadian registry on 2 July. Planes are therefore not entitled to carry Canadian markings Canadian goverment are making further enquiries and have assured us that they will take every justifiable step in their power to prevent any illegal use of planes of Canadian registration as well as irregular practices by Canadian pilots.'

Usually the Lancastrians took a circuitous route, flying due south across the Arabian Sea turning east at a point at right angles to Hyderabad then overflying Indian territory. They were only over India for about twenty minutes. While forces conspired against him in London, Cotton now dared the Indian air force to shoot his aircraft down.

On one occasion he purposefully flew over an Indian airfield in broad daylight knowing that their Hawker Tempest fighters were in the air looking for him—then he sent a radio message to Pandit Jawahalarl Nehru, the Indian prime minister, asking: 'Where are your Tempests?' It was deliberately provocative. But then Sidney and Nehru would not have had a lot in common.

Sidney seemed to delight in seeing just how far he could go. In Karachi he strolled into the office of the Indian High Commissioner, Sri Prakasha, and admitted that he had just been flying low over the Indian ordnance factories and that no harm had come to him. The High Commissioner promptly threatened to arrest him as he was technically on Indian soil. Unfortunately he realised that if he did so he had no way of transporting him to Delhi. Prakasha wrote: 'I left him in no doubt that I thought he was doing a shameful thing worsening the relations between Pakistan and ourselves and doing no good to anyone.' Afterwards the High Commissioner saw Sidney lolling about in the Palace Hotel as if he were lord of the place. 'He was certainly a great favourite of the Pakistanis,' he wrote.

The Indians had their spies on the airfields but because Cotton's planes were guarded by armed sepoys it was not easy to get close to the action. One man posed as a farmer collecting grass for his cattle but he was so badly beaten up by the guards he had to crawl home.

Sidney's luck could not hold forever. As early as February 1948 New Delhi had been preparing for police action in Hyderabad. It was given the name Operation Polo.

The Indian army planned a two-pronged attack on Hyderabad. It would commit a force of 20 000 troops including tanks and a battalion of Gurkhas. Hyderabad was doomed from the outset. Even the Nizam had gloomily forecast that his country could only hold out for two days against the might of the Indian army. The Hyderabadis were strong in numbers but poor in training. By April 1948 Hyderabad had a force of 22 000 regular troops. In the first day's fighting the Indian army lost seven dead and nine wounded. The Hyderabadis lost 623 dead and fourteen wounded.

The war in the air was non-existent. The Hyderabadis had no independent air force. Two decoy aircraft sat on the ground at Bidar and an old biplane at Warangal. Quite apart from the crash of the Lancastrian with the loss of four lives Cotton's operation in Hyderabad was not without its casualties.

The chief engineer at Bidar airfield, Frederick Rowan, was shot in the back and his body dumped into a ditch. Curiously, his assassin was not one of the invading Indian army but a Hyderabadi brigadier, Syed Habib Ahmed. The *Cape Argus* in South Africa reported that Rowan was shot because it was feared he would give the advancing Indian army details of Sidney's arms shipping operation.

A witness said that he was taken into a field of tombs guarded by three sepoys and shot as he was sitting on a stone. 'Rowan was a clever technician who was in charge of the landing base at Bidar,' wrote Sidney. 'We tried to get him back to Karachi. Flying over the airfield we flashed signals to him from the air but to no avail.'

At 3 o'clock on the morning of 16 September Sidney Cotton was getting ready to make his final flight from Hakimpet airport on the outskirts of Hyderabad to Karachi. This time the cargo was human. The Nizam had been cultivating a fanatical Muslim called Kasim Razvi who had decided that it was time to leave.

Razvi was the titular head of a private army called the Razakars who were devoted to achieving Muslim supremacy in southern India, no matter what the cost. Razvi knew that if Hyderabad fell he would probably be for the chop. He implored the Nizam to help him escape. 'Your Exalted Highness,' he pleaded, 'Please arrange for me to escape with the flier Cotton. And please persuade Pakistan to attack India.'

The early hours of 16 September found Kasim Razvi in the office of the Nizam's chief of staff, Afsar Ali Baig. Razvi was deeply agitated and strode nervously about the office glancing repeatedly at the telephone on Afsar's desk. A phone call from the airport meant that Sidney Cotton was ready to take off.

The heavy uniform he was wearing added to his discomfort and he was sweating profusely. The uniform was ridiculously ostentatious, like something out of a Gilbert and Sullivan operetta. On his hip he carried a revolver and across his shoulders a bandolier of bullets. As chief of the Razakars he had designed the uniform himself.

Fearing that wearing it might make him rather too much of a target he asked to be excused and reappeared shortly in simple civilian clothes. He was no longer armed with a pistol but a copy of the *Koran*.

Next to Ali Baig's desk, where it had lain for three days, was an ordinary wooden box. It had been left there unattended, Ali Baig having been told that its contents were of no interest, and was simply full of papers being sent abroad. In fact the box contained almost four million pounds in rupees. Ali Baig had arranged for a military convoy to take the Razakar chief and the box to the airport.

At Hakimpet airport Sidney was waiting for the weather to improve before taking off. Already above the clouds he could hear the high revving Bristol Centaurus engines of the Indian air force's Hawker Tempest fighters. This time the Indians weren't going to let him get away. Suddenly the sky cleared and the stars were visible. Sidney ordered the Lancastrian pushed out of the camouflaged hangar. The first grey in the east appeared. Now the big machine was a sitting duck for fighters. The airfield soon reverberated to the sound of the Lancastrian's engines being warmed up.

Sidney Cotton strode about the airfield like Errol Flynn, brandishing a revolver and threatening to use it on anyone who tried to stop him. The aircraft taxied onto the apron and luggage was slung into the rear door, the large wooden box having priority. In the semi darkness, there was confusion and the aircraft started moving slowly forward before all the passengers had boarded. Razvi was not the only VIP seeking a way of escape, and as the plane gathered speed he was pushed out of the way. Running as fast as he could he could not make it into the open door. One of Ali Baig's lieutenants telephoned from the airport.

'The plane has gone! It's gone!' he said exploding with laughter. 'And that damned fool Razvi is still on the ground running after it!' But Razvi had a charmed life. The invading Indians decided that he would keep his head and he served a brief term of imprisonment in Hyderabad.

Reg Chasney tells the same story about one of the planes he crewed. Sidney's loyal Pathan guards had loaded the aircraft with long wooden boxes which looked like coffins. Chasney boarded the plane to lind one of the guards stretched out on top of one of the boxes, asleep. 'The planes were full of wooden boxes stuffed with money guarded by a Pathan guard with an antique rifle,' he said. 'The boxes were crammed with one hundred rupee notes stapled together in bundles of a hundred—so each bundle was worth £750 and the box was as big as you could get into a Lancastrian.' There was to be one last flight before Sidney quit Hyderabad for good. He had left another Lancastrian at Hakimpet in case it was needed to evacuate the Nizam and his precious jewel collection.

Sidney by this time had already made arrangements with contacts in Egypt to have the Nizam accommodated in one of King Farouk's spare palaces. King Farouk's terms for having the Nizam as his guest was 25 per cent of all that he brought out of Hyderabad, and as someone pointed out 25 per cent of a £100 million was a lot of money.

As it happened the Nizam didn't leave. Being a devout Muslim he was staying behind to say a last prayer when the Indian Army took over the palace.

As the sole remaining Lancastrian taxied out to take off, an

Indian air force Tempest swooped in and dropped a bomb on the neighbouring airstrip. The pilot could not have missed seeing the big aircraft so the attack was at best half-hearted. The Avro droned off into the evening without its distinguished passenger and his jewels. Hyderabad was incorporated into the state of India and the revolution was at an end.

The episode had a strange twist for Reg Chasney. When he arrived back in London he realised that his pilot's licence might be confiscated if it was discovered he had been carrying munitions in a civilian aircraft. So he went to Rhodesia to start a flying school—something he would not have been able to do had he not been so handsomely rewarded by Cotton. 'I decided to leave the country and lie low for a bit until the heat was off,' he said.

Some of the other members of the crews were having difficulty getting back to England. The police confined the movements of Sidney's Irish navigator E. G. Patterson to Bombay despite his protestations that he had come from London expressly to take up a job with an Indian airline. A car that Sidney had loaned him was impounded. Operation Polo had lasted just four days. The spectacular Asaf Jah dynasty which had lasted for more than three hundred years was over. And Sidney Cotton was richer by at least ten million pounds. But he was not to get away that easily.

Jill Cotton had been staying with her father at the flat in Curzon Place and was aware of the comings and goings of Sidney and his new friends from Hyderabad. One of them was General El Edroos, the commander in chief of the army.

'It was very hush-hush,' she said. 'I was aware once or twice that these people were coming to the house but El Edroos was closeted away with my father.'

Sid had been in England when Hyderabad fell. He hurried back to Karachi to find that the Hyderabad government had given notice that the airlift was to cease. But just as the Hyderabad airlift ended another was in the process of being organised—to fly food and coal to Berlin. The Russians had blockaded the city and Sidney's Lancastrians were in demand.

The Pakistanis were interested in Sidney's aircraft as well. Ghulam Muhammad, the Pakistani finance minister and an old enemy of Sid's, was a director of the Pakistani airline, Pakair. He suggested to the Prime Minister, Aly Khan, that the planes be impounded. The Pakistanis were embarrassed. Having given tacit approval to the gun running operation they were now under pressure from Britain, Canada and India to provide information about who was involved and how it had been run.

Sidney was hated by the Indians, an embarrassment to the British and now some of his friends in Pakistan would desert him. It was inevitable that sooner or later someone would try to remove him from the picture altogether.

Sidney Cotton was dressing for dinner when there was a discreet knock at the door of his rented villa on the outskirts of Karachi.

Outside was a Muslim who had helped Sidney at the height of the gun running. He was distraught. 'Master, master, you are to meet with an accident tonight. I have seen the orders and I have come to warn you.'

He had, he said, taken the precaution of placing an armed guard around the villa—the same loyal Pathan guards that Sidney had hired to guard the boxes of money on the aircraft. Sidney had hired fifty of the Pathan troops when the blockade on Hyderabad had been imposed and they had been refused permission to cross Indian territory.

'They guarded our planes, our stores, our offices and our villas and they even guarded our persons as I had been warned that my life was in danger.' It might be wise, he surmised, not to leave the villa without an armed guard.

Sidney needed an escape plan. That day he had lunched with an Australian pilot who was flying out to Cairo that night. He made up his mind to be on that aircraft. He decided to throw a party at the villa. 'I remembered that in a thriller I had once read the intended victim gave a party on the principle that nothing was likely to happen while the party was in progress.'

Sidney had always been a generous host and invited everyone he could think of. At half past ten that night the band was playing, champagne was flowing and everyone was having a good time. Sidney moved easily among the guests chatting amiably. Suddenly in mid-conversation he said, 'Will you excuse me for a moment. I have some business to attend to.'

Sidney slipped out of the house and into a waiting car which drove him to the airport. The first person he saw at the airport was the pilot with whom he had had lunch. He agreed to get Sidney a seat on the plane. It was nearly midnight when the plane took off. Back at the villa his guests were wondering when Sidney was going to return. As it happened he was destined never to return to Karachi.

Cotton himself had to face the music when he returned to London in 1949 charged under the Air Navigation Act 1928 with carrying arms and ammunition. The court appearance was potentially damaging to his reputation but Sidney did not seem unduly concerned about it. While waiting for his case to be heard at the Bow Street Court, Sidney sat outside in the hall surrounded by prostitutes, drunks and other n'er-do-wells. He thought this hugely entertaining. The rest of the court list for the day was fairly mundane stuff—drunken driving, breaking and entering, petty larceny.

Sidney's case, however, was more complicated than it seemed. He had enraged Jahawaral Nehru, India's first Prime Minister by his insolent cable in which he had dared the Indian air force to shoot his planes down.

Now it was time to even the score. Nehru had paid for seven prosecution witnesses to fly to London; Colonel Haneef Rahat, Major Henry Luschwitz, Major S. A. K. Ali Razvi, Major M. S. Qureshi, Mr Mohamed Ali Abbasi, Mr Shoukat Ali Khan and Nawab Najmuddin Khan. Sidney was on friendly terms with many of these men and knew that if some of them appeared as witnesses they would give evidence that could go against them when they returned to India. If they gave evidence that implicated them in the airlift they could lose their estates—or even worse.

Sidney was advised to plead guilty to charges in breach of the air navigation regulations. He got off two other charges because of a technicality. His counsel, Russell Vick KC, produced certificates from the office of the Pakistan High Commissioner which proved that the aircraft was under charter to them at the time it had been carrying weapons. The flight had been undertaken by them and therefore no offence had been committed.

Russell Vick was a famous advocate with an impressive track record. Also standing in the wings was Sir Walter Monckton, one of the architects of the original scheme to send arms to the Nizam. And Monckton in turn was in direct contact with Winston Churchill.

Mr Vick said that Sidney was an ex-serviceman of two world wars and had won the OBE for his RAF service. He also claimed that Sidney had lost money on the deal. Sidney's case, said the prosecutor, Mr B. M. Stephenson, was a fantastic story in which arms and munitions were described as fruit and vegetables and the Oerlikon anti-aircraft guns as 'cheese'.

The official charge was that Sid was carrying arms and munitions of war in a Lancastrian aircraft at Warangal, Hyderabad on 10 July 1948. Two other summonses alleging a similar offence at Basle-Mulhouse, France, were withdrawn. Mr Stephenson said that as far as that flight was concerned it had been ascertained that no offence had been committed.

Sidney was described as of an 'adventurous nature particularly when it meant bringing money into his pocket or to his company; and extremely large amounts of money have passed in connection with this matter.' Cotton went to Hyderabad in March 1948 and had an interview with General El Edroos. Arrangements were made between Cotton and the general who gave him a letter to officials in the Pakistani government asking them to assist by providing landing facilities for aeroplanes, and a tentative arrangement was made with officials of the Hyderabad government for Cotton to run aeroplanes from Karachi into Hyderabad carrying munitions of war. After discussion in Karachi Major Luschwitz, director of music in the Hyderabad army and 'a gentleman in the Pakistan government', flew to London and with a Mr Shoaib—who was something to do with the Pakistan government—met in Cotton's office.

'Further details were arranged at Secunderabad with two other gentlemen: a civilian, Najmuddin Khan, who was known to the prime minister of Hyderabad, and Mr Abbasi, deputy finance secretary to the Hyderabad government.

'Mr Abbasi had with him the terms of a contract drawn up in London in which £400 000 was to be paid to the account of Mr. Cotton. Before the operation started £200 000 was to be paid in advance to enable Cotton to establish the necessary organisation and to buy aeroplanes. Finally on 27 May they met in Karachi and in the house of the agent general for Hyderabad the contract was signed by Khan and Cotton.'

Mr Stephenson said that after the contract was signed Mr Khan was handed a quarter of a million rupees, which were banked and used to pay Cotton; a hundred thousand pounds was paid out of the Hyderabad state account by the Westminster Bank London.

Fifty men of the Nizam's army, under a major, loaded up the aeroplanes at Karachi and from the start of the operation an average of two a day ran guns into Hyderabad at £4000 a trip for each aeroplane. Then Hyderabad complained that the weapons weren't coming fast enough and speeded up the ferry service. 'Cotton himself flew in one of the aeroplanes,' said Mr Stephenson, 'and Major Luschwitz and Mr Khan also made a trip in a Lancastrian which flew in 920 rifles or sten guns and 64 boxes of ammunition each containing 1000 rounds. They had cause to remember that trip,' continued Mr Stephenson, 'as they later complained that the aeroplane was in charge of a mad pilot who when told there were tigers in the jungles below decided to swoop down and see if there were any.' The Lancastrian was a big aeroplane—not exactly the sort of machine in which you flew close to the ground to look for wildlife!

Sidney and the Aeronautical and Industrial Research

Corporation were each fined £200, with £600 costs making a total of £1000 in all. He had his pilot's licence cancelled for two years. Winston Churchill was said to have intervened so that he got off lightly. To the waiting reporters Cotton said: 'I am no villain. All I want is somewhere in the world where I can use my imagination.'

A writer in the the *Deccan Chronicle* did not see it quite that way: 'Even though the punishment meted out to Cotton and his Aeronautical Corporation by the Bow Street court has been trivial, when compared to the magnitude of the transaction and the dangerous implications of his illegal gun running, it is at least a censure on Sidney Cotton and his gang of adventurers for tampering with international politics. Cotton's gang had only one criterion; namely, making money. For they had neither the excuse of patriotism flaunted by Kasim Razvi nor the religious affinity paraded by Zafrullah.'

After the affair blew over, an RAF pilot called Edward O'Farrell was having a drink in the bar of the Semiramis Hotel in Cairo when Sidney walked in. O'Farrell had met Cotton at Heston in 1939 and recalled that Sidney had been very kind to him. Sidney was smarting after the Hyderabad debacle and asked quite seriously if there was an extradition treaty between Britain and Brazil. 'I might have to go and live there,' he said grimly.

Meanwhile the Canadian registered Lancastrians were impounded by the Pakistani government. Cotton finally got £50 000 for the four of them but it took him fourteen years to get the rest of the money for the properties he owned in Karachi.

Like the fish who waits in the hole in the bank, Sid had got the big one. But among friends he always denied that he had made any serious money out of the Hyderabad adventure. After he had paid off his crews and his helpers, how much had Sidney made from Hyderabad? He told Joan Henry he had just on a million pounds.

'I said to him why don't you put something away for yourself. You don't have to make it over to Jill or to Johnny. He said to me "I want at least two million before I think of settling down."'

## Chapter 12

# A Whisky for the Prince

The flag of Saudi Arabia is a luxuriant green with the script in Arabic picked out in white. The writing above a white horizontal sabre may be translated as: 'There is no God but God; Muhammad is the Messenger of God.'

For the next decade, Sidney Cotton was to see quite a lot of that flag.

Arlington House in Mayfair, where Sidney had his luxury flat, was home to many rich men. One of them was the Armenian Nubar Gulbenkian. The eccentric, bearded son of the oil magnate Calouste Gulbenkian, was conservatively worth three hundred million pounds. Gulbenkian senior had earned the nickname of Mr Five Per Cent because of his holding of one-twentieth of the shares of the Anglo Iranian Petroleum Company. Nubar and Sidney were friends. The Gulbenkians' success in the exploitation and marketing of oil was the inspiration for Sidney's next great adventure.

By 1950 most people would have thought that Sidney Cotton could have started to take it easy. He had made a fortune out of the Hyderabad venture; he had a luxury yacht the *Amazone*, as well as his Lockheed 12 the *Caprice*. After he bought *Amazone* in 1949 Sidney sailed to Malta to have the yacht completely refitted. Malta was to be another turning point in his life.

Sidney had remained married to Joan Henry until 1944 when they divorced. He had been a bachelor for five years. 'I had no thought of marrying again. I had always had an ideal about marriage and I had begun to feel that the possibility of finding someone who fitted harmoniously into my way of life was too remote to be considered further.'

As it happened he was wrong. In Malta he was to meet an Englishwoman called Bunty Brooke-Smith. He was fifty-five, she was twenty-five. He asked her to become his secretary. Two years later in 1951 they were married at the British Consulate General's office at Nice in the South of France. The first two years of their marriage was spent almost entirely afloat, on the *Amazone*.

It was not a new experience for Bunty.

She had made her first sea voyage at the age of three months and her family had lived in Liverpool, Bristol, Shanghai, Yokohama, Tokyo, South Africa and France. Her father had been the Lloyd's Register agent in Malta and Bunty often spent the summer holidays there. During the war she had lived in South Africa where she had finished her schooling and had then worked as a secretary at the British High Commission.

As the social pages put it in 1955: 'Slim, attractive and charming, Mrs Sidney Cotton, English wife of a rich Australian businessman, certainly did not look as if she had spent the last four years of her life on a yacht in the Red Sea when she sat sipping tea with her husband at the Dorchester hotel in London this week. No sign of parched skin, sunbleached hair or rough hands.'

Joan Henry was interested to meet Sidney's new bride, and Bunty invited her to tea at the Dorchester. 'I was looking a bit dowdy,' Joan said, 'But Bunty came in wearing baby pink. I thought: "Poor old Sidney. What have you gone and done this time."' Joan was amused by Sidney's continued taste for younger women. 'He collected young women like other people collect stamps. He would say: "Get 'em young enough and you can teach them your ways." But a strong woman would have sunk him.' Bunty was only seven years older than Sidney's daughter, Jill.

Jill joined the cruise on the *Amazone* and got to know Bunty well, finding her 'very good fun but rather managing'. I think she felt she could change Sidney once she married him and they had children, but she didn't have a hope.'

It might have seemed a decadent life sailing around the Mediterranean, but for some time Sidney had not been well and he needed to take it easy. The yacht was the means of escape from things that had been troubling him. In Jiddah he had two heart attacks. The first was at the airfield, the second on board the *Amazone*. 'A strangling pain seized me across the back and right up both arms from the wrists.' His doctor diagnosed angina and said that he would have to slow down. There was no reason why he could not carry on flying his beloved Lockheed—but he always had to take a heart pill before he came in to land. He also had an operation to have his gallbladder removed. Eight days after the operation he had a blood clot on one lung which kept him in hospital for several months.

This did not stop Sidney enjoying himself. Wearing a white tuxedo he would stroll into the bar of the Carlton Hotel in Cannes and ask the barman: 'Anyone of any importance here tonight?'

'Only you, Major Cotton,' the barman would reply diplomatically.

Sidney would spend his days strolling along the Croisette or sitting in the sunshine on his yacht reading the British newspapapers. One story caught his eye. In 1950 petrol was still rationed in both Britain and Australia. Australia, however, had decided to go off petrol rationing without consulting the mother country and this had upset Clement Attlee, the British Prime Minister. In 1950 Australia had yet to develop its oilfields in the Bass Street and was still dependent on oil from the Middle East.

Getting their hands on Saudi oil had been the goal of many nations since the early twenties. One of the first to try was a New

Zealander, Major Frank Holmes, who had been granted a concession in 1922 after plying the King with elaborate gifts, including guns. His syndicate, the Eastern and General, specialised in buying oil concessions and selling them on to others. The concession expired in 1927.

In the 1930s the British already had more oil than they could handle in Iraq; they weren't especially interested in Saudi Arabia but they wanted to keep the Americans out. Britain had made a half-hearted survey of Saudi Arabia in the 1930s and decided there was no oil there. The Saudi Royal family neither knew nor cared.

So in 1933, Standard Oil of California (later to become Aramco, the Arabian American Oil Company) acquired the search rights to four hundred thousand square miles of Saudi Arabia. The King, Ibn Saud, gave his blessing to the deal but said quite openly he did not think there was any oil there and thought he was receiving £50 000 in gold for nothing. There was still, however, a large area of the western district, known as the Hejaz, which had not been taken up. Sidney thought there could be oil there and spent the next eight years of his life trying to clinch the deal. It was to prove a time-consuming, frustrating and ultimately a very expensive venture.

Eleven years before, Sidney had acted as a go-between for Britain and Germany. Now he was to act as an intermediary between Britain and Saudi Arabia. In July 1950 the Foreign Office gave cautious approval to the scheme, presumably because Sidney had asserted that he was interested in securing the concession for the Empire.

Britain was now anxious to get a foothold in Saudi Arabia 'and Mr Cotton's method of doing so seemed as likely to succeed as any other and possibly more likely than direct bidding by Shell. He refused however (and has continued to refuse) to disclose the names of his financial backers—if he has any.'

Sidney played up the fact that there was a good deal of anti-British feeling in Saudi Arabia and that this deal, if there was to be any sort of deal, would be better handled by an Australian. 'Daily, the Mecca radio is blasting Britain to high heaven. It is making it very difficult down here for everybody,' he said.

To make any sort of progress with the Saudis, Sidney knew he would have to impress. He flew the Lockheed to Cairo so that it was 'in striking distance of Saudi Arabia'. It was starting to sound like one of the spying missions from 1939.

Sidney then sailed the *Amazone* to Jiddah, cruising through the Suez Canal and the Red Sea. On 14 December 1950 they dropped anchor off Jiddah. Jill Cotton was on board. 'It was a magnificent yacht. Tied up at the wharf in Jiddah it sparkled in the sunshine compared to the ubiquitous dhows and rusty cargo ships. I think the Saudis were fairly impressed,' she said. 'If he had just arrived and stayed in a hotel it wouldn't have been the same.' Sidney had had the yacht air-conditioned while it was being refitted in Malta. He had also gone to a great deal of trouble with the interior decor.

He had been told that blue was the colour most favoured by Muslims so he had the yacht carpeted in Malta weave matting. Blue carpets, blue curtains, and a blue tablecloth. But green is the traditional colour of Islam so at the last moment, to Sidney's intense irritation, it all had to be changed.

The Saudi Arabia that Cotton came to in 1950 was still shackled to the Middle Ages. True, King Ibn Saud now rode around in a Rolls Royce given to him by Winston Churchill, but at day's end he drove out of town to the edge of the desert, lay a rug on the sand and faced Mecca to pray.

There was now a railway from the oil wells at Dhahran to Riyadh, a new jetty in Jiddah and a few tarmac roads, but water was still drawn from public wells using leather buckets. The King spent six times more on entertaining and hospitality than he did on schools and education. There were public executions and public canings. People could be arrested for singing, or smoking in public. The bedouin still lived off dates and camels' milk and a plate of sheep's eyes was a luxury.

Sidney went ashore and made a courtesy call on the British Ambassador. There was no car waiting for him at the jetty and no taxis. He had to walk from the jetty to the embassy in temperatures of forty degrees. It was over a mile.

The Ambassador Sir George Pelham was polite but lukewarm. 'I really don't know what you are doing here, old boy,' he said. Sidney told him in confidence about his mission to acquire an oil concession. Sir George wanted nothing to do with it or him. Later he was to confide in the French ambassador that he thought Sidney was up to no good and on the verge of committing a breach of the exchange control regulations. Perhaps it was the fallout from the Hyderabad episode but the Foreign Office was still wary of Sidney.

While Sidney was doing business, Bunty and her friend Sadika Tancred had gone ashore to see if they could find a hairdresser. 'At that time there was really nothing in Jiddah—one or two hotels, no cinemas no drinking—but there were some lovely old Arab houses. Bunty asked one of the women from the British Embassy if there was a hairdresser anywhere and was told that she had her hair cut by the King's executioner. So we decided to let our hair grow.'

The meetings were interminable. Sidney shuttled back and forth between the Middle East and London; one minute he was in an office in Whitehall being lectured by a group of diffident civil servants, the next he was sitting cross-legged on the floor drinking tea with the Saudis.

Mr R. M. B King from the Bank of England wrote: 'I found Mr Cotton to be a plausible gentleman, not without personal charm and obviously with great faith in his ability to come to terms with the Saudis. But he is difficult to tie down in an argument and readily strays from the point.'

Sidney remained firm in his belief that you had to spend money to make money. Certainly he would have to continue to spend a lot if he was to impress the Saudis. The Foreign Exchange Control department at the Bank of England granted him £3000 a month in foreign exchange. Part of the deal was that if Sidney obtained an oil concession he would give first refusal to British firms in its subsequent development. He was closely watched by British

Intelligence during his time in Jiddah. On 15 April 1953, Pelham wrote this confidential letter to the Foreign Office about Sidney's comings and goings: 'Cotton turned up again in Jiddah in the middle of February, having been promised, as he said, the signature of the Ministry of Finance to his oil concession in Hejaz. He left yesterday for Port Said with no signed agreement and without apparently having had any success whatsoever with the Saudis.'

Pelham said that Sidney's arrival had hardly been auspicious. It took him three days and a telegram to the Crown Prince before he was allowed by the port authorities to moor at the customs pier and take on water. 'The customs authorities knew he had liquor on board and in their suspicious minded way they were taking no chances until they were certain that every single bottle was under lock and key.'

Sidney kicked his heels in Jiddah for a few more weeks before being told that the oil concession would not be specifically granted to anyone but would be put up to auction and that Sidney would be granted first option. 'Even Cotton is not so sanguine about his future chances after this,' said Pelham.

Sidney's last two weeks in Jiddah were dogged by continual trouble with members of the cosmopolitan crew of his yacht. He sacked two Egyptian stewards for selling brandy off the ship; to get rid of the evidence, they had dumped the bottles overboard.

Sidney ordered the captain, who was also Egyptian to lower the ship's boat to find the evidence; when he refused he sacked him too. Sidney had given his personal assurance to Prince Abdullah Faisal that no liquor had left the ship. A Saudi committee of enquiry decided that Sidney would have to pay the hotel expenses for the sacked members of the crew and pay their first first class passages back to Port Said before the *Amazone* would be allowed to leave Jiddah.

'Cotton, having had several heart attacks in the process, paid up vowing that after such a travesty of justice he would never come back again to Saudi Arabia,' said Pelham.

The liquor smuggling charge was serious. In 1950, it had still been possible for foreigners to consume alcohol in their own homes. Cyril Ousman the British pro Vice-Consul who had made many friends among the Saudis, regularly entertained them in his home and served them alcohol.

One night a row developed involving Prince Mishari bin Abdul Aziz, the eighteenth surviving son of the King. Aziz left the house and returned with a gun with which he shot the Vice Consul dead. So in 1952 Ibn Saud had banned alcohol completely from his kingdom.

All these petty, but potentially damaging incidents were very irksome to a man brokering a major international deal. Sidney's parting shot, said Pelham, was to now tell everyone who would listen that the Saudis had sold out to the Americans and that it was only a matter of time before the United States government would be asked to take over the running of the country.

'Of course,' wrote Pelham, 'This is the exaggeration of a peeved man.'

By July, much to the chagrin of Sir George Pelham, Sidney was back in Jiddah. 'It seems pretty clear that Cotton's eternal optimism, which seemed somewhat shattered when he left here in April, has now returned to him. Cotton of course is wildly exaggerating the position when he says that he was advised to leave Saudi Arabia to avoid possible incidents arising from the Buraymi dispute. He went of his own accord on being told that the Crown Prince had no reason for wishing him to stay.'

The main reason for Sidney's optimism was the return of Najib Salha, who was, according to Pelham, a man of calibre. 'He has the reputation of being one of the few Saudi officials who is prepared to make a decision and stick to it.'

Meanwhile Sidney was once again in trouble with the *Amazone*, which had been impounded in Beirut by the Lebanese at the request of the Egyptian authorities. The Egyptians accused him of smuggling gold and currency worth £250 000 from Egypt to the Lebanon. 'Apparently Cotton himself is free to come and go as he pleases but there is a guard over the yacht,' said Pelham.

Sidney had first made overtures to the Saudi finance minister, Abdullah Suleiman. Now he invited Prince Abdullah Faisal, the second son of King Ibn Saud to dine with him on the yacht. Sidney admitted to Faisal he was naive in matters of Arab custom. How should the guests be seated?

Faisal suggested that Sidney give a buffet dinner rather than a set dinner. Those that thought they were important would sit where they thought they should be. Those who were important would sit where they liked and enjoy the dinner.

During the meal, Sidney produced a Polaroid camera and asked if he could take a picture. The King's son agreed, then while Sidney was lining up the shot quickly removed the glass of whisky he had been drinking and had set on the table in front of him. Dumping liquor in the ocean was one thing. Drinking it while a guest on board the *Amazone* was another. Sidney's photograph shows that in 1952 Faisal was plumper than the hawk-billed monarch who would later topple his older brother. The Prince was a friend; he had at least provided Sidney with a car and driver whereas the British Ambassador had let him walk.

News of the Australian entrepreneur had filtered through to the Saudi capital Riyadh, and Sidney was now to meet King Ibn Saud, but there were dress rules. Sidney had always dressed well; the dark business suit for the city; the white tropical rig for the Middle East. This time he would have to wear a keffiyeh and Bunty the black sack known as the ayabeh. It was all a bit like dressing up for an amateur production of the *Arabian Nights*. 'Oh well,' said Sidney slipping on the headgear and securing it with the head ropes, 'Whatever it takes.'

Sidney looked patrician and rather fine towering over Bunty who grinned shyly behind a rectangle that was her only view of the world. But if the veil did anything it enhanced a lovely smile.

The flight from Jiddah to Riyadh was a long way in a propeller plane; if you were wearing an ayabeh it was suffocating and Bunty was dripping with perspiration by the time they arrived at the airport. Najib Salha greeted them at the steps to the plane,

'I thought you were bringing your wife?' he said to Sidney. 'Yes,' said Sidney. 'This should be her in the ayabeh.'

Next day they were received in the palace by Ibn Saud. The frail monarch had now been on the throne for more than a quarter of a century. Sidney did not know it at the time but the 73-year-old king had less than a year to live. Sidney and Bunty walked on expensive Persian carpets up the centre of the long room to where the King was sitting on his throne talking quietly to his secretary. The Lion of Nejd was crippled by arthritis and blind in one eye. He was immobile from the waist down and wore thick woollen socks to improve the circulation in his ankles. The royal voice had been reduced to a hoarse whisper.

'We bowed in front of the King and we shook hands. It was plain that both physically and mentally he was beginning to fail,' said Sidney.

In the 1930s, Ibn Saud had personally granted oil concessions to the Americans. Now he left that business to his ministers. In fact it was unlikely that he knew or cared what Aramco were doing in his name. He would grant anything to anyone so long as they could do something about the crippling pain in his knees. 'I am aware of why you are here,' he said to Sidney, without interest. 'The Finance Minister will talk to you and I wish you luck.'

Ibn Saud offered a withered claw and the two men again shook hands. The audience was over. The next day Sidney was locked in discussions with Najib Salha and the Finance Minister Abdullah Suleiman.

Sidney was now being offered a concession for the whole of the Hejaz from the Jordanian border in the north to the Yemen in the south, including all the islands in the Red Sea and preferences for all the inland areas which had been relinquished by Aramco. There was just one catch. They wanted an advance payment of five million pounds ($15m) for the Hejaz concession alone. No one, said Sidney, would pay that sort of money for the concession until the geologists were satisfied there was oil there. Still, it was the first thing that had resembled a proper deal. A gamble maybe, but Sidney agreed to take it. The Saudis granted him six months to raise the money. What he did not know was the Saudis had brought in their own geologists to survey the Hejaz, and they had struck oil. Suddenly there was no need for a middle-man like Sidney.

After several weeks Sidney had still not received the final agreement. In an attempt to find out what was happening he went to see Ahmed Fakri, the Minister of Mines, who told him quite confidentially that he would never clinch the deal unless he was prepared to pay a bribe of one million pounds.

It was beginning to look hopeless. In London the Treasury refused to allow him any more foreign exchange.

> It was made quite clear to him that he must if he wished to continue being granted foreign exchange be prepared to come clean with us and show some prospect of achieving tangible results.
>
> We also understood that this was to be a two year exploration concession with no down payment and that Mr Cotton was to submit a draft concession agreement within six months. Mr Cotton led us to believe that Shell and various other firms were interested in his negotiations. On investigation however the suggestion that Shell had expressed interest was found to be without foundation.
>
> After spending large sums of foreign exchange (on his own estimate £2–3000 a month) on entertaining the Emir Faisal on the Riviera and his yacht without anything more tangible than a report that he had an oral offer of agreement, Mr Cotton found in March 1952 that his allotments of foreign exchange ceased and he was informed by his bank that the Treasury would grant no further currency without having a report on his progress and evidence of success.

Sidney meanwhile did not have enough money to pay the crew of the *Amazone*. 'The Foreign Exchange Control have not been very helpful,' he wrote. 'I am under obligation to pay my crew monthly and they took exception to some small figures in my requirements for January, February, March and April and instead of sending me a substantial amount on account, only sent the personal expense account and refused crew's wages and food costs until I answered their questions. I have sent a letter to my bank today hoping that they can clear the matter, but it is really most depressing to have been working on the difficult problems I have been working and to have these little niggley obstructions and worries given to me by the Foreign Exchange Control.'

On 24 July 1953, Mr R. M. B. King at the Treasury wrote: 'Despite expenditure of about £50 000 over the past two and half years nothing has been achieved by Cotton. In fact in some ways he now appears to be considerably less likely to obtain a concession than he was when he started. We cannot help thinking that if there was really anything in this scheme of Cotton's the well established oil companies would not be letting the grass grow under their feet.'

On 21 October 1953 King wrote again, this time to the Bank of England. 'We are not impressed by his story of the *volte face* on the part of the Saudi government. If they are now so anxious for him to sign the agreement presumably they could arrange for it to be done through the Embassy in London. Cotton has now negotiated a loan of £10 000 from the British Bank of the Middle East in connection with his Distol and Asbestopol projects—this would appear to constitute an offence against Section 1 of the Exchange Control Act.'

Sidney could not stay any longer in Saudi Arabia. He had agreed to loan the *Amazone* to the Duke and Duchess of Windsor and it had to be delivered to Cannes by 1 August 1952. Before that he had to sail it to the Italian port of Genoa to be refitted.

Jill Cotton was twenty years old, and having a wonderful holiday on the *Amazone*. She was not privy to the Saudi oil adventure but she was aware of the high profile Saudi ministers who dined on the yacht and the business meetings behind locked doors in Sidney's office: 'If he had been able to pull off the Red Sea oil rights it was would have been an incredible coup—but it was so huge as to be unrealistic and he was up against Aramco and the enigmatic "If God Wills It" of the Arabs. He had not the patience to outwait them or the cunning to outwit them.'

Taking his turn at the wheel as they sailed back to Italy, Sidney considered his options. The Saudi affair had cost him a fortune and his health had suffered. He had already had two heart attacks. His doctor, Tom Creighton, had diagnosed angina and repeatedly advised him to slow down the whole tempo of his life. Bunty also was keen for him to abandon the Saudi project. It had been one of the most exciting times of her life but they had been spending money like water and there didn't seem to be much coming back. Sidney spent all night in the wheelhouse.

Sidney was still at the wheel of the *Amazone* when dawn broke. By then he had decided to have just one more try at Saudi Arabia.

Sidney had met the Duke but not the Duchess of Windsor before he invited them to borrow the *Amazone*.

'What purpose cultivating them was meant to serve was a mystery, if not a downright error of judgment,' said Brian Brooke-Smith, Sidney's brother in law. Jill Cotton said: 'My father was very happy to have the Duke of Windsor on the yacht because he was a bit of a snob.'

Edward and Mrs Simpson avoided England in the fifties, chosing to spend most of their time at their mansion in Paris or in the South of France. Edward had not had a good year. In February he had gone to London to attend the funeral of his brother George VI and his first meeting in many years with the young Queen Elizabeth. The new Queen was beautiful and radiant and the House of Windsor had never been in better shape. This was the dawn of a new Elizabethan age and people did not to wish to be reminded of a grubby scandal from before the war. Edward, said many people, had deserted Britain in her darkest hour.

People did not want to know about the playboy Prince and the help and support of the woman he loved. Many referred to Wallis as *that woman*.

And there were those servicemen who had suffered at the hands of the Germans who clearly recalled the picture of Wallis Simpson shaking hands with Hitler. Why Sidney decided to give his yacht free, gratis and for nothing to these irrelevant people is anyone's guess. But Sidney had to have his contacts. The Windsors thought they needed a holiday; others might have wondered what they had done to deserve one.

The *Amazone* made a leisurely cruise to Genoa, Portofino and other Italian coastal towns. Finally the Windsors ended up in Rome where they had an audience with Pope Pius XII. On the next leg of the cruise the Duke came down with a severe case of gastroenteritis and had to be taken back to Paris for treatment. He was approaching sixty and feeling his age. The Duchess continued the voyage alone and was clearly not having much fun.

Nicholas, a Swiss steward, had asked if he could stay on after the Windsors took over the vessel and lived to regret it. The Duchess was most demanding, ringing the bell by her bedside at all hours of the night. She specified that she would not rest her head on a pillow with a crown embroidered on it. And although the *Amazone* had a fully equipped laundry, she insisted on all her clothes being sent to a laundry in Paris. Bunty's sheets meanwhile were hidden away in a cupboard.

When the Windsors left the boat in Cannes, the crew breathed a sigh of relief.

The Windsors had borrowed the yacht for the best part of a month. Bunty was furious that Sidney had lent it to them for nothing but they were still in contact with the Windsors after the cruise.

One night when they came to dinner the Duchess was sitting on Sidney's right and she was the first to be served. A large bowl of what she assumed to be mashed potato arrived in front of her and she helped herself to a generous serving only to discover that it was horseradish sauce.

At a house they rented in Porchester Terrace, Rhoda, nanny to the Cotton children, answered the phone one day to a man with a soft and cultured voice. It was the Duke of Windsor. Bunty completed doing her lipstick and combing her hair before answering the telephone. Wallis Simpson had been in London having an operation at the London Clinic. Sidney had sent her flowers. The Duke wished to thank him.

The Buraymi Oasis, or to give it its Arabic name Al Buraymi, is a collection of small Arab villages on the border between what is today the United Arab Emirates and Oman. The boundaries had been drawn up in 1913 and again in 1930. A number of vague lines in violet, brown, green and yellow had been marked on the map but matters had been further complicated by the fact the British minister responsible for the boundaries was colour blind.

Nobody was much interested in Al Buraymi until oil was found in nearby Abu Dhabi, then it became disputed territory. It was claimed by three rulers. Shaikh Shakbut of Abu Dhabi, the Sultan of Muscat and King Saud of Saudi Arabia. Behind the Saudi claim was the Arabian American Oil Company. The Americans shrewdly hired some Arab scholars to delve into Saudi history so that a convincing claim could be made to the area, including not just the oasis but the beaches, banks and islands along the Trucial Coast.

Nearly eighteen months after the Saudis made a formal claim to the oasis they invaded it. Riding in trucks supplied by Aramco and stocked with Aramco supplies, forty Saudi bureaucrats and armed policemen occupied Al Buraymi and immediately threw a feast for the bedouin, persuading them to put their thumb prints on documents which would make them Saudi citizens.

The disputed oasis went to international arbitration in 1955, then in October a party of British led troops, the Trucial Oman Scouts, occupied Buraymi and expelled the Saudi garrison. The next year after the Suez crisis, King Saud broke off relations with Britain. The Saudis said they would only resume negotiations with Britain if the oasis dispute was resolved in their favour.

Sidney had been living in Beirut for four years when the Suez crisis blew up. In October 1956 British and French troops invaded Egypt to take control of the Canal Zone.

Now Sidney saw a way of renegotiating an oil concession with the Saudis, this time for the Buraymi oasis. Sidney had known King

Saud when he had been Crown Prince. He now decided that he would act as a mediator between Saudi Arabia and Britain and behind the scenes he would also bring Australia into the loop.

'My experience of the previous years and my friendship with King Saud left me in a position where I might be able to do something towards repairing the damage,' he wrote. He cabled King Saud to arrange a meeting then flew to London to see his old friend Lord Bruce.

By May 1957 Sidney was again in Jiddah preparing for his second audience with the Saudi royal family. The last time it had been King Faisal. Now it was his son King Saud. Since he had assumed power in November 1953 Saud had been spending money like a drunken sailor. He had demolished the old royal palace at Nasriyah and built a new one costing ten million pounds. The Lebanese architects who had designed it had been given their heads and the new palace was described as being half Granada-Moorish, half Beverley Hills. It was a symbol of all that had gone wrong with the reign of King Saud—vulgar, gaudy, and excessive.

But the Saudi deal looked to Sidney as if it might be on again. He wrote this optimistic letter to his family in Australia about the trip to Riyadh:

> Well, here I am again, Fidelitas Vincit (Faith Conquers) and all that. I arrived here on 29th April. The King had left for Riyadh. The Bahreim (Holy week) holidays and feasts were on. Eventually he received a note taken by hand that I was awaiting his pleasure—and despite the fact that he was about to leave for Baghdad on a state visit he cabled instructions to his Foreign Minister Prince Faisal—a friend of Buntys' and mine—that I was to be his guest and taken to Riyadh immediately.
>
> It's the nearest I know to a magic carpet. Somebody presses button K.G—'Kings Guest' and everything is laid on like magic. I was called at 3 a.m. the next morning and taken over to the airport—outside the door of the hotel almost—and my baggage and everything handled by a foreign office official.
>
> While this is going on I'm led into a private waiting room.

Eventually, after coffee and sweet tea—then coffee and sweet tea—the number depending on how long it takes to get the plane away I was ushered into a plane where everybody had already taken their seats—and two seats had been reserved for me so I should not be jostled on the trip.

After a smooth delightful flight of 2 hrs 20 minutes we circled over Riyadh, the capital. I was met at the airport by a senior Foreign Office or royal protocol official and another one as an interpreter. I gave my baggage slips to the lesser one and was whisked off to the Hotel Yamamah—new and air conditioned but the latter is not yet working. Very comfortable and good food.

Very, very different from when Bunty and I went there four years ago. We can now wear normal clothes and women go about without the black sackcloth affair. European women that is. I was left at the hotel to rest and take it easy—and was told a car would be at my door all day, in case I needed one—A Chrysler Windsor 1957 and chauffeur. So I turned in and slept. Then lazed all afternoon.

A telephone message came through after lunch asking me to come to the palace for dinner—normal suit. So I put on a white dinner jacket and looking my snappiest adjourned to the new palace. Cost $172 000 000 (not my suit)—Chandeliers alone cost $8 000 000. What a fabulous palace—and in really good taste—if such cost can ever be considered good taste these days.

The throne room is at least seven hundred feet long with twelve of the most beautifully made chandeliers I have ever seen. They are hanging down the full length of the throne room—and the floor is covered with the most exquisite Persian carpets, made to fit the room.

The walls have 250 chairs lined along them on each side. The palace seats at least 500. The King and his principal guests, after dinner walk in up the full length of the room followed by all the courtiers and others.

The room is so beautifully proportioned with high ceilings that nothing looks out of place.

After an ‘exquisitely balanced’ meal, the King rose to leave.

> We were ushered to meet him in our protocol positions as he went out the main door. Then we marched along acros the large extrance hall and into the Throne Room. A number of councillors and Princes who I met previously came up to me during this route march to shake hands including old St John Philby, who has written several books on Arabia.

Sidney had got that name wrong. Philby was not a Sir he was a St John. Harry St John Philby had been doing what Sidney wanted to do except that he had a head start of more than forty years. Philby had been in Saudi Arabia since 1917. He had been an intermediary between the old King and the modern world, Ibn Saud's favourite infidel.

He spoke the language, he embraced the religion and from the early days he had been the go-between in dealings about oil. In fact he had been receiving a thousand dollars a month retainer from the Americans during the Socal deal in the 1930s.

He was also the father of Kim Philby, later to achieve lasting fame by the revelation that while employed by MI6 he had been in the pay of the KGB for a quarter of a century. Father and son had both turned their backs on their country.

Harry St John Philby had converted to Islam and had married Marriam, a slave girl from the King's harem. He regularly visited Mecca.

> While coffee was being served the King kept smelling a pink rose with its stem wrapped in silver paper. He stood up and the Chief de Protocol whispered 'Take leave of His Majesty now, please.'
>
> The General Tumeg said goodbye, then the other general, then the US Ambassador then I stepped forward.
>
> As the US Ambassador turned to move away, the King stepped up to me and with a naughty boy look on his face gave me a lovely beaming smile and handed me his rose.
>
> As I was walking down the room several courtiers came up to me and said: 'You were much honoured by His Majesty. That means you are the honoured guest tonight.' As I walked down the

full length of the room a number of courtiers and counsellors came up to me and introduced themselves most politely.

Did the handing of the royal rose mean that Sidney had been given the nod? It was hard to tell whether this obsequious fawning to the Saudi Royal house was getting him anywhere.

Shuttling once again between the Middle East and England Sidney worked out the details. He would acquire an oil concession for Buraymi oasis, then: 'The proposal was to let me have a go at forming a Saudi Arabian oil company with Australia showing a moral interest and letting me have the right to export only one million pounds worth of capital.' Once the concession was signed Sidney proposed to get the funds from the International Money Market. 'Then we'd develop the Saudi oil area, and once big quantities of oil were found in Australia we could have taken over the American control and let them have the Saudi fields instead.'

Cotton bombarded the Australian government with correspondence over the Buraymi dispute, with letters to the Prime Minister Robert Menzies, Richard Casey (later Lord Casey) the Minister for External Affairs, Sir Eric Harrison the Australian High Commissioner in London and other prominent figures.

He wanted two things from Australia. The first was that the Australian government should put up one million pounds sterling to Cotton's company to exploit an oil concession granted by King Saud. The second was that Australia should set up an embassy or at very least a trade commissioner in Saudi Arabia.

Casey in a confidential letter to the Cabinet wrote: 'I would not expect the Cabinet to agree to the use of government funds in a speculative enterprise in a distant and little known country. Such a project, would I believe be more a matter for private investment. The Department of Trade had no interest in establishing a trade commissioner in Saudi Arabia. This could best be done by the commissioner in Karachi making regular visits to Bahrain and other places in the Gulf.'

By 1958, Sidney had been out of the country for twenty years and everybody had forgotten him. It would not be long before people in Australia started asking who he was. In London, however, he still had friends.

Lord Lambton, a Conservative MP, wrote in glowing terms in the *Evening Standard*: 'Mr Cotton is a figure one would have thought no longer existed in the century of the common man. He would seem to step straight out of the pages of E. Phillips Oppenheim. [Oppenheim was a popular thriller writer of the thirties.] During this period he has constantly flown to and fro between this country and Saudi Arabia and lest it might be doubted that he is very seriously regarded, he has carried messages direct from the King to the Prime Minister and Mr Selwyn Lloyd.'

Back in Australia, ASIO were alerted. Who was this man Cotton, and was there a file on him? D. V. O'Leary, the regional director of the Attorney General's Department wrote to the director of the Australian Security Intelligence Organisation (ASIO). What was known about Sidney Cotton?

The enquiry had originally come from Arthur Cutler, later Sir Roden Cutler a distinguished soldier who had won the Victoria Cross in Syria. After the war, Cutler had served as Australian representative in Cairo. Some idea of Sidney's anonymity can be gauged from the fact that Cutler thought that Cotton's full correct name was Sydney O'Grady Cotton [*sic*] and that he was born in Melbourne about 1885!

'Cotton has now put up certain propositions to the Australian government and because of this it was desired to know whether ASIO had any record of him.' Cutler had known Cotton when he was Australian representative in Cairo after the war and was not impressed. He had heard many 'sticky' stories concerning his activities. These included the death of a pilot and that Cotton was involved in gun running in Hyderabad. He had also heard of numerous nefarious and well paid deals in the Middle East. 'In recent years, however, Cotton had surrounded himself with an aura of respectability.'

The letter is dated 8 April 1958 and marked 'Secret'. Sections of it are still exempt from public access after thirty years. A reply from ASIO was dated 15 May 1958. ASIO established that Sydney O'Grady Cotton was not the man! Frederick Sidney Cotton had been born at Bowen in Queensland on 17 June 1894.

ASIO enclosed some newspaper cuttings detailing Sid's wartime exploits. 'Because of the persons and negotiations involved in and referred to in this case we request that correspondence concerning it be classified "Top Secret".'

By 27 May, the ASIO director was expressing some concern. 'It is evident that our efforts to assist Mr Cutler have given rise to some perturbation and anxiety lest our enquiries concerning Cotton should become too widely known in External Affairs.'

By 6 June Cutler had all he needed to know about Sidney. 'His Minister (Richard Casey) was very well aware of Cotton's background and: "*Would not trust him as a mediator on behalf of this country on any matter*"'. Then, as now, ASIO worked closely with British Intelligence.

In February 1958 King Saud had handed Sidney a personal message to the British Prime Minister Harold Macmillan which Sidney duly delivered. King Saud was keen to have a secret meeting with the British on neutral territory, say Bahrain, but it was destined never to happen. Sidney meanwhile thought that Britain had betrayed the trust placed by the Saudis. Without the peace deal over Buraymi there would be no oil concession.

It was up to Selwyn Lloyd, the British Foreign Secretary to drop the final bombshell. At the Foreign Office he produced a telegram from the Saudis which said that Sidney had no authority to discuss anything on their behalf.

Sidney's amateur diplomacy had once again come to nothing. He was refused a visa to return to Jiddah and had become a pariah in both England and his native Australia. If it was any consolation Sidney's exit from Saudi Arabia had at least been more dignified than that meted out to an earlier intermediary, Harry St John Philby.

After Philby had written an article critical of the behaviour of the young princes who were he said, 'picking up their morals in the gutters of the West', he was invited to the palace where he was publicly spat upon by Saud and his courtiers. Then he was driven to the border with Lebanon and dumped there, spending the rest of his life in exile.

Sidney had been close to King Saud but clearly not close enough. But Saud was not to remain King for much longer. Six years later he was to be deposed by Abdullah Faisal the young prince who had drunk whisky on Sidney's yacht the *Amazone*.

## Chapter 13

# Amazone *Days*

In 1948, assuming you had ten million pounds how long would it take you to spend it? If you owned a motor yacht and a private plane and rented a house in Cannes probably not very long.

Sidney consistently denied that he made any money from the Hyderabad adventure and when asked said he had been paid in carpets. That may or may not have been be true; it was certainly a convenient line with which to bamboozle the Inland Revenue but with a floating office and no permanent address in Britain they would have trouble catching him anyway.

Sidney had always been a competent sailor and was as comfortable afloat as he was in the air. In Australia he had taken part in the Sydney to Hobart yacht race. In St Moritz he had raced power boats with Joan. In the 1930s he had regularly attended Cowes week in the Isle of Wight hiring a yacht called the *Golzar*. At sundown he would moor as close to the Royal yacht as possible. 'We would all dress for dinner and go up on deck in our best clothes. He liked to be close to the King,' said Joan.

After the Hyderabad adventure he was rich enough to buy a

luxury motor yacht. The *Amazone* fitted the bill perfectly. It was oceangoing and provided a luxurious alternative to the cramped cabin of an aeroplane. It enabled Sidney to cruise the Mediterranean and the Red Sea at his leisure while entertaining guests and business associates. Moreover as his floating office it was rarely in any port long enough for Sidney to be liable to pay any taxes. He had shrewdly registered *Amazone* in another tax haven, Jersey in the Channel Islands.

The yacht had been built by Thorneycrofts in England and had previously been registered as the M.Y. *Evangeline*. It weighed 250 tons had six guest rooms and a crew of thirteen. It was his home for the next four years. He would carry a car as deck cargo—sometimes a Rolls Royce but later a little Fiat. He always had a car when he went ashore.

He became a member of the prestigious Royal Thames Yacht Club and so the *Amazone* was entitled to fly the undefaced Blue Ensign. This had its advantages as it meant they could enjoy the hospitality of the Royal Navy. In the cabins was special writing paper embossed with the words M.Y. *Amazone* and the RTYC burgee in full colour, with envelopes to match.

Sidney's little office had a big window rather than a porthole. It was lined with bookshelves so Sidney contacted a bookstore and said, 'Send me some books to fill up the spaces just to make it look lived in.' But according to Jill the books were all completely unreadable.

Cannes in the 1950s was a dizzy scene. The grim wartime days and the Nazi occupation were a distant memory and the port was teeming with every sort of opportunist and entrepreneur. People were out to have fun.

'There was Dawson the scrap king with his huge yacht and the odd people who were in and out of it. Freddy Dexter who died in a storm in the Med—up to the eyes in loot—having tied his French girlfriend to the mast in an effort to protect her from drowning.'

The harbour was full of celebrities: Greek tycoons, film stars, night club owners and Mafiosi. Sidney's crew were something of a United Nations. After he had sacked the Egyptian for peddling liquor he had engaged a new captain, a man called Monti who came from Trieste. The chief engineer was a German, Von Fischer. There were two young German deckhands who had served on a German U-boat. The Maltese steward, Secluda, and a Maltese cook, Borge, used to fight like two dogs.

Jill Cotton recalls: 'We used to get visited by drunken American sailors in Cannes harbour. They would go ashore from an American warship, get drunk and then wander along the Croisette looking at the names on the yachts. When they got to ours they would only see the name Jersey (where the yacht was registered) and think it was New Jersey and try to come on board. We met it in Port Said and went down through the Suez Canal which was wonderful. If it was under 250 tons you didn't need a pilot.

'Sadika Tancred and her husband joined the cruise in Athens on the way to Jiddah. 'Life on board *Amazone* was extremely comfortable. When the sea was rough we could not eat in the dining room as the table was screwed down so we had to put a damp cloth on the floor of the saloon where we put our food and plates. It was sometimes quite fun rolling around.'

In Jiddah, Sidney was busy seeing the King and other important people. Although my husband and I spent nearly five months on board *Amazone* we did not get to know Sidney very well. He was a very kind generous and private man but not a great talker, certainly not about himself. He was really a very modest man. He did not drink except for a glass of wine and did not go for exotic food. One thing I noticed was that he had very blue eyes that could look right through you. I once asked him how it was that he was so successful with all his inventions and he said: "Intuition and a little luck".

'Unfortunately, luck did run out for him in the end'.

The days on board the *Amazone* were spent fishing, or ashore shopping in the local *souq*. In the evening the party played bridge on the top deck. and sometimes watched a movie. 'But we never played for money as the wind often blew our trumps overboard,' said Sadika.

Sidney had gone ashore and was having a business meeting at an office in Jiddah when the British pro-vice consul Cyril Ousman put his head around the door. A yacht had run aground on a coral reef further up the coast. Four people had escaped from the vessel. Six more were trapped on board. Could Mr Cotton assist? There was nothing Sidney liked better than to organise a rescue mission. He drove to the airport and took off in the Lockheed. An hour later he was circling around the *Bessie*.

The yacht was stuck fast on the reef and Sidney could see waves breaking over the stern. He flew low over the vessel and saw six people on deck waving. They seemed to be in good spirits but the boat was breaking up and would not last forever. If they were to be rescued there was no time to lose. Back in Jiddah the British Ambassador thought that this was a matter for the coastguard.

Sidney decided to put to sea anyway knowing that it would be a risky business manoeuvring the 250 ton *Amazone* through uncharted reefs. He had a Saudi pilot, Mohammad, but even he was unsure whether he could safely navigate the reef. The *Amazone* was about six yards wide—the gap in the reef was about seven yards. Miraculously they made it through the gap, and headed into deeper waters.

'There was only three or four feet of water on either side and the rippling of the water made it seem as though the coral was stretching out long fingers to clutch us and rip our plates open,' wrote Sidney. Finally only a half an hour before dark they found the *Bessie* and anchored one hundred yards away from her in a pool on the lee side of the reef. Sidney decided to launch the tender and take everyone off the yacht before it got dark.

Every time the waves came in the tender was lifted two metres into the air. The problem was to get the small boat close enough to the *Bessie* without smashing it to pieces against the hull. Sidney shouted to the crew to stand next to the rail and launch themselves into the boat as soon as the next roller brought them level.

It worked. It was almost dark by the time the last passenger was taken off. Sidney noticed that some of them were the worse for wear. The *Bessie* had run out of drinking water so the crew had been forced to drink the spirits from the bar.

The *Amazone* dropped anchor in Jiddah the next day. Sidney had offered the shipwrecked party accommodation on the yacht until they could find something ashore. As it happened they stayed for three weeks. Sidney, as ever, was an exemplary host and would give his guests fistfuls of money to spend ashore.

'He was not an accumulator of wealth. He would just give it away. He had no real interest in money. What was more important was the adventure and the journey,' Sally Anne Cotton recalls.

The rescue attempt had taken Sidney's mind off the more serious matter of doing a deal with the Saudis. While he was waiting for developments he decided to go fishing. He hooked a fish almost immediately but this in turn was swallowed by a big shark. Sidney did not want to lose his expensive rod and line, so he put a hook through the shark's head and hung it from a rope, still thrashing, against the hull. One of the guests suggested drowning the shark by putting a few buckets of water down its throat.

Sidney gloomily reflected that water was more expensive than petrol in Saudi Arabia. He paid thirty pounds a week for water. In maintaining the *Amazone* and keeping his guests in comfort he was spending money fast, with so far very little to show for it.

The *Amazone* made its lazy way back to Suez. There were dances and dinner parties, cocktails and fishing. The Saudi finance minister, Abdul Suleiman, was a regular dinner guest but after the death of the old King he fell out of favour with the new one and went to live in exile in the Lebanon taking his money with him in gold coins.

Sometimes the monotony of English breakfasts on board the ship was relieved by American waffles in the air conditioned company dining room of Aramco, where most of the food was imported from America.

Bunty and Sadika went ashore to a dinner party hosted by Palestinians composed entirely of women. It was slightly unnerving. Some were wearing the latest Paris fashions, others were in full evening dress, but there were no men. The food as always was exquisite but there was no alcohol. After dinner somebody produced a record player and several women got up and danced. 'I saw one of the women looking at me and Bunty. We decided it was time to go home. We shook our heads and left.'

Back in the Mediterranean en route to Malta the Italian captain inadvertently steered the ship towards a British aircraft carrier and they were suddenly buzzed by Royal Navy fighter aircraft. They had sailed into the path of HMS *Eagle* which was on manoeuvres. The *Amazone's* radio had broken down. Unknown to them the *Eagle* had been trying to tell them to get out of the way.

Jill Cotton spent the winter of 1950 at Jiddah and sailed back up the Italian coast to Genoa. On the way up they ran into a terrible storm. 'The boat was practically standing on its end.'

Sidney was not on the *Amazone* at the time. He had decided instead to fly the Lockheed from Jiddah to Suez. The trip could have been a disaster: unknown to Sidney, when it had been refuelled at Jiddah the ground crew mistakenly filled it with American gallons instead of Imperial. Sidney was running so low on fuel that he had to land at an Egyptian military airport. When he taxied to stop he found himself looking down the barrel of a gun. 'They nearly shot him,' said Jill, 'But he managed to talk his way out of it.'

In Cairo Jill asked him for five pounds so that she could buy him a birthday present. 'I remember he turned to me and said, "You have no idea of the value of money". I said, "Can you wonder? You've never given me any".' He was bankrupt quite often. He went up and down. He didn't know where the next deal was coming from. 'It wasn't so much that he was mean, it meant making a commitment. He never planned for the future.'

Jill didn't particularly like flying and to combat air sickness used to sit in the back of the aircraft and eat biscuits. Sidney however would fly the Lockheed as casually as if he had wings sprouting from his shoulders. He had invited ex-wife Joan and her new husband Peter to fly to a race meeting in Ireland. Joan was asleep in the back of the aircraft and woke up to find Sidney reading the papers with his feet up.

'That's all right, Joey,' he said, 'I've got her.' The plane was on automatic pilot.

Once the Lockheed was accelerating to take off when Sidney realised that there was some stiffness with the controls. 'We came to a grinding halt. My father realised that something was wrong and we pulled up just before the end of the runway. The clamps had been left in the elevators.'

Sidney would always try to land short so that he didn't have to taxi too far to the terminal building. This meant he would have to come over the fence at the end of the runway. Landing at Pisa in Italy the Lockheed came down so low that the undercarriage caught in the night lighting system at the end of the runway. 'Luckily the lights were quite primitive,' said Jill. 'We ended up in front of the terminal building dragging yards and yards of little light bulbs behind us popping. The Italians were very upset. I don't know whether he had to pay for it but there was quite a stink about it.'

Not everyone enjoyed flying with Sidney. He would carry two pairs of glasses—one for reading and one for distance. When the Lockheed was committed to land, Sidney would switch glasses when the plane was on the glidepath.

Captain Barry Riley was also lucky enough to fly the Lockheed. In 1951 he had the job of ferrying the plane back to Croydon from Nice. 'I had seen the shining silver and two tone green Lockheed gracing the apron of many a European airport. Compared with most of the twin engined planes I was currently flying, it was very modern.'

Riley had left Croydon on a civilian flight early in the morning but it was evening by the time he arrived in Nice.

Sidney Cotton had thoughtfully sent his chauffeur and car to meet me. I was rapidly whisked along the Corniche road to Cannes. The car came to a stop alongside the fabulous Cotton yacht, *Amazone*. I went aboard and introduced myself. He greeted me as one would a casual but respected friend and it wasn't long before I was holding a glass of champagne and wondering where I would be spending the night. My worries were short lived. A steward showed me to my cabin for a shower and a change of clothes before dinner. I took a chance and washed out the shirt I had been wearing and put on a clean one I had been saving for the flight back to Croydon. Any change in the rest of my clothes would been in the eyes of the beholder.

Dinner was a relatively formal affair. The ladies were dressed impeccably. The men wore white linen jackets and bow ties. I wore a blue blazer and grey slacks with a white shirt and RAF tie. Sidney was resplendent in a short sleeved open necked shirt and a pair of casual slacks and sandals.

He impressed me as a person who succeeded in life by the sheer force of his domineering personality and a scant regard for protocol, artificial etiquette, regulations and the Establishment. I was simultaneously attracted to, and repelled by this man who had so much to show that his was a successful formula and yet flew in the face of everything that I had been taught was right and proper.

We talked into the night and my host skilfully manoeuvred the conversation away from any topic that he wanted to avoid. His ability to dictate the subjects of discussion was cleverly disguised but one only talked about the things that interested Sidney Cotton.

Captain Riley went to bed dreaming of being rich one day and thinking about the next morning when Sidney was going to teach him to fly the Lockheed. At breakfast Riley tried to bring the conversation around to talking about the aircraft. But Sidney seemed preoccupied with other matters and left the table without giving any clue as to his plans.

'I went back to my cabin and put my clothes in my bag. I didn't intend to be caught out by somebody so volatile as Sidney Cotton and I was ready for anything.'

When the order was finally given to move Sidney gave him fifteen seconds to be on deck and ready to go. At Cannes airport in Mandelieu he was introduced to a small man wearing a trilby hat. This was the faithful Mroszczak, Sidney's Polish radio engineer who before the war had flown for Polish Airlines LOT. 'Mroszczak (pron. Muroshak) obviously loved his machine and knew far more about it than I ever would.'

Riley eased himself into the pilot's seat and looked around the instrument panel. He had flown a variety of American aircraft so it was largely familiar. To reassure himself he ran through the mnemonic check list: HTTMPFFCGGGGS: Hydraulics, Trim, Throttle Nut, Mixture, Pitch, Fuel, Flaps, Compass, Gills 'George', Gyros, Gauges and Switches. Riley felt honoured to be flying the Lockheed. He didn't want to make a mess of it.

But Sidney was impatient. He thrust his head between the two and said: 'Why don't you start her up. She is really quite simple to fly and you are in good hands if you need any help. Your flight plan is filed so you might as well be on your way—Goodbye!'

Sidney left the cabin, closed the door and gave the all clear to taxi. This infuriated Riley. That decision was his to make and he was not ready. Typically, Sidney had assessed the situation and pre-empted that decision. 'In a fit of pique I called the tower and asked for clearance to taxi for an immediate take-off.'

He asked Mroszczak to check the engines and perform the pre-flight checks as they taxied. 'As he set the various controls I monitored his movements and made sure that at least we had accomplished the vital actions. As we lined up to take off my companion advanced the throttles and performed the ignition checks.

'"Ready to go," he called, and we were on our way. This was the last time I saw Sidney Cotton. The loss was mine.'

Later, Riley wondered whether Cotton had been secretly laughing at him for exercising caution. In fact Sidney had been submitting him to a test—and he had passed it. Only the most experienced pilots got to fly the Lockheed.

Sidney would fly off in the Lockheed as casually as others would catch a subway train. In postwar Britain, many commodities were impossible to find so Sidney used the plane for smuggling into the country little luxuries like chocolates, cheeses, and liquor. In France he flew the aircraft a hundred miles to buy a tin of Nescafé and on another occasion he smuggled tennis balls from Ireland. The postwar Lockheed was more sophisticated than the one Sidney flew before the war, fitted with blind flying aids which enabled the aircraft to land unaided in fog.

But aeroplanes are costing money even when they are standing on airfields doing nothing. It would not be long before Sidney would be travelling by commercial airliner like everyone else. There were the occasional business trips to London when Sidney would check into the Grosvenor House Hotel and call to see his brother in law, Brian Brooke-Smith. Brian was a penniless law student and had just got married. Sidney was unfailingly warm and friendly to the impecunious newlyweds.

'The call would come "Hi kids, how about a movie?" and off we'd all trundle (Sid spending more on the West End cinema tickets than we spent to live for a week!) followed by Baked Alaska at the hotel—a favourite of Sid's specially prepared for him to round off the evening.'

Brian got the impression that he was often lonely and at something of a loose end—with quite an extraordinary need for company. 'The business schemes he was nurturing in the early years of his marriage to Bunty seemed to us fanciful beyond belief—but he was prepared to outlay vast amounts of money on these fantasies. Little did any of us know.'

In December 1953 Sidney ordered the yacht to Southampton to be laid up for the winter. The London *Evening Standard* sent a reporter to the Dorchester Hotel to interview him and reported: 'Mr Cotton has been conducting his business from the yacht with the help of two secretaries. He has been building interests in the

Arab countries. Mr Cotton is fifty-nine, tall and white haired. He has been flying since 1915 and used to own a fleet of aeroplanes. Now he has only one, a four passenger aircraft which he pilots himself.

'"I like to be in control," he said.'

## Chapter 14

# The Bitter End

Sidney had two children by his previous marriages—John who was by now living in Australia, and Jill, who had married and gone to live in Canada. His restless life had meant that he was to see very little of either of them.

In 1954 he was to have a daughter Sally Anne and two years later a son, Charles. Never before in the true sense had he ever been a family man. Now he loved being surrounded by his young children.

In 1956 Sidney and Bunty moved to Beirut and lived in a luxury flat in the suburb of Ras-Beirut. It had four bedrooms, an office, a library and a day nursery. The *Amazone* and the Lockheed were too expensive to maintain so he sold them both. Sidney still adored flying but his heart problem was such that Bunty did not like him taking unnecessary risks.

Sidney had not completely abandoned the idea of getting an oil concession—but it was time to move on. He was always working on at least half a dozen projects at the same time.

In Egypt he had discovered a seemingly endless supply of

naturally occurring building material which when mixed with water could be made into adobe style building blocks without adding straw. He called the stuff Tectonite and took out a patent on it. In theory it was ideal for low cost housing and it was tough enough to build runways. In his Beirut office he had a wall built of the material and he tried to get the Lebanese and the Saudis interested in it.

Sidney was still working on Tectonite when in 1962 they moved yet again, this time to Switzerland, selected because of its low rates of income tax. 'Sidney used to say that taxes were for the peasants,' said Brian Brooke-Smith, his brother-in-law.

The Cotton family rented a house at Mont sur Rolle near Geneva, and the children went to local schools. Sidney was still speculating on projects which were not bringing any returns.

The children had a nanny, Rhoda Fraser, a cheerful Scotswoman. 'I was aware that there wasn't a lot of money,' she said. This was already starting to generate friction between husband and wife.

Sidney would enrage Bunty by buying expensive gadgets like cameras and record players when there was no food in the house. He always had to have the best of everything. He was besotted with Sally Anne and Charles and even from the time they were tiny babies lavished upon them extravagant presents. When Charles was only four Sidney bought him a complete model railway from the leading toyshop in Mont sur Rolle. Fortunately the rented house had a room big enough to take it even though Charles was not yet old enough to play with it.

Nor was the Swiss retreat as free from bureaucracy as Sid might have wished. Even the Swiss, after all, pay some taxes. Sidney was declared persona non grata and asked to leave the country. The Swiss confiscated Bunty's dark green Jaguar which Sidney had bought for her in Beirut.

Sidney did not like living in England but there was nowhere else to go. He had not lived in Australia for nearly forty years; now it was starting to look attractive. In London they rented houses first in Porchester Terrace and then Sloane Square. Bunty was keen to buy a house but Sidney was still not anxious to put down roots.

In July 1966 the Cottons moved to a rented house on the Ford Manor estate at Lingfield in Surrey. The address might have given the impression that the Cottons were living in the splendid manor house. In fact they rented a more modest property, a wooden house in the grounds for twenty-two guineas a week. 'We had reached the stage in London,' wrote Sidney, 'after hunting for houses for several years, where we were prepared to pay as much as forty pounds a week then this place turned up.' The Cottons and their children had the full use of a thousand acres of the most beautiful rough garden and woods, with acres of cut lawns. 'All of which we enjoy,' wrote Sidney, 'but it is at the expense of the owner. He maintains two gardeners to keep the place looking nice, which costs him more than the rent I am paying.'

If Sidney Cotton was a prolific letter writer during the war he excelled himself in peacetime. Until his death in 1969 he wrote a weekly aerogramme to his brother Victor in Queensland. In almost all of them he is telling Victor about his latest deal.

There was the contract with British Petroleum to purchase crude oil for a new oil refinery in Italy. The Italians promised Sid a generous royalty which would have guaranteed him £1.5 million a year from the oil and the sale of the products from the refinery. But the Italian government fell and the licence for the refinery was never granted.

By 1968 Sidney had taken up the patent on another invention, the Vortex tube, and set up a company, Indural. Significantly the company headquarters were in the Aeulestrasse in Vaduz, capital of the European tax haven of Liechtenstein. The Vortex tube was a heat exchange device invented by a Frenchman, Marcel Ranque, and was designed to be used in refrigerators or air conditioning systems for aircraft and cars. It worked on the principle of blowing air at high pressure through a tube which produced cold air from one end and hot air from the other. By 1968, Sidney was hoping to sell fifty thousand tubes a year in the United States alone, but he was still looking for backers. An American investor had offered to put five thousand pounds into the Vortair project and Sid triumphantly went up to London to collect the cheque. Sid's change in fortunes had not come a moment too soon.

'If the Vortex business gets going well we might have to consider living abroad somewhere,' he wrote. 'Switzerland would be the best locality but we've both had our fill of the Swiss and may consider somewhere else so that the taxman cannot put his hands on all I hope to make out of Vortex.'

He wrote to Victor: 'We have thought of you today on your birthday and it has brought me some good luck at last.' Before the war Sidney had met R. H. Naylor the great British astrologer, who offered to read his horoscope for nothing. Naylor told him that his horoscope was the most interesting he had ever read but that he was in the wrong part of the world to get a favourable action from his stars.

'That I should go West and if I did I would make millions. "If you stay in the unfavourable area you will develop some big propositions and they will all fall through at the last moment for a small reason which no one could foresee." You have no idea how right he was,' Sidney wrote to Vic, 'I have been on the point of pulling off fabulous deals for the last fifteen years or even twenty years. The King of Saudi Arabia gave orders for the oil concession agreement to be signed, twice.'

The prophesies that Sidney would acquire fantastic wealth, but that he would have to go West to achieve it—had played on his mind. Somewhere in the Australian outback was a fabulous gold mine called Lasseter's Reef. In England Sidney met a man who claimed to have acquired Lasseter's diaries and knew how to decipher them. Sidney in a letter to Victor recalled how in 1915 an old man had ridden into the Brunette Downs station and took several large nuggets from his saddlebag. When Sidney and his father had asked where he had found them he had pointed vaguely in the direction of the MacDonnell Ranges.

The strange man with the diaries said he could accurately

predict the location of the reef, which was thirty miles long. The only problem was that the reef lay on Aboriginal land. 'The samples we saw of the gold in the quartz were thicker than my little finger,' wrote Sid. He said he would use his influence with the Minister for Aboriginal Affairs in Adelaide to get permission. 'I told him the story of Lasseter coming to Brunette Downs and that I knew Menzies and Casey and others who might be able to help get permission. The Minister of Mines there has offered all help if we can get permission to prospect. Perhaps this is the prophesy of R. H. Naylor. As ever yet another golden goose.'

Nothing was ever heard of the matter again. The golden goose had turned into a wild goose chase.

In his letters back to Australia in the last two years of his life Sidney made constant references to his declining health. The damage he had caused to his ears during his World War I flying days was starting to catch up with him. If Sidney seemed uninterested in other people's affairs it was simply that he could not hear them. He had become increasingly dependent on hearing aids and found the effort of wrestling with other people's trivia too much.

On 1 October 1966 he wrote: 'The doctor tells me that I must not have any upsets or tensions, for they give me spasms in my heart muscles, and now with the ulcer and diaphragmitic hernia, I am on a very tight diet. It gives Bunty a good opportunity of deliberately upsetting me to get her own back. I have seriously thought of walking out on her but that would undoubtedly affect the children so I must take it and smile as much as possible.'

16 May 1968: 'My doctor gave me a very thorough overhaul and pronounced that my condition was no worse than when he first examined me in 1963. My weight is down to fourteen stone from fifteen stone five pounds and I would continue to get the pains but I must take things very easily, not worry, not get excited. Then his pretty secretary walks in with skirts that show most of everything and I grab for a pill, not that sort but the one which is to stop my heart from beating so fast. Anyway that is something

but it does not enable him to do anything to prevent the heart pains which I get—too often to my mind.'

By 21 March 1968 Sidney was turning to old friends in America to help bail out his precarious financial state. In the 1930s he had sold his interest in an electronics company making piezo crystals to a man called Wiggs Williams, who had since made a million pounds out of it. He wrote and asked him for twenty thousand pounds—Wiggs cabled him five thousand pounds. 'Thank God for an honest decent man,' he wrote to Victor.

About the same time Sidney was making occasional visits to Germany to see a heart specialist. He noted with interest that one of the streets near the clinic in Bad Nauheim bore the name of Bodenstrasse or Bode Street. The Baroness Bode was a Cotton ancestor.

His condition did not prevent him having the occasional evening out. On 27 May 1968 he was invited to the Royal Air Force Club in Piccadilly for a 30th anniversary reunion of the founding of the Photographic Reconnaissance Unit. For Sid it was a harrowing experience and reaffirmed his distrust of the RAF hierarchy. 'It has become very much an Air Force affair now and everything to do with those awful colonials who started it is brushed under the table,' he wrote.

The evening started disastrously for Sid, with the presentation of a portrait to Geoffrey Tuttle—not Sidney—as 'The unit's first Commanding Officer'. 'It really made my blood boil,' wrote Sidney. 'Geoffrey, perhaps knowing what was about to happen, made an excuse and left before they presented a painting of him.'

Towards the end of the evening, Sid could not swallow any more and decided to slip away. He was sneaking out of the door when one of his friends, an Air Commodore Wheeler came over to him. 'Please do not go', he said, 'We are about to put these monkeys in their place.'

Sidney, more than ever, wanted to leave. 'But several others came over and as they were my old boys I stayed. Then Wheeler really put the screws on, telling that if it had not been for Sidney

Cotton, who was with them tonight, there would not have been a PRU and there would not have been this party tonight . . . that I had completely revolutionised the art of photographic intelligence which had contributed to us winning the war and had saved countless lives of our crews.'

When they vacated their flat in Beirut, Bunty had placed their furniture in storage intending to ship it to England when they had found a house. By October 1966, although the furniture was in the country, Sid could still not afford to retrieve it from storage. 'How much better if we had sold it all in Beirut five years ago when we would have got a very good price for it,' he lamented.

Now Thomas Cook were threatening to sell it unless the storage bill was paid. On 29 June the bailiffs turned up at Ford Manor hoping to repossess the furniture only to discover that the house was rented fully furnished! Sid's big air-conditioned Oldsmobile car had become too expensive to repair. He bought a secondhand Austin A 40 and Bunty a Triumph Herald.

The last six months of Sidney Cotton's life were desperate. His heart condition was deteriorating and his marriage was in tatters. Life with Bunty was a series of debilitating rows. They had occupied separate bedrooms since Switzerland. 'I daily have exhibitions of unbalanced temper. Bunty . . . cannot control her shrieking vulgarity. She is quite unable to control herself. I expect her to froth at the mouth any minute.'

Sally Anne and Charles saw a lot of the world in the first years of their lives—Beirut, Switzerland, France, Spain and England. Both of them boarded at private schools but Sidney loved it when they came home to the house at Ford Manor during the holidays. Sidney had mellowed. He was in many ways a Victorian father. But he genuinely delighted in telling stories at bedtime when the two children would compete for positions on his knee. He was a good storyteller. These were the 'and so . . . ' times. He loved to tell Sally Anne and Charles about the days in Newfoundland looking for seals, but seemed reluctant to talk about the war.

He became reclusive, locking himself in his study for hours

working on his memoirs. Ralph Barker his biographer had virtually completed the book ten years before but Sidney could not prevent himself from tampering with it:

> I started work on Sidney's book in November 1958 and worked on it right through my two years in Aden and and had it virtually ready when I returned to England in April 1961.
>
> Had the book come out that autumn, as it should have done, it might have earned some money.
>
> But Sidney dragged it out for another eight years giving me enormous trouble, immense irritation and frustration which at one period landed me in hospital.

Barker was aware that many would read the book and wonder where Sid got the money for many of his adventures. But: 'Whenever I questioned Sidney about finance and suggested to him that we could not write a book which purported to be his life story without going into some detail on money, I always got evasive answers. I concluded that most of the money came from his father.'

The book finally ended up in the bookshops twenty-eight days before Sidney died.

Sometimes there were flashes of the old Sidney in his letters. 'What man has the confidence and the will to do he can usually achieve. I have done things which everyone thought impossible in the past on a number of occasions, but I have proved that there is no such word as cannot. It may require great faith and patience and I have always felt that Providence helps those who have faith and help themselves.'

Realistically even if Sidney had not lost his job in the RAF would he have been content to be in a uniformed service? Probably not. Even to the end, Sidney was bitter about the way he had been treated. 'I will never get any recognition for it . . . in this country because . . . it was done by an outsider, i.e. an Australian.'

When the aircraft designer Barnes Wallis was knighted, Sidney wrote to congratulate him. In a reply Wallis said that Sidney should have got a knighthood for his war work. Bunty sniffed: 'Sidney did get a K. It stood for kicked out.'

To the end he was hoping to pull off a big deal which would enable him to return to Australia. 'I have always been fascinated by new things,' he wrote, 'and at the age of seventy-four I am developing a business which I hope may go some way to recoup my losses and provide for my wife and our two young children. Then I may be able to return with them, as I have always hoped to do, to the country of my birth.'

On 20 October 1968, four months before he died a creditor journeyed out to Lingfield Manor to serve a bankruptcy writ on Sidney Cotton. Sidney was mortified. Things were bad but they were about to get worse. A man who Sidney had considered to be a close friend had put a thousand pounds in the Vortex project, and he wanted his money back. Sidney borrowed the money from a scientist friend to pay him off.

The week that Sidney Cotton died it was bitterly cold at Ford Manor and the grounds of the house were covered in snow. Sally Anne had been home for the half term holidays and was reluctant to leave. There was a long drive to the house; she loved arriving but hated driving away. The tall figure of her father filled the frame of the door as he waved goodbye. She was not to see him again.

'He was a gentleman, and a gentle man, a giant of a man. He had a kind of persona about him so that people would turn and look. He had some energy that was charismatic. The kids at school would ask what did your father do? I could never put a finger on what Dad did. What did your dad do in Beirut? I don't know; he kind of worked undercover.'

Sidney spent the days sitting in front of the fire in the drawing room waiting to hear from the exchange control office that he could set up his new Vortair company in Liechtenstein. It never came. On Tuesday he spent the day in his office writing a few letters and making plans to go to London the following day.

Early on Wednesday morning Sidney called Bunty and told her he was in great pain. He had in fact suffered the first of a number of heart attacks which left him paralysed. An ambulance took him to the Queen Victoria hospital in East Grinstead where he was given oxygen and morphine.

Sidney survived the night but by morning his condition had worsened and Bunty was called to his bedside. 'Suddenly a nurse came and said "quick, he is worse". I dashed to his bed and he was staring in the direction in which I had been standing. After several little gasps he just stopped breathing. Poor, dear handsome Sid, the peace on his face was wonderful.'

The funeral was set for the following Monday at Dormansland Parish Church and the weather, to everyone's surprise, was bright and sunny. Sir Geoffrey Tuttle, Sidney's loyal successor at the Photographic Reconnaissance Unit made a moving speech paying tribute to his pioneering work in World War II. It was a hero's funeral. An obituary in *The Times* recorded his passing. A month later his solicitor broke the bad news. Bunty had to face the grim reality that Sidney was broke.The gross value of his will was £455.19 shillings. The net value was nil. It was clear that she could not go on living at Ford Manor and there were many debts to be paid.

There was at least a way out. The Royal Air Force Benevolent Fund provides for widows of servicemen who have fallen upon hard times. Sidney's career with the air force had lasted less than a year but even so he was considered to have done his bit.

Sir Geoffrey Tuttle had a few words in the right places and the RAF Benevolent Fund found Bunty a modest cottage at Ashtead in Surrey. It was not the luxury she was used to but it was better than nothing.

Bunty wrote a bitter letter to Barker:

> The final chapter of your book was never written. Perhaps you do not realise that we were left completely destitute without a shilling in this world—only debts, some of which were joint account and had to be met by my father. There is no State pension for me as a widow, for no stamps were ever paid—and there is no Air Force

pension—there was nothing but a zero, and the memory of the MOST selfish and thoughtless man who ever lived.

In my marriage I was taken for the most appalling ride, and despite being a good wife in the face of shocking odds, I was let down in a way that no people can believe. No normal man could have treated a good wife and two lovely children the way we were treated—so perhaps it is best to excuse him on the grounds that he was not normal.

I only pray that the bad blood does not course through the veins of my children—for I could say a lot that has never been said—and I earnestly pray that my son does not emulate his father. I cannot subscribe to any more lies about Sidney Cotton—I lived with them for 18 years of marriage—and see how I was repaid.

I'm sorry if I shock you. But I am weary of my struggle—and I am even more weary of the lies.

Brian Brooke-Smith recalled the last days:

Towards the end of his life Sidney suffered the desperation of a gambler who has passed the point of no return with all his chips and who has no alternative except to go on until he has lost them all—in the hope that the winning number must finally come up.

When he did finally reveal to Bunty that his resources were not as inexhaustible as he had led her to believe, whenever she sought to question his extravagance, she was appalled. Bear in mind that they consorted with many people whose resources did indeed seem to be inexhaustible though few tried to match Sid's extravagance.

At the end they turned to family and friends to raise funds when Sid was seriously threatened with bankruptcy avoided only by his death.

What a tragedy—and really pathetically irresponsible to leave Bunty and his two adored children absolutely penniless.

I was sad that Bunty seemed unable after Sidney's death to cope with the problem better than she did but her resilience must have been destroyed by the thought (with which I know she was obsessed) that what had been squandered in any one year of their marriage might have kept them all, Sid included, in modest comfort for the rest of their days.

Sidney's ashes were brought back to Australia and placed in a niche in the family grave at Tallegalla cemetery, not far from the old homestead at Hidden Vale. But those expecting a splendid mausoleum to the father of aerial intelligence would be disappointed.

The simple metal plate is almost impossible to find, being let into the wall surrounding the grave and almost hidden by the headstone of Alfred Cotton and his wife Annie Bode. Sidney had achieved much in the fifty years he had been away from Australia, but it was almost as if the family had been embarrassed by his success. The simple metal plate has no mention of his skills as a pioneering aviator, reading simply:

'Frederick Sidney Cotton 1894–1969.' In June 2000 the surviving members of the Cotton family in Australia held a family reunion at the Hidden Vale. Most of the old house was burned down during World War II and was rebuilt as a hotel and convention centre. A. J. Cotton's wooden paymaster's cottage, looking vaguely like a small Chinese temple still stands as does the mantlepiece in the dining room but apart from that the property is unrecognisable from the country mansion where Sidney spent his happiest days.

On Sunday the family gathered at the Tallegalla cemetery to witness the reburial of Sidney's ashes. For thirty years they had lain in a niche in the concrete wall. Now the rectangular brass urn was prised from its resting place and reburied in a more prominent site. There are plans for a more imposing memorial.

Alongside him was buried Alick John, Sidney's son by Joan MacLean who had survived his father by thirty-one years and ended up as a gardener and odd job man on Hayman Island on the Great Barrier Reef.

He would regale anyone who would listen with stories about

how his father had virtually won World War II single handed, but John was a strange fellow and few were inclined to listen.

Intelligence is still gathered by men in shabby raincoats and seductive blondes but the most successful technique, as Sidney Cotton discovered, is to look down from above. That is his legacy.

In the autumn of 1964 the President of the United States announced the existence of the fastest aeroplane in the world—The SR-71 Blackbird. The Blackbird had been built by Lockheed, the same company who thirty years earlier had built Sidney Cotton's Electra. It could fly at nearly 3200 kilometres an hour and its cameras were good enough to read a car numberplate from a height of 26 kilometres. It did not have to be painted pale blue because it flew so high that nothing could touch it. For fifteen years it ranged unchallenged in the skies above the Soviet Union, China, North Korea and Vietnam.

The SR-71 has now been superseded by satellites whose cameras view the earth from deep space. These were used to great effect during the Gulf War in 1991 and during the war against terrorism in Afghanistan.

In 2001, the United States Air Force flew the Global Hawk, an unmanned photographic aircraft from Edwards Air Force Base in California to Adelaide in South Australia, a distance of twelve thousand kilometres. On the way it loitered over Australia to take some pictures with a variety of sophisticated cameras. Its thermal imaging cameras could detect the warmth from human bodies and show how many people were inside a room.

The clandestine photographic unit which Sidney Cotton established at Heston in 1939 survives today. Its direct descendant is JARIC, the Joint Air Reconnaissance Intelligence Centre, and its headquarters are at RAF Brampton near Huntingdon in England. On 12 June 2000, the unit celebrated sixty years of aerial intelligence.

Most people in England had long forgotten Sidney and his conflict with the military hierarchy but a modest exhibition was staged which included a photograph and a plaque. At long last Sidney was belatedly acknowledged as the paterfamilias of photographic intelligence. Not a bad effort for a man who started out in life mustering cattle in outback Australia.

Sidney Cotton was single-minded and obsessive and had the force of personality often to will things to happen in the way he wanted. By his own admission he was an opportunist and an adventurer.

Many people would have wondered where he got the money to pursue some of his fantastic schemes. Although his second wife darkly hinted that he was not above using privileged information to his own ends there was never any hard evidence that he was involved in blackmail. If this was true, however, it may have explained some of the decisions made in his favour.

Sidney was incapable of using the proper channels and disliked all bureaucratic systems. He cultivated public figures and his connections with the moneyed classes in Australia meant that he slipped easily into the British Establishment. He had his contacts and his connections; whether he had any special power over them is open to speculation.

He always said that he lived by an unorthodox but strict moral code. But how did he reconcile that with the Hyderabad episode? Indian independence had been proclaimed. By running guns Sidney was deliberately helping to prop up a rogue state run by a feudal dictator who was despised by the majority of his people.

Hyderabad was not about morality it was about money.

The days of the Maharajahs were over whether Churchill and Monckton liked it or not. Their support for the Nizam can only be seen as squaring the account.

In Kauai, Hawaii, Pat Martin looks out from her balcony at a paddock where her sole surviving horse is grazing. She still considers that Sidney was at the zenith of his creative ability during the World War II.

'I had his best years,' she says again.

Three time zones away in Perth, Ontario, it is now late in the afternoon and Joan Cotton is getting a little tired. It is three-quarters of a century since she first met Frederick Sidney Cotton, and sixty years since they went their separate ways. He was not exactly an ideal husband but they had some great adventures together.

On reflection she may have been a little hard on him and there is the barest suggestion of a catch in her voice.

'Oh Sid, poor old Sid. Still today I'm very fond of him. There was nothing I wouldn't have done for him.'

At the bottom of the garden the freight train sighs on its way to Ottawa.

# Postscript

And what happened to the other famous men who passed through Cotton's life?

Hermann Goering, the popular Deputy Führer and minister for forests and hunting who preferred the company of art dealers to his Luftwaffe pilots, descended into a fantasy world fuelled by morphine, chocolates and champagne.

Goering's country mansion, the Karinhalle was dynamited in the face of the advancing Red Army in 1945. Goering had eighty aircraft bombs placed in the cellars. When he left the house for the last time on 21 April he gave instructions to the caretaker that the house was to be destroyed.

Russian troops were entering the estate when there were a series of explosions. The house disappeared in a cloud of dust. Train loads of art treasures were shipped out. Goering fled to Berchtesgaden and was captured by the Americans. He was sentenced to death at the Nuremberg War Crimes tribunal but took his own life with a phial of cyanide.

Fred Winterbotham, 'Cloak and Dagger Fred', died in 1981 after writing three books.

Albert Kesselring was sentenced to death at Nuremberg but he was released after serving a short sentence and died in 1960.

Major Rudolf Bottger commandant of Tempelhof airport from 1925 to 1945, who Cotton literally took for a ride in the Lockheed, committed suicide on 29 April 1945 as Russian troops occupied the airport.

Geoffrey Tuttle was knighted for his services to aviation. He oversaw the expansion of the PRU unit and its move to Benson in Oxfordshire. Later he was to become one of the driving forces behind the Anglo–French Concorde project. He died on 11 January 1989.

Heston aerodrome closed down in 1947 and is today an industrial estate.

The Nizam of Hyderabad died in 1967 and was succeeded by his grandson who now lives in exile in Istanbul.

Maurice 'Shorty' Longbottom survived the war but was killed testing a Vickers Warwick in 1946.

Joan Henry died in Perth Ontario on 22 September 2001 aged 94.

Bob Niven, the lanky Canadian, continued to serve in the Royal Air Force and became commanding officer of 59 Squadron. He was killed in 1942 during a raid on German shipping.

Ian Fleming died in 1964 from a heart attack. He and Sidney remained friends to the end. In fact it was Sidney who recommended his German heart specialist Dr Ottomar Mechow in the Hessen town of Bad Nauheim.

Both of Sidney's Lockheed 12s are still flying sixty years after they were built.

G-AFTL, the wartime aircraft, was shipped back to the Lockheed plant in California to be repaired. It did not fly again until November 1942 when it was sold to a New Zealander, Lowell Yerex, and was flown to the British Honduras.

In 1943 it was sold again, this time to British West Indian

Airways in Trinidad, Jamaica. After the war it had eight owners and moved all over the United States, finally ending up as the property of Steve Oliver of Forest Grove Oregon. The cameras have gone and so have the sliding panels but the removable panels in the floor are still there.

This aeroplane has starred in a number of films and television programmes including *Doc Savage* and *The A Team*. In 2001 it has flown at Oshkosh air shows.

Sidney's postwar aircraft G-AGTL *Caprice* is also still airworthy. It is based in France but is a regular visitor to England.

# Acknowledgments

The help of a number of people is acknowledged in the Author's Note—and to those names I would like to add the following:

Georges van Acker, David Austin, Patricia Beck, Vic Bloxome, Kathy Buckley, Andrea Cameron, Bruce Connell, Connie Cotton, Victor Cotton, Reg Chasney, James Cullington, the late Sir Roden Cutler VC, Denis Dewar, Don Dinnie, Lana Dopper, Gill Drake, Paul Dunstan, Jane Fish, David Gardner, Frank Haines, Naomi Hall, Estate of the Late Lord Halifax, Hans Joachim Heidrich, Alex Henshaw, Brian Johnson, Howard Knox, Jean Lagarde, Steffi Lamla, G. Stewart Leslie, Margaret Lewis, John Maynard, Michael Mockford, Geoffrey Morrell, Jim Muncie, Eileen Naseby, Arnold Naylor, Roy Connors Nesbit, Robert Niven, Laurie Ogle, Steve Oliver, Michael Ross, Ian Smith, Christopher Tuttle, Nancy Bird Walton, Tony Winterbotham. There are also others who helped in many ways—some of whom did not wish to be named.

Thanks are also due to the Australian War Memorial for access to Sidney Cotton's papers; the Australian National Library; National Archives of Australia; the Public Record Office, London; Bundersarchiv, Koblenz; Stadtarchiv, Frankfurt; the Probate Registry, London; Hickleton Papers, Borthwick Institute, York

University; and L'Armée de L'Air Service Historique, Château Vincennes, France.

The photo of the River Rhine from the air is courtesy of the Australian War Memorial, and the following are courtesy of the Imperial War Museum: Beaufighters attacking the Gestapo Headquarters in Trieste, War Council Meeting with Kingsley Wood, Sir Cyril Newall, Sir Richard Peirse, Constance Babington Smith, Sidney Cotton with Arthur Barratt.